MIKE MOONEYHAM

Legends of the Mat Remembered

EVENING POST
BOOKS

Published by
Evening Post Books
Charleston, South Carolina

Editor: Kenneth Mihalik
Designer: Gill Guerry
Cover: Chad Dunbar

First printing 2019
Printed in the United States of America

A CIP catalog record for this book has been applied
for from the Library of Congress.

ISBN: 978-1-929647-40-8

Contents

Part I – CHAMPIONS

Part II – ORIGINALS

Introduction

"As long as one is remembered with love and reverence, they are never truly gone." — Anonymous

"Who's going to write my obituary when it's time?"

I've been asked that question more than once during my three decades writing a weekly pro wrestling column for The Post and Courier. Over those years I've written dozens of tributes dedicated to some of wrestling's greatest personalities. While I've always considered it an honor to "send off" these larger-than-life characters, it's a heart-wrenching exercise to say goodbye to men and women who have had such an impact on your life.

Finding the words to say goodbye is never easy, but the profound imprint these unique individuals left on the profession, and on my life, never failed to inspire me.

Many were my sports heroes growing up, but they became much more than that over the years. Some became confidantes and friends, and we would share an unbreakable bond that would forever tie us together.

The task of coming up with a theme for a compilation of some of my best columns over the years was a relatively easy one, yet they had been the hardest to write at the time. I thought about a recent request from a friend of mine in the business, who once again posed the question, "Who's going to write my obituary when it's time?" Sadly, that time came, and the answer was simple: I would. It would also be a reason why I decided to continue writing my weekly column even after retiring from the paper.

It is my wish to bring these sung and unsung giants of the ring to life once again on these pages. At the time these columns were published in print and online, they had been the toughest, at least emotionally, to write. In my way, I was saying goodbye. While tinged with grief and sadness, they also were stories of perseverance and triumph, celebrating the lives and careers of wrestling stars who lived by the credo that "the show must go on."

Ultimately this collection of columns is a tribute to the men and women who provided memories to last a lifetime.

– Mike Mooneyham

Comments

"Mike has been a friend of the wrestling business for a long time and no better friend could a business have. His honest and accurate reporting will enshrine Mike into the hearts of everyone that loves and respects our business."

– Jerry Jarrett

"It is wonderful that you have so much knowledge of our rich history and help to keep the memories alive. Thank you for your support, your friendship and your fine work over the years on behalf of professional wrestling. The ghosts in Township Auditorium will always smile upon us."

– J.J. Dillon

"There are few writers in the sport of wrestling that are true journalists. That is, those who have the talent, training, professionalism and understanding of the sport to tell compelling stories that beat to the heart of those in the ring and the impact they have had on wrestling. It is no wonder that Mike has gained the trust and respect that he has throughout the years. He is without a doubt wrestling's greatest asset and most intelligent writer."

– William Murdock

Forewords

I'm honored to have been asked to write the foreword to anything written by my longtime friend Mike Mooneyham.

I have known Mike since the '70s and though to my knowledge he has never taken a "bump." I still tend to look at him as "one of the boys" because he has always seemed to understand the crazy business of professional wrestling more as an insider then a fan.

He remembers and reminds me from time to time of a match I had with Ronnie Garvin years ago not because we did anything crazy, but for the technical excellence he saw in it.

To call Mike a wordsmith is a slight, because he is more an artist with verbs and hammerlocks. I understand the title of this book "Final Bell," but with the Mooneyham twist on the articles herein it's not anything final because my friends, peers and mentors enshrined here will never be forgotten.

It's not just the biggest stars, in the biggest matches, in the most famous arenas that come to life in these stories, but also the blue collar performers that made the top guys look good. It's the minds behind the scenes that brought the personalities together to make the in-ring magic, and the voices whose rich tones embellished those in-ring heroics for the television viewers.

I have been blessed to have wrestled, befriended or been mentored by most everyone in this book. So join Mike and a colorful cast of characters on a journey through some of the greatest times in pro wrestling history with many of the giants that blazed the trail and wrote the history which is here in "Final Bell."

– Les Thatcher

For my money, Mike Mooneyham is the most trusted, pro wrestling newspaper journalist to ever cover the wacky genre of 'rasslin' that many of us still love for our own crazy reasons.

Mike did it for generations with class, professionalism and honesty and with no political agendas.

What a novel concept, to have a media member report the hard to come by facts with no "dog in the hunt."

Mike made reading about the business of pro wrestling and the many amazing personalities that drove the engine, with the accuracy that few of his peers have ever accomplished.

When this old school, pro wrestling fan thinks of true, 'rasslin' journalists who made these bigger than life characters come to life, I think of these names....

Solie, Caudle, Russell, and Mooneyham.

None better…

– Jim Ross

Part I
CHAMPIONS

Jack Brisco

Verne Gagne

Ivan Koloff

Fabulous Moolah

Dusty Rhodes

Bruno Sammartino

Randy Savage

Lou Thesz

Jack Brisco
All-American hero

Feb. 7, 2010

J ack Brisco was one of the greatest wrestlers in the history of the business.

But make no mistake about it. Jack Brisco also was a hero. An honest-to-goodness hero who pulled himself up by his bootstraps as a rawboned youngster in Oklahoma, worked incredibly hard to beat the odds, and went on to live his dream as a world-class athlete in both amateur and professional wrestling.

Brisco, who died Monday at the age of 68 due to complications following open heart surgery, leaves behind a legacy in wrestling only a select few can share.

A three-time state high school champion in wrestling-rich Oklahoma. An All-American collegiate wrestler and NCAA heavyweight champ at Oklahoma State where he lost only one match during his career. A two-time NWA world heavyweight champion in the professional ranks who was regarded as one of the greatest technical wrestlers of our time.

But Brisco also knew when to call it quits. Unlike many who had come before and many who came after, he was able to leave the business on his own terms, and never looked back.

Jack Brisco was only 43 years old when he realized, in the midst of a fierce 1984 snowstorm in Newark, N.J., and unable to feel his face or his hands, that he was physically — and mentally — ready to leave pro wrestling's long and grueling road behind. He decided then and there to cancel his future engagements, catch the next plane, and call it a day.

"I went home and thawed out," he later joked.

And he never came back.

"I feel like I got out at the right time. I felt myself slowing down," Brisco recalled. "My mind was still there and I knew what to do, but my body was flagging behind, and that's one thing that I never wanted to do, to outstay my ability."

Brisco also did something he never thought he'd be able to do. For the previous 22 years, he had lived by the watch, always living by somebody else's timetable, be it plane schedules, check-in times, match times or television tapings. But when he returned home to Florida, he took his big gold Rolex off, and he never wore one again.

But that was Jack Brisco. Devoid of ego and humble to a fault, Brisco was a man's man who rose above childhood poverty and his hardscrabble station in life to succeed in a sport where one's worth is measured by his mental and physical toughness.

Jack Brisco was born for the wrestling business. With natural, God-given skills, handsome features and an All-American background, he was tailor-made for the sport. Longtime Florida star and promoter Eddie Graham, who championed amateur wrestling, immediately made the young star his top babyface attraction.

Graham's creative genius as a booker, paired with legendary announcer Gordon Solie's astute commentary and ability to sell angles and characters, helped put Brisco, with his boyish good looks, innate ability and charisma, on a fast track for the world heavyweight title.

Before he could get to the title, however, he had to get through then-champion Dory Funk Jr. And those battles, waged over a period of several years, would result in one of the most classic series of matches in modern-day pro wrestling.

Gold standard

Considered by many the gold standard in technical wrestling, the Funk-Brisco program spelled sellout business throughout the country, firmly cementing the names Funk and Brisco in wrestling lore.

The travel was grueling, the matches usually lasted an hour to 90 minutes, but it was the apex of two tremendous careers.

"I never had a bad match with Jack," said Funk, who estimates he and Brisco engaged in several hundred bouts together over the years. "Every single match was spectacular for the wrestling fans. He was an ideal challenger for me to work with. It was always a pleasure to be in the ring with him. And he always had a super attitude. The opportunity for me to have Jack to work with was tremendous."

Neither ever took a night off. Even when a ring once broke down in Funk's home territory of West Texas, and he was in the position of challenger for Brisco's world title, the two continued the match.

"We were running the ropes, and I noticed Jack was going down in the valley," jokes Funk. "Jack was trying to do everything right even though the ring was busted. It was so funny. He was still trying to continue the wrestling match."

But with a pair of exceptional athletes the likes of Brisco and Funk, both of whom could make a broomstick look good in the ring, it was business as usual.

"We went ahead and worked the match in a busted ring," said Funk. "We returned the match, and the publicity was around a 'reinforced' ring. We actually worked a return out of it."

It was like that everywhere they wrestled. Every night of the week with capacity crowds clamoring to see these two rivals in action.

"We were working without national TV," said Funk. "But it was the match to see. It was pretty much an automatic sellout. Fans all over the country loved to watch that match."

And forget modern technology. The only communication back then happened in the ring.

"In those days, everybody dressed in separate dressing rooms," said Funk. "If you wanted to see your opponent, it was nearly impossible. First time I'd see Jack was in the ring, and it was always terrific."

"It was a blast working with Jack," added Funk. "You'd just push him a little bit, and he was going to push back. To really get a competitive match, all you had to do was just push Jack a bit and he'd fire back, and the people knew it was real."

And was there a secret way to get under Brisco's skin and raise his dander?

"I could get him excited," laughed Funk. "All I'd have to do was mess his hair a little bit."

Working with Brisco was the highlight of Funk's four-and-a-half-year reign as world heavyweight champion.

"He was a ball to work with. It became a real pleasure to be able to stay in the ring and have that spotlight for an hour. All the hard work in professional wrestling is getting there, but once you're there the thrill of being able to perform in front of the wrestling fans is really something."

Quiet confidence

Pro wrestling Hall of Famer Bob Roop, a heavyweight Greco-Roman wrestler at the 1968 Summer Olympics, fondly recalls meeting Brisco in Florida during the early '70s.

"When I broke into the business, Jack and I took an immediate liking to one another," said Roop. "He was Championship Wrestling From Florida's star baby-face, an experienced hand, and to have him treat me like a peer was especially gratifying. My attitude at the time was that a newcomer like myself had dues to pay and deserved no notice from the veterans, so having Jack treat me as an equal was special. We had a lot of fun together for most of my first year in the business. Once I became a heel, we weren't able to pal around much."

Strangely enough, says Roop, it wasn't until he recently read wrestling historian Bill Murdock's 2004 book on Brisco that he realized just how little he knew of this intensely private, yet self-assured, individual.

"What an eye opener," said Roop. "Jack never talked of his background with me, not one word about his family origins. He was an eight-year veteran when I began and perhaps had left his amateur days far behind him, but I think it interesting that I spent so much time on the road with him and knew so little about where he came from, and heard so little about his amateur days. After reading the book, I realized Jack was a very private man."

Roop says it made him respect Brisco even more.

"He was a great amateur wrestler. I had no idea of his struggle just to stay in school, how he managed to do family, school, work and athletics at the same time is a real testament to character and steadfastness. I was a decent amateur, succeeding at every level, state champ, varsity heavyweight in college, AAU national champion and Olympian. My background provides credibility in saying Jack was a truly great amateur. It was an important part of his life, perhaps a major driving force for his early years, and my accomplishments pale compared to the success created by his focus, dedication and effort."

No one, says Dory Funk Jr., appreciated a strong amateur background more than his father, Dory Funk Sr., who was an Indiana high school state champion wrestler for three years, as well as an Indiana State University Amateur Athletic Union champion.

"Jack brought so much credibility to the wrestling business," said Funk. "Being an NCAA wrestling champion at such a young age was unbelievable. To bring all that credibility and become such a great worker was awesome. My dad always thought the NCAA style of wrestling was the best. He thought the collegiate wrestlers were the best, and I've always tended to think the same thing."

There were no pretenses. What you saw was what you got with Jack Brisco.

Murdock, author of "Brisco," says the wrestler was everything he was advertised to be.

"You grow up and you have these idols and heroes, and you think you know who they are. Many times they turn out to be just the opposite of who you think they are. But Jack was who I thought he was … who I wanted him to be. He was the same guy."

Jack and Jerry

One of Jack's most enjoyable runs in his pro career was teaming with younger brother Gerald. "Jerry" Brisco was an accomplished amateur and pro in his own right, and his tag-team combination with Jack garnered a number of titles, from Texas to Florida to the Carolinas.

"Jack told me that he had more fun working with Jerry — working the tag teams and working heel — than he had at any time in his career," said Murdock. "He said it was such a great way to end his career. Teaming with his brother meant more to him than the world title.

"That's what impressed me so much about Jack. I always had been a fan of Jack, and he had always been an idol to me, but to see how close his family was … how much they loved their mom and their brothers and sisters, and overcoming the hardscrabble life they had early on."

As great a role as Brisco played inside the squared circle, he also would play an influential role in a pair of unrelated events that would change the direction of the wrestling business in the 1980s.

As a part owner of the Florida and Georgia promotions, Brisco was a key player in the 1984 acquisition of WTBS wrestling programming rights by WWE owner Vince McMahon, a pivotal point in wrestling history commonly referred to as "Black Saturday." Brisco, along with brother Jerry, covertly sold Georgia Championship Wrestling to McMahon, claiming business partner Ole Anderson (Al "Rock" Rogowski) was running the company into the ground. The transaction helped give McMahon a valued cable time slot on TBS as WWE began its national expansion.

Brisco also was responsible for helping launch the career of Terry "Hulk Hogan" Bollea in the late 1970s. Brisco spotted Bollea playing bass in a rock band at a local Tampa bar and arranged for him to train with Hiro Matsuda. And the rest was history.

Brisco finished out his career as a headliner, teaming with Jerry in the Mid-Atlantic area for a memorable series of matches with Ricky Steamboat and Jay Youngblood, and winding down in the World Wrestling Federation (now WWE).

Unlike many stars who went to the well once too often, Brisco retired from the business and never looked back, refusing to return for a retirement match or one last shot at the brass ring.

Even when he had relinquished the world title in the '70s, it was on Brisco's terms, not the National Wrestling Alliance.

"When he knew it was time for him to go, time for him to drop the title, Jack was the one who decided that," said Murdock. "It wasn't the NWA. It was Jack Brisco. They weren't moving him down the card when he relinquished the title. He was still the main event. But it was time to go."

Always a wrestler

Jack Brisco was a far cry from today's overly privileged and overly pampered star athletes. He didn't crave the spotlight, was happy for others' success and always seemed to be, for whatever reason, just happy to be part of the group. He was happy in his own skin, and it showed.

He was grateful to be part of a business that afforded him the opportunity to see the world, to perform at the highest level and to be a member of a special fraternity. The business gave him a good life, along with the love of his life, his wife Jan.

Always willing to make a sacrifice, he never forgot the path that led him there. Whether it was working in a coal mine, serving as a carpenter's helper, or putting in after-practice hours as a janitor while, at the same time, Sports Illustrated was hailing him as one of the greatest collegiate wrestlers in the country. Or as a young star in the pro ranks, working the small towns in Arkansas that paid twenty-five bucks a shot, giving it 100 percent when fans stayed home due to a snowstorm.

Full throttle was the only gear Jack Brisco ever knew.

And in later years, when he could have just as easily picked up a quick paycheck in the wrestling business serving as a consultant, he was content with staying home and helping run the Brisco Brothers Body Shop, a local Tampa business he and his brother Jerry, a longtime WWE talent scout, operated.

He also was a traditionalist who believed that wrestlers should be athletes first, entertainers second, yet he didn't begrudge today's stars the big-money contracts and less-taxing schedules that didn't exist in Brisco's era. He was as honored and excited as anyone when he and Jerry were inducted into the WWE Hall of Fame in March 2008.

"If he had wanted to, he could have, upon retiring as a pro, trotted out his amateur background and been welcomed to any and all national tournaments as an honored guest," said Roop. "Again I come back to the fact that Jack was a private person. Therefore it is left to us to invade that privacy to substantiate that Jack was much more than former NCAA and NWA champion ... he was also a champion human being — decent, honest and a man of character. His memory will, for me, be greeted with fondness, respect and regret that he's gone."

"Jack was a great champion who held the title with so much dignity," said Murdock. "Great champions are rare, but good men are even more so."

Dory Funk recalls that the last time he saw Brisco was at Wrestlemania 25 in Houston.

"I had kind of been under the impression that Jack had been through the worst of his medical problems. I just didn't imagine anything like that would happen."

Funk's voice trails off when he thinks about the old days. He had hoped to do another loop with his revered rival somewhere down the line.

"He was such a fun guy to know. I really will miss him. It's disappointing the medical things he had to go through. I would love to still have a Jack Brisco around to make these events with."

Murdock, recalling the last lines in his book, believes that Jack Brisco remained true to the essence of what — and who — he was.

"The ring gets in your blood and once it's there it courses through your veins and deep into your heart. That is why I am happily reminded with every beat of my heart, that I am, and will be while I breathe, a wrestler."

"Jack was a hero to everybody," said Funk.

Verne Gagne

Verne Gagne helped shape mat industry

May 3, 2015

One of wrestling's most iconic figures, Verne Gagne also worked as a major promoter and helped shape the careers of some of the profession's biggest stars.

The impact of Verne Gagne's influence on professional wrestling may never be fully known.

But it can be said that if there had never been a Verne Gagne, pro wrestling most certainly would be the poorer for it.

Gagne, who passed away last week at the age of 89 after an extended battle with Alzheimer's disease, was an Olympic-caliber athlete who excelled in football and wrestling in college, and parlayed those skills to the pro wrestling arena where for decades he was one of the sport's most celebrated performers and promoters.

The straight-laced, no-nonsense Gagne wore many hats during his lengthy career in the Midwest-based American Wrestling Association — as president, owner and main-event star. He held the AWA world title 10 times between 1960 and 1981 and was champion for a record 10 years during that period.

Even into his '70s, only Father Time and the changing tide of the wrestling business were able to slow him down. And later, but much more cruelly, Alzheimer's disease robbed him of his mind and bountiful memories.

"Verne was one of the pioneers," said Hall of Fame announcer Gene Okerlund, 72. "He put (pro wrestling) on the map in the early days when no one had seen it before."

"He was a wrestler's wrestler," said Sean "X-Pac" Waltman, who grew up in Minnesota watching Gagne and the stars of the AWA.

The lives he touched in the wrestling business are far too numerous to mention. From those he trained and mentored, to those he wrestled and helped launch to stardom, for decades Gagne was one of the most influential players in the wrestling profession.

Had it not been for Gagne, chances are there never would have been a "Nature Boy" Ric Flair.

Former wrestler and weight-lifter Ken Patera, once known as "the world's strongest man" and a gold medalist in the 1971 Pan American Games, recalled rooming with Flair during the early '70s in southern Minnesota before either got into the mat game.

He knew that Flair, then known as Richard Fliehr, wanted to break into the wrestling business.

"He never stopped bugging me about introducing him to Verne Gagne," says Patera.

Flair had attended the University of Minnesota with Gagne's son, Greg, and Jim Brunzell, both future wrestlers.

Patera obliged and took the then-23-year-old Flair to Gagne's wrestling office. Initially Gagne refused to take Flair since he already had his limit of students at his training camp.

Patera, though, recalls doing a sales job on the veteran promoter, telling him about "the stack of wrestling magazines four feet high" that Flair had collected. ("I saw the pile at his parents' house. It was actually four feet high," Patera verified.)

"You gotta take this kid," he implored Gagne. "He knows Greg, he knows Jim. "We're roommates, he's a good, big, athletic kid. He's a natural for this business. He can do all the spots and moves like Ray Stevens."

Gagne agreed to consider Patera's request despite the fact that his camp was at capacity.

"Trust me, he won't be in the way," Patera assured Gagne, who trained the aspiring grapplers on his sprawling, 120-acre farm.

Gagne eventually consented, and the rest is history.

That class of trainees included the likes of Flair, Greg Gagne, Brunzell, Hossein Khosrow Vaziri (later known as The Iron Sheik) and former NFL linebacker Bob Bruggers. Patera would join the camp a couple of weeks after returning from the ill-fated 1972 Summer Olympics in Munich.

Out of the 150 or so wrestlers who were trained by Gagne, most had strong amateur backgrounds and most reached main-event status in the pro ranks.

Flair would later admit that he had never worked so hard in his life as he did during that harsh Midwestern winter, with Gagne and trainer Billy Robinson putting him through the paces of 500 free squats, 200 push-ups and 200 sit-ups.

The training, Greg Gagne told the Minneapolis Star-Tribune, was grueling.

"Wrestling was going strong and we had a huge number of guys show up … over 100," said Gagne. "The daily workout was six hours. The first hour was calisthenics. We lost half of the guys in the first hour of the first day."

The ring, notes Patera, was inside one of Gagne's unheated horse barns.

Along with learning the basics, trainees might even find themselves chopping wood and doing other physically taxing chores around the farm.

"He was a taskmaster without a question," said Okerlund, who got his start in the business working for Gagne. "He demanded a lot out of people and he got a lot out of people."

Those grueling workouts, though, would set the stage for Flair's future reputation of being one of the most well-conditioned performers in the business.

"That was Ric's role in life. He was meant to be in this business. He was meant to be the Nature Boy," says Patera.

To Flair, Gagne was the man who instilled a never-say-die attitude in him. And, more than anything else, Gagne taught Flair and countless others to respect the business.

"Everyone needs someone to instill that type of attitude in them. For me it was Verne Gagne," says Flair. "Verne took a green, raw kid who wanted to quit after two days of wrestling camp, and made me believe in myself. He made me who I am."

Flair, indeed, tried to quit the camp, but Gagne convinced him otherwise.

"The sheer brutality of wrestling training made me want to quit a second time, but even more brutal was the thought of Verne coming for me and dragging me back like he had done once before," recalls Flair. "Thank God I never had to find out. But that experience gave me tremendous respect for the business early on, and a respect I still have to this day. He instilled the basics and the toughness in me that I would be able to take throughout my career. I will always thank him for that."

Former NWA world champion Dory Funk Jr. recalls getting his feet wet in the business in the early '60s when his father and trainer, Dory Funk Sr., brought Gagne to the Amarillo territory to wrestle his son.

"You will never learn to be a great worker unless you have the opportunity to wrestle the best in the business," Funk Sr. told his son.

"Learning from Verne Gagne impacted my whole life in such a positive way," said Funk Jr. "Verne Gagne was a man of his word, a great professional wrestler and a world-class athlete."

Funk says he earned a true wrestling education that night in the ring with Gagne.

"That night I had the privilege of wrestling Verne Gagne to a 60-minute draw for the AWA world championship in front of a capacity crowd at the Amarillo Sports Arena," said Funk.

"Dad always said that the really great amateur wrestlers within the wrestling business always had respect for each other. Verne Gagne was a friend of my father born of admiration for each other in business, professional wrestling and amateur wrestling."

Folk legend status

Just how good was Gagne?

A statement attributed to the legendary Jim Londos provides a pretty good clue.

"You take this kid Verne Gagne. Well, he could have tied most of the wrestlers of 20 years ago in knots."

Now that was high praise.

LaVerne Clarence "Verne" Gagne was one of the most decorated athletes in Minnesota sports history.

The essence of sportsmanship and epitome of wholesomeness, the clean-cut, personable Gagne became an institution in his native Minnesota.

Gagne, whose name is engraved on the school's wall of champions, won four Big Ten championships and was the program's first three-time All-America (1947, 1948 and 1949) and first two-time NCAA champion (1948 and 1949).

He was an alternate for the U.S. freestyle wrestling team at the 1948 Olympics in London, and won the AAU championship in 1949.

"Verne represents what's great about the University of Minnesota and our wrestling program," Director of Athletics Norwood Teague said in a school release. "He was an incredible athlete — Big Ten champ, national champ, Olympian — but he also selflessly served his country, took academics seriously and used the opportunity provided through college athletics to lead a successful life and give back to his alma mater. Verne's legacy is a lasting example our student-athletes can all aspire to achieve."

Although the bulk of his collegiate success came on the mat, Gagne also earned All-Big Ten honors in football at Minnesota.

Gagne, a product of a hardscrabble upbringing that would help him develop the physical and mental toughness for which he became famous, received a football scholarship from the University of Minnesota where he joined coach George Hauser's Golden Gophers and became the youngest man ever to start for the university's football team.

He left after one year, however, to join the Marines at the end of World War II, but returned to school in 1946, winning three more conference titles and a pair of NCAA championships and earning a spot on the 1948 Olympic wrestling team.

When his collegiate career was over, and after discovering that he could make more money and have greater longevity in pro wrestling than with George Halas' Chicago Bears or Curly Lambeau's Green Bay Packers, Gagne turned to pro wrestling in 1950 and never looked back.

During his prime Gagne was one of the best in-ring workers in the sport. With his good looks and impressive physique, he became a matinee idol in the '50s during the Golden Age of televised wrestling, earning widespread exposure and one of the first six-figure salaries in the business.

Gagne was, indeed, the gold standard in an era when credibility, believability and pure skill were hallmarks of the profession.

In later years, though, Gagne and his AWA promotion would become a casualty of Vince McMahon's national expansion. Gagne refused to adapt to the changing industry, and stars left en masse, business sharply declined, and the AWA closed its doors in 1991. Gagne left the profession he had loved, and eventually sold the AWA video library to WWE in 2003.

Gagne had been living with his daughter in Chanhassen, Minn., ever since a fatal confrontation in 2009 in a Bloomington retirement home.

Gagne, then 82, pushed Helmut Gutmann, a 97-year-old fellow resident in the memory-loss unit of the facility. Gutmann fell to the floor, broke his hip and later died.

While the death was ruled a homicide, Gagne was never charged due to his mental condition as he had no recollection any such thing happened.

Gagne had been diagnosed with Alzheimer's, although some speculated that his condition could have been a result of or worsened by CTE (chronic traumatic encephalopathy), a degenerative brain disease found in athletes (and others) with a history of repetitive brain trauma.

His wife of 56 years, Mary, died in 2002.

Ivan Koloff
WWE, Ivan Koloff and an opportunity missed

Feb. 26, 2017

He was a champion in every territory he appeared, headlined Madison Square Garden 13 times, and scored one of the biggest upsets in pro wrestling history when he dethroned Bruno Sammartino in 1971.

Yet Ivan Koloff, who passed away Feb. 18 at the age of 74, never made WWE's Hall of Fame. Reserved for wrestling greats, particularly those who made valuable contributions to WWE, the Hall was established in 1993 and since then has inducted more than 150 men and women. Koloff is not among them.

And that's an injustice. Not only to Koloff, but to an organization and a profession that is damaged by his omission. While many might argue that the WWE Hall is politically driven and there are other mat shrines that rightfully honor Koloff, the fact is that the "Russian Bear" deserved his spot in the sun and for years had hoped that honor would find him.

Could WWE have been possibly waiting for a more opportune time? There was no better time than several years ago when Sammartino, the man Koloff defeated for the organization's most coveted crown, was finally inducted following a lengthy impasse with the company. Four years have passed since then, and the Hall has inducted many others far less deserving than Koloff, who will go down in pro wrestling history as one of the greatest heels ever.

Every passing year, however, made it less likely that Koloff would ever get the nod. Battling liver disease for the past decade, Koloff's health had deteriorated. Even if WWE had come to its senses and inducted him in this year's class, it would have been too late. "He wouldn't have the strength to make it," Renae Koloff said several weeks before her husband's passing.

Koloff's name was attached to a class-action concussion lawsuit against WWE several years ago. It would be fair to surmise it could have kept WWE at arm's length in the past couple of years. But what about the 20-plus previous years the Hall has been in existence? What possible reason could WWE claim to keep out one of the top stars in its history?

WWE went through the obligatory motions and recognized his passing with a brief graphic on last week's Monday Night Raw. The company might even try to remove some of that ample egg off its face by honoring Koloff with an induction at a later time. But at that point it would only come across as self-serving. A matter of too little, too late.

Saving souls

Ivan Koloff's accomplishments are many. During a full-time three-decade ring career he made a living out of collecting championships. But to the mild-mannered, Canadian-born wrestler, what he did during the ensuing years meant even more. And that was saving souls.

Koloff became a born-again Christian in 1996. He always enjoyed talking about his conversion and his faith. The wrestling career had taken a heavy emotional and physical toll on him. While achieving success in the wrestling business, he had battled a litany of injuries, the most serious being a ruptured disc he suffered in 1973 that plagued him for most of his career. There also were broken shoulders, torn biceps, knee injuries and dislocations. In his role as a world-class villain, the "Russian Bear" whom fans loved to hate as the Cold War stand-in for the Soviet Union, he had been attacked by rabid fans who assaulted him with knives, bent nails, and chairs.

The sheer intensity of the business was grueling enough. But there also were the constant distractions and temptations on the road, and the consequences that went with them.

But he knew something was missing. He was a champion many times and made lots of money, he says, but he was "lost." That all changed in 1996. Ivan's introduction to his new life occurred when protégé Nikita Koloff, who had left wrestling several years earlier to become a part-time evangelist, asked him to attend a revival at an Assembly of God church in Kannapolis, N.C.

Koloff, who was raised Roman Catholic in his native Canada, had left the church when he was 17 years old and had drifted. But when the preacher asked him to repeat a prayer to accept the Lord, he says, he fell backwards as if he had been knocked down by Andre The Giant. Like a good partner, though, Nikita was there to catch him.

"I guess that was the Lord's way of just letting me know through the Holy Spirit that 'I'm for real, man' ... I realized it was more of a relationship than the action of just going to church."

From that point on, life dramatically changed for the menacing grappler who made a living by making millions hate him. But the soft-spoken man with the gentle soul maintained the shaved pate and beard for effect. "People come up to me and ask me if I'm really Ivan Koloff. They eye me up and down. Especially old ladies. They're not sure if they've forgiven me or not," he'd joke.

Koloff's last 20 years were spent as an ordained minister who visited churches and prisons, presided over wedding ceremonies, and served a number of charitable organizations that included the Children's Miracle Network, St. Jude's Children's Hospital and Toys for Tots.

It was a far cry from his previous life. "We'd travel 250, 300 miles a night going from town to town, and sometimes we'd have a little party after the match," he would recall. "Fights, tearing hotels up, crazy stuff. You'd be put in jail for that kind of thing today."

His new life, though, was ministering to those suffering from addictions that went along with the challenges of life. "I wanted to let everyone know what the Lord has done to me and how he delivered me from drugs and alcohol. He gave me the strength to overcome that when I turned my life over to him."

He also attended a number of fan festivals and conventions, never forgetting his fans who never forgot him.

Always brought up was that iconic moment in wrestling history when Ivan Koloff stunned a sold-out crowd at the sport's most storied venue on Jan. 18, 1971.

"I'm as excited today as I was when I walked into Madison Square Garden and won the belt from Bruno Sammartino and that was my big dream back then," he'd say. "Now my dream is to reach people for the Lord Jesus Christ."

To many, including friend Nikita Koloff, "Uncle Ivan" achieved the greatness he had sought.

"He didn't make the Hall of Fame, but he did make the Hall of Faith."

Fabulous Moolah
Moolah enjoyed Fabulous career

Nov. 18, 2007

For as long as I can remember, Mary Lillian Ellison has been "one of us." Born in the small Kershaw County town of Tookiedoo, and living most of her life in Columbia, she was as much a part of the state as the palmetto trees that line its landscape and the history that surrounds its every corner.

She was, in fact, a piece of history herself, becoming one of the greatest female performers to ever step into a professional wrestling ring and the most powerful woman outside the squared circle.

With her recent passing at the age of 84, Lillian Ellison, better known to millions of fans around the world as The Fabulous Moolah, takes that next step into immortality, leaving behind a half-century of monumental accomplishments and lasting memories.

She was alternately known as Lil, Lillian, Nana and other names of endearment, but to me, she was and always will be simply "Moolah." It was the perfect name she picked out for herself shortly after becoming a wrestler nearly six decades ago, and the one that really fit her the most. It was back then that promoter Jack Pfeffer told her that her real name wasn't memorable or flashy enough and asked her why she even wanted to wrestle. Annoyed, she blurted out, "For the money. I want to wrestle for the moolah."

It was one of those rare seminal moments that help define a career. A star was born, and a legend had begun.

Simply fabulous

It can be debated whether The Fabulous Moolah was the greatest professional women's wrestler of all time. She stands alone, though, being the most influential female figure in the history of the industry, having maintained an ironclad control over women's wrestling in this country for decades.

"In the world of women's wrestling, there will always be one irrefutable legend that stands head and shoulders above the rest: The Fabulous Moolah," WWE said in a statement. Moolah, who had been connected with the McMahon family for a half century, was considered a part of that storied dynasty.

The rough, rowdy and raucous women's wrestling of Moolah's era was, of course, a far cry from silicon-inflated divas and over-the-top theatrics. But there's little argument that Moolah paved the way for the girls. She was the face of women's wrestling for many years, and her credentials were lofty.

Moolah was the longest reigning champion (1956-1984) in the history of the business, and was the first woman allowed to wrestle at Madison Square Garden. Along with Vince McMahon Sr., she reinstated women's pro wrestling back into New York after it had been banned. And, 35 years after breaking into the business, it was her feud with Wendi Richter, which involved pop superstar Cyndi Lauper, which was the catalyst behind the first Wrestlemania.

At age 61, Moolah found herself smack dab in the middle of the "Rock 'n' Wrestling Connection," a boom period of unprecedented success and newfound mainstream popularity for the World Wrestling Federation.

Moolah continued to wrestle on special occasions, including her 80th birthday, when she worked a short match with WWE diva Victoria (Lisa Varon), fulfilling a personal goal by taking part in a WWE match as an octogenarian in 2002.

"I'd like to thank Moolah for paving the way to make the divas what we are today," Victoria told the WWE website. "We're wrestlers, not just beautiful bodies. She sacrificed herself and her well-being to make it possible for us to go out there and be respected. I miss her and I loved her."

Moolah, the first female inductee into the WWE Hall of Fame, also was a central figure in the 2005 documentary "Lipstick and Dynamite" which chronicled the rise of women's professional wrestling throughout the last century. Admittedly she had her share of detractors in the business. Having trained the majority of women wrestlers who came up through the '60s and '70s, Moolah was widely criticized by many of her charges for taking what they claimed were inordinate booking fees, along with taking the best bookings for herself as the perennial world champion.

But Moolah, with her wonderfully fearless personality, was a strong woman in a man's business, and always maintained that she was protecting her girls and putting them in a position to succeed in a male-oriented arena.

"Lillian was strong. She was a shining role model and example for women everywhere," Stephanie McMahon-Levesque, daughter of WWE chief Vince McMahon, said at Moolah's funeral. "Lillian was all about fighting for what she believed in. She was full of life and full of passion, and she wanted that life, love and passion to go on."

Perhaps her most endearing quality was her love for the wrestling business. It was a passion rarely seen in this profession. Many performers love the business for what it brings them — fame, fortune, glory. Moolah loved the business for no other reason than it was the biggest part of her.

"Wrestling has meant everything to me. It's got me what I dreamed of," she once said. "I know if I had a regular job as a secretary, I would never had gotten what I have now. Wrestling has been my love and my life."

She loved the business so much that she remained a part of it until her death. She won a world title in 1999 at the age of 76 and, along with best friend Johnnie Mae Young, took part in a number of WWE shows over the past decade, mostly in comedy skits, with her last appearance being at the SummerSlam pay-per-view.

"Lil loved wrestling fans and she loved wrestling," said Young. "There wasn't a day or night that went by that she didn't think of wrestling. She was already looking forward to going to the Hall of Fame (ceremony) next year. She was a wrestling fan and a wrestler for all her life."

A well-worn life

Moolah's career has been well documented in this space and elsewhere over the years. She even penned her own autobiography, "Moolah: First Goddess of the Squared Circle," several years ago. To be fair, however, Moolah's real life story could never fit into the confines of a 250-page book, nor could her best tales ever see the light of day, for a variety of reasons. She led far too complex a life and traveled far too many miles.

But that was the thing about Moolah. For as intriguing and colorful a life as she led, she could also be the most genteel, down-to-earth creature, oozing sultry, Southern charm, with a humble unpretentiousness that belied her gaudy image. Whether she knew your name or not, you were either "Honey," "Baby" or "Darlin," and the words dripped from her mouth like sweet maple syrup.

Her early life, though, had been far from easy. She was the youngest of 13 children and the only girl. Her mother died of cancer when she was 8, and the youngster nearly suffered a nervous breakdown. Her dad, in an attempt to break her out of the depression, took her to the weekly wrestling shows at the Township Auditorium in Columbia, and she became hooked after watching then-women's champion Mildred Burke, the top female of that era.

Ellison, who labored as a dollar-a-day cotton picker at the age of 10, knew she could do the things she saw in the ring. In 1956, she cashed in, winning a world championship she would hold 28 years.

She began her career in 1949 under the banner of infamous women's wrestling promoter Billy Wolfe, Burke's husband, in Columbus, Ohio. Wolfe, though, considered Ellison too small and discouraged her from seeking a ring career, so she moved on to work with Pfeffer, an eccentric promoter who loved freakish wrestlers and outlandish gimmicks.

"Billy Wolfe, the guy who all the girls at that time were wrestling for, told me that I was too small to wrestle and told me to go sit on some lawyer's knee and be a secretary. "I said, `No, I'm going to be a wrestler, and I'm going to be the best,'" she once said.

Pfeffer had "Nature Boy" Buddy Rogers in his stable at the time, and the future world champion needed a valet. Ellison took the gig as the leopard skin-clad "Slave Girl" Moolah and later formed a partnership with The Elephant Boy (Tony Olivas) and worked with him for nearly two years.

Moolah won a 13-woman battle royal to win the vacant women's world title in 1956, although June Byers still held claim to the NWA women's championship after having beaten Burke three years earlier. After Byers retired in 1964, Moolah was subsequently recognized as the NWA champion, making her the undisputed world champion.

With pouty red lips and smoldering eyes and sporting flashy, decadent jewelry, the brash and brassy Moolah quickly climbed to stardom as the most recognized female athlete in the business. A performer the fans loved to hate, she was a heel of the first order and liked to stomp, choke and gouge her opponents with a foreign object she kept secreted in her ample bra.

She wore sequined robes, and her trademark wrestling boots were inscribed with a dollar mark. She was a tigress in the ring and a shrewd businesswoman outside it.

It was lifelong friend Young who first hooked Moolah up with the McMahon family.

"Vince (Jr.) is a great man. He loved Lil," said Young. "I was one of the first girls to work for Vince Sr. when he opened up Joe Turner Arena in Washington, D.C. At that time Lil had never worked for Vince Sr. She had been calling me and writing me to use some of her girls. Mildred (Burke) and Billy (Wolfe) had split up at that time, and Vince asked me what I thought about getting Lil and his girls. I told Vince that would be the greatest thing that ever happened. And Lil has been with the family ever since."

Moolah, in fact, sold the rights to her championship to Vince McMahon in 1983.

Lillian Ellison, whose birth name was Ellisor, was married, at best count, five times, and numbered among her close friends Elvis Presley, Jerry Lee Lewis and Hank Williams Sr., who she once claimed proposed marriage to her. The late wrestler Buddy Lee (Joseph Pino), with whom she shared a common-law relationship and a pro wrestling promotion, would later become one of the most successful music promoters in Nashville. Their marriage ended when Moolah caught him in a compromising position with 18-year-old Rita Cortez, whom the two were training, in a wrestling ring at their facility. Her relationship with Lee had lasted nine years, and together they had started Girl Wrestling Enterprises, which filled the void left by Wolfe's death in 1962, booking most of the girls in the business.

With Lee no longer in the picture, Moolah never wavered, becoming a hard-nosed, iron-fisted woman in a profession that had been dominated by men. She was, in fact, so tough that she gained the respect of promoters throughout the country. They knew that Moolah trained her girls well, and they never had any second thoughts about using any of the women she had booked.

Camp Moolah

To newer fans of the wrestling business, a trip to Wrestlemania might be their version of the sport's Holy Grail. To an old-school follower, however, being a guest at 101 Moolah Drive was the best ticket in town.

Moolah lived on a 42-acre estate in north Columbia — appropriately dubbed "Camp Moolah" — that included a 13-room home, eight- and 12-acre lakes, a row of lake houses and a gym equipped with a wrestling ring where she had taught hundreds of men and women to wrestle. She had bought the land nearly 40 years ago, with only a lake house occupying the area at the time, and later decided to build her home there, with her estate located in the back of a tranquil neighborhood in the suburbs of Columbia. Her land had once extended even further until Interstate 77 was built, and she sold several acres to the state to accommodate the highway.

"The Amazing" Mae Young, who started wrestling in the late '30s and helped break Moolah into the sport, had shared the home with Moolah for years. "She was in California and had lost all of her family, and I told her this big place was just sitting here and she could have the whole upstairs," Moolah once explained.

The two, both members of the Pro Wrestling Hall of Fame, were delightful hosts and reservoirs of grappling history. A couple of ordinary senior citizens they weren't.

In many ways a visit inside the gates at the end of Moolah Drive was akin to a trip to a very cool grandmother's house. In this case, though, a pair of grannies who could whip you and your posse if it ever came down to it. And if you needed proof, you only had to venture a few hundred feet away to watch the old girls in action, training (and stretching) aspiring young women (and men) grapplers with ease at their official training facility, a cramped building that resembled a little red barn.

Back at headquarters, though, was a treasure trove of wrestling history and a pair of hostesses who were true pioneers of women's wrestling and blazed paths through a business that wasn't always welcoming to the fairer sex. There were tales of 500-mile nightly trips from town to town, with five girls to a car, along with $10 payoffs. Mae, three months Moolah's senior, was wrestling professionally when World War II broke out. More than 60 years later, she was still taking bumps in WWE rings, going through tables and and proving that age is only in one's mind. Her longevity promoted WWE announcer Jerry Lawler to once quip: "When God said let there be light, Mae Young threw the switch."

Moolah and Mae truly were wrestling's version of The Golden Girls. They could, as an observer once noted, "still take a punch, spit out a tooth and mop the mat with your sorry backside."

To the uninitiated, a visit to the compound might be like a trip to The Twilight Zone, or something out of The Wizard of Oz.

Part of the fun would be watching a new visitor's reaction when a third occupant of the house would make an appearance. "Oh, don't worry about her, that's just my damn midget," Moolah would laugh with her endearing Southern drawl.

Moolah, of course, would be referring to Katie Glass, whom she adopted years ago when the 17-year-old knocked on her door looking for work in the wrestling business. Since Moolah loved diamonds, and her nickname was Lil, she gave the pint-sized performer the name "Diamond Lil," and she became one of the top midget performers of that era. Glass lived with Moolah for more than 40 years and called her "Ma," while Moolah affectionately dubbed her "my damn midget."

"She came to me when she was just 17. She calls me mom," Ellison once explained. "The first day I picked her up at the bus station, I felt so sorry for her. She asked if she could call me mom. I said, 'When you throw that damn cigarette away, you can call me mom if you want to, but my daughter doesn't smoke cigarettes.' She threw it out of the window, and that was it. She's called me mom ever since. She's a sweetheart."

The finish for this grand lady of wrestling came on the evening of Nov. 2. Moolah had undergone shoulder replacement surgery several days earlier. It was a procedure she had put off for years, because doctors had told her it would mean she could never wrestle again. It also would have jeopardized the fulfillment of a dream match Vince McMahon had promised her on her 100th birthday.

But there were post-surgery complications. She died three days later from either a heart attack or a blood clot stemming from the surgery.

"We thought she was going to be able to go through the operation fine. And she did go through it," said Young. "I was up at the hospital for two days and nights with her. When I left up there, I told her, 'I love you, Lil, I'll see you tomorrow.' And she said, 'I love you too.' Those were the last words that were spoken. They called us about an hour after we got home, and they said she'd gone. She was my dear friend. And you don't have many friends in this life. Your friend is gone forever, and it's hard."

The two were bookends, Mae and Moolah, and it's hard to imagine a wrestling world without them. But, just like in wrestling, all good storylines must come to an end.

"I've known Lil since 1949, and I taught her to wrestle. It breaks my heart, but what can you say? We have all to go," reconciled Young. "We're not guaranteed the next day. The old saying is that you were born to die. And that's the truth. When your number is called, you're going to have to go. It's not going to make any difference who you are, how big you are or how small you are. So many people think that you're going to live forever, but you never know when your last day will be."

Along with the health issues, said Young, the past few months had been particularly difficult ones for her friend. The last of her 12 remaining brothers, Chip, had died two months earlier.

"Chip was a real sweetheart," said Young. "Lil was real close to him. I thought an awful lot of him. I loved Chip. I used to take him grocery shopping. His wife had passed away about 15 years ago. He was a sweet guy, and Lil loved Chip."

"She was famous, but I never looked at her that way," Mary "Flossy" Austin, Moolah's only natural daughter who wrestled briefly in the '60s as Darlin' Pat Sherry, told The State newspaper in Columbia. "She was just Mom, someone that was always there for me. Someone I could turn to."

The loss also will be difficult for the 63-year-old Glass. Both Glass and Young have burial plots reserved on either side of Moolah's tomb at a mausoleum in Columbia's Greenlawn Memorial Park.

"Lil took her (Glass) in when she was 17 years old," recalled Young. "She called her 'Ma,' and Lil called her 'her damn midget.' She loved Lil. She waited on her hand and foot."

Young said she always thought she'd go before her friend because she was three months older.

"Vince McMahon promised us a wrestling match on her 100th birthday. I really thought we were going to make it. I know Vince thought we were going to make it. It looks like it's up to me now. I'll carry the ball ... I'll tell you that. I sure will."

Although her physical condition had worsened over the past several years, including a near-death heart scare and a pair of stents put in, Moolah was considered invincible among her family, friends and fans. She had knee surgery and had lost 30 pounds in late 2005.

The loss shook not only the community, where she had become a local celebrity and a beloved fixture over many years, but also to a wrestling industry where her name had become synonymous with the glory days.

Moolah's final earthly appearance was at a chapel in Columbia.

"The Old Rugged Cross" accompanied a white casket with gold accents down the aisle, while a crowd of a couple hundred friends and family paid tribute.

Stephanie McMahon described the love her father and grandfather had for Moolah during a eulogy.

"She felt like she was a part of the McMahon family. And I'd like to say that she is very much a part of the McMahon family. She always will be."

"She loved life and she loved wrestling," said Young. "And she was surrounded by people who loved her. When she left this world, she knew she was loved."

The daughter of Vincent Kennedy McMahon later sat reverently at graveside as the last mourners filed by to pay their final respects. I hugged her and thanked her and her family for taking care of and loving Moolah all these years.

"That wasn't hard," she replied. "It was so easy loving Lillian."

The Fabulous Moolah belonged to everybody. She belonged to the wrestling business. She wouldn't have had it any other way.

Dusty Rhodes
Sweet dreams to an American icon

June 13, 2015

I've wined and dined with kings and queens, and I've slept in alleys and ate pork and beans."

— "American Dream" Dusty Rhodes.

As Jerry Brisco pulled into the parking lot of what was once known as the Fort Homer Hesterly Armory — at one time one of the Southeast's premier wrestling venues — he couldn't help but smile.

There for an event to help raise money to create a memorial at the storied Tampa building that for decades hosted Championship Wrestling from Florida, Brisco thought about the many Tuesday nights when the area's biggest celebrity sold out the arena with regularity.

Just like in the old days, the event was a sellout. But this time, it would be without Dusty Rhodes, the legend who came in with a splash during the early '70s and rode out on the end of a lightning bolt earlier that day.

"What a tribute to the Dream," said Brisco. "He was advertised to be here, and he sold out his last event. When I drove up, I saw the 'sold out' sign, and said to myself, 'Dream, you did it again.'"

Virgil Riley Runnels Jr., better known to millions of fans worldwide as "The American Dream" Dusty Rhodes, passed away last Thursday at the age of 69.

And a little bit of the business died with him.

"I'll love him and miss him forever," said Brisco, who made sure to take a selfie with Dusty just days earlier in what would be their final meeting. It's now a photograph that holds even greater meaning for Brisco.

"We didn't talk business, we just talked family and friendship," he said. "We've known each other for nearly 50 years. Now that I look back on it, those were the greatest two hours I ever had."

Common man hero

Reports say that Rhodes died from complications suffered after a fall Wednesday morning at his residence. His family was by his side when it was time for The Dream, one last time, to go home.

"He was our hero and the greatest father in the world," said eldest son and WWE performer Dustin Runnels. "He is the reason why I am who I am today. He taught me so many lessons in life. He was my mentor, my hero and a dad that I strive to be like."

His passing left not only the wrestling community — but millions of fans around the world who knew and loved The Dream — in shock and mourning.

Dusty Rhodes was much more than a wrestling icon. He was a household name that had long transcended the wrestling business. He was, simply put, a force of nature.

Nobody loved his job more than Dusty. "He doesn't want the magic to end," son Cody once said. "He loves it so much."

The Texas native really was "the son of a plumber," a legitimate hero to the blue-collar crowd who paid their hard-earned money each week to see Dusty do battle with the forces of evil, back in the days when wrestling was clearly split between good and bad, with no shades of grey.

An everyman with a less-than-stellar physique but armed with a surplus of charisma, he didn't look like the typical athlete, but embraced the "working class man" persona with a lisp-tinged spiel that could talk fans into the building while promising to lay the smack down and "take care of bidness."

"My belly's just a little big, my hiney's just a little big," he said during his famous "Hard Times" promo in 1985. "But brother, I am bad and they know I'm bad."

Didn't matter that Dusty didn't have a chiseled physique or a fancy ring entrance. He knew what his audience wanted. And they wanted a taste of that very dream he symbolized.

Today's wrestling "superstars," as they are commonly referred to, owe a lot to

Dusty. Many, such as WWE world champion Seth Rollins, expressed their gratitude last week.

"I was ever so fortunate to be a friend to this man, to learn from him as a performer and as a human being."

"Shocked. Honored to have performed in front of him," tweeted Rusev.

"The Dream will live forever in my heart. Thank you for the wisdom and for always making me smile. The stratosphere is reserved for you," echoed Samoa Joe.

Dusty Rhodes paved the road for them and hundreds of others who watched him over the years, trained with him, or merely studied tapes.

The list goes on and on, but there really wasn't anyone worth his or her salt who hadn't learned from The Dream.

Even a young Ric Flair emulated Rhodes.

"All I wanted to be is Rambling Ricky Rhodes," said the future 16-time world champion. "He was the guy I idolized."

"You can make it on your own," Rhodes encouraged Flair, whose early career preference was eventually overturned by booker George Scott, who thought the flamboyant Minnesotan might be better suited for a robe and "Nature Boy" moniker.

"He mentored me and taught me how to be a star," said Flair. "Dusty used to say, 'If you are going to pass by ... why not in a Cadillac?'"

Dusty Rhodes was one of those rarest of performers who had that intangible quality that can't be taught and can't be replicated. Few ever came close to matching his ability to speak into a microphone and entertain an audience.

"If Dusty came along today, he'd be as big a star now as he was back then," said Flair. "He knew how to sell, he had a comeback, he had fire in his interviews. He could walk out in his robe right now, or he could walk out in his jeans and cowboy boots. He was way ahead of his time."

Hard times

It'll take a while before the shock and sadness begin to subside. It's almost as if folks expected Dusty Rhodes to live forever. Many have lost a piece of their childhood

It's a more pleasant thought, however, to imagine The Dream exiting as he had arrived — on the end of that lightning bolt, on a silver-studded saddle, riding off into the stratosphere.

After all, that's what The Dream was really all about. He was the ultimate good guy, like his hero, the late John Wayne, whom he quoted in his masterful "Hard Times" promo as he bucked the odds and challenged the bad guys to a showdown.

"There were two bad people ... One was John Wayne, and he's dead, brother, and the other's right here."

But even heroes are mortal. Now, sadly for his legion of fans and friends and the many lives he touched, those "Hard Times" are now.

No amount of words could ever adequately describe what Dusty Rhodes meant to the wrestling business. Wrestler, performer, entertainer, booker, promoter, power broker, innovator, teacher, trainer, friend. He was all of them, and he left lasting impressions and memories that will become part of wrestling lore for decades to come.

"There will never be another Dusty Rhodes," said Flair. "He was a true original."

"The Dream taught me so much in this life and I will be forever grateful for his friendship and his great big heart. He taught me that family is more than the blood in our veins but the people that grow in our hearts," said longtime friend Janie Engle.

Indeed, as Gordon Solie might say, Dusty Rhodes was many things to many people.

But to his children, who loved him unconditionally, he was everything they had ever dreamed of.

"He had one thing that he wanted to be, and that was he wanted to be forever young. Now he is. Now he is dancing with angels in heaven," said son Dustin.

How prophetic that just one week before his sudden and untimely passing, Dusty Rhodes posted a message to his four children on Facebook. To them, no doubt, it will be his greatest promo ever.

"Sometimes you must think ... what thing you have to be most proud of? It's your kids ... They are truly God's gift to you. Put nothing above them, take care, don't leave them hanging. My kids are and always will be my life. We are blessed."

Bruno Sammartino
An incredible life: Bruno Sammartino was the real people's champion

April 28, 2018

"Where we are going, there is no pain, no hunger, no suffering."

– Emilia Sammartino

Bruno Sammartino never forgot those poignant words spoken to him by his mother three quarters of a century ago. They were words of encouragement during the bleakest of times.

Adolf Hitler's Nazi forces had invaded their small Italian village during World War II, and Emilia Sammartino was forced to flee to the mountains during the German occupation with her two sons and daughter.

They survived by eating snow in the winter and dandelions in the summer.

The starvation and deprivation left the youngest, Bruno, frail and weak. A brother and sister had both passed away at young ages, and his father, Alfonso, had been cut off from his family due to the war, having moved to Pittsburgh in 1936 in hopes of setting a foundation to bring the rest of the family.

Risking her life, Bruno's mother often had to make grueling and dangerous day-long treks down the mountain and into the German-occupied village at night to snatch food she had hidden in the family home. She was captured once, but escaped, and another time she was shot in the shoulder by a Nazi soldier who caught her leaving the house, and nearly bled to death while finding her way back to her family.

Many were not as lucky, with scores of villagers lined up and executed.

But Emilia Sammartino, fearlessly protecting her children, refused to give up hope.

Barely surviving the elements, the family spent 14 treacherous months in a secret refugee camp before returning to their ravaged homeland after German troops moved out.

Bruno fought off rheumatic fever before World War II ended, and his mother nursed him back to health after doctors told her that her youngest son had only a day or two to live. But he was so sickly that it took three years before medical authorities would clear him to travel and reunite with his dad.

When the family immigrated to the United States in 1950, and Bruno met his father for the first time, he weighed 80 pounds.

Drawn to the gym and weightlifting, within 10 years the proverbial "98-pound weakling" bulked up and built himself into a 275-pound powerhouse who would be considered one of the strongest men on the planet.

It was only through hard work and sheer determination that Bruno made that remarkable transformation. Frail, sickly and able to speak little English, Bruno was an easy target for schoolyard bullies. But he dedicated himself to bodybuilding, built up his physique, and would eventually push his bony 80-pound frame as a teenager to an Olympic-style weightlifter.

In 1960, he set a world record by bench-pressing 565 pounds, earning the title of North American weightlifting champion. Not long after he would begin an amazing journey in the world of professional wrestling.

While he became a hero to millions, it was his mother, he would always maintain, who was the real hero.

"She was absolutely my hero," Bruno said in a 2015 interview. "She would do without if she could help somebody else. My mom showed the courage of the lion to keep her kids alive, and the sacrifices she made were incredible. I don't know if I would have been man enough to do what she did."

"Where we are going, there is no pain, no hunger, no suffering."

"I remember my mother holding me up and all she kept saying was not to be afraid, that we were going to be happy and no more suffering, no more hunger, no more cold," recalled Bruno. Lined up and looking at a machine gun, they were saved by men from their village who overpowered the would-be executioners.

Nearly 75 years later those same words of hope, suggested Frank Costa, Bruno's close friend and longtime doctor, were surely the same ones she used welcoming her son to his eternal home.

Emilia Sammartino died in 1995 at the age of 97, but her son would never forget her courage and sacrifice.

She was, Costa told the Pittsburgh Post-Gazette, "the driving force in his life."

"Everything that I am, everything that I've done, everything that I hope to be is because of my mom," said Bruno.

It's what drove him to be a champion.

Stuff of legend

Bruno Leopoldo Francesco Sammartino, who passed away on April 18 at the age of 82, was one of the pillars of professional wrestling over the past half century. Not only was he a hero to millions of fans, he was a bonafide hero outside the ring as well.

While the words icon and legend are grossly overused, in the case of Bruno Sammartino, no other words better describe an individual who truly personified the American Dream. His nickname, "The Living Legend," was fitting.

A man of unquestioned integrity and unshakable faith, Bruno "no last name is needed" was a rags-to-riches story. He was a survivor.

He was professional wrestling's ultimate good guy, achieving a status that few others in the history of the industry ever came close to attaining. His blue-collar style attracted the sizable and fiercely loyal immigrant and ethnic populations in one of the biggest markets in the country. Bruno connected with not only fellow Italians, but also Latinos, Greeks and Jews, and he became their champion, fighting for everyone who rooted him on.

But to simply label him a "good guy" doesn't go far enough in describing Bruno.

"The image of Bruno has actually grown stronger over the years, to the point that "good guy" is too weak to depict his role in pro wrestling," explained Larry Matysik in his book "The 50 Greatest Wrestlers of All Time." Placing him fifth on his list, Matysik describes Bruno thusly: "Stalwart, reliable, as honest as is likely in this shady business. A picture of health. Try using the word "hero," trite though it be, and maybe that's more truly descriptive."

It was an era before the sports entertainment wave crashed across the wrestling landscape. Bruno was a wrestler, and to be called a sports entertainer would have been perceived as an insult.

"Bruno came along in the '60s and he reflected what was going on in terms of the American Dream story," said WWE Hall of Famer Larry Zbyszko. "Poor, starving immigrant kid who escaped Nazis. His mother was shot over the mountains and he came to this country starving and achieved the American Dream. He became the beloved heavyweight champion of the world. People saw that, they felt that. He was a real guy. Everybody believed in him."

He accomplished records that will never be broken.

Just eight days after the official opening of Madison Square Garden, widely considered the "mecca of pro wrestling," Bruno headlined the first wrestling show the Garden ever hosted. As the marquee attraction and centerpiece of Vince McMahon Sr.'s Northeast territory, Bruno sold out Madison Square Garden more than any wrestler in history (although not the often-reported number of 187 times), and not surprisingly that storied venue became known as "The House That Bruno Built."

The "Italian Superman" owns one of the most untouchable records in company history as he held the WWWF championship for nearly eight years (2,803 consecutive days) starting in 1963. The World Wide Wrestling Federation was born on May 17, 1963, when Bruno, at the age of 27, dethroned Buddy Rogers in only 47 seconds, setting the foundation for today's WWE.

For the next seven years and eight months, Bruno defended the title all over the world against challengers such as Gorilla Monsoon, Killer Kowalski and "Big Cat" Ernie Ladd.

But his remarkable run would come to a stunning end with a defeat at the hands of "The Russian Bear" Ivan Koloff on Jan. 18, 1971.

Known as "the night the Garden went silent," it was a seminal moment in professional wrestling and the most shocking event in the history of the building. Fearful of a riot, the referee didn't present Koloff with the title while he was still in the ring. Not taking any chances, Koloff wisely decided to claim his championship out of sight of the fans.

The quintessential hero had been dethroned. Many wept as they left the building that night.

"I remember seeing Bruno's fan club president, Georgian Orsi, sitting in the front row, crying. Many other fans wept as well. I felt like we were all at a funeral as Bruno left the ring," longtime wrestling journalist Bill Apter told the WWE website.

It was the only time Bruno was ever pinned at Madison Square Garden.

Bruno's second reign lasted from 1973 until he was beaten by "Superstar" Billy Graham in 1977 in Baltimore. But wanting to be home more with his family, he grew increasingly weary of the demanding schedule he worked as a champion. Four years later Bruno retired as a full-time performer.

Bruno would come back as an announcer in 1984, and even return to compete part-time for two years.

Pittsburgh proud

Nowhere was Bruno more revered than his American hometown of Pittsburgh, where he had lived since 1950 and had provided the launching pad for his road to wrestling stardom.

He and his wife, Carol, moved into a house in Ross Township, a suburb just north of Pittsburgh, in 1962, the year before Bruno won his first world title. They would live in that same house for the next 56 years.

Despite being the highest-paid wrestler in the profession for a near-10-year stretch, Bruno never flaunted it. He was ethical and genuine, and it showed. He was an everyman, working-class sports hero who lived a regular life. His old-school humility endeared him to his legion of fans.

Stardom's trappings were for someone else, not for Bruno.

"If I was a so-called star, they (the fans) made me that star," he'd say.

Pittsburgh was a place Bruno loved, and the people loved him back. In a city with no shortage of sports heroes, Bruno Sammartino ranked at the top of the list.

According to Sports Illustrated, Bruno, Willie Mays and Mickey Mantle were the top-paid athletes of the 1960s. Bruno received a lifetime achievement award in 2010 from the Dapper Dan organization, the city's premier sporting organization.

Pittsburgh Mayor William Peduto called Bruno Sammartino one of the city's greatest ambassadors.

"Bruno Sammartino was one of the greatest ambassadors the city of Pittsburgh ever had," he said. "Like so many of us, his immigrant family moved here to build a new life, and through his uncommon strength and surprising grace, he embodied the spirit of Pittsburgh on the world stage. Some of the fondest memories of my childhood are of sitting in the basement with my grandfather on Saturday mornings and watching Bruno wrestle."

Many of Bruno's millions of followers over the years got their first taste of the sport in that same fashion: watching the Italian strongman battle the bad guys on black and white television sets with their parents or grandparents.

Pittsburgh-area native Ken Mihalik was one of those.

"It was very much a family affair," said Mihalik, a retired communications director at Trident Technical College. "My siblings and my mom and dad. Tuning in was a weekly ritual. The Steelers were not winners then, and the Pirates were so-so in the mid-1960s. So, Studio Wrestling was must-see TV, though we didn't have a color set until the late "60s.

"My cousins with us, along with their dads, would drive to the Civic Arena in Pittsburgh if the main event was a big draw. We had quite a crew my first time. July 1964 is still a vivid memory. I was seven years old, and super-excited. My grandfather accompanied us to Forbes Field, not an ideal venue for the matches, but it lent to the event's significance, to see Bruno defend against, and defeat, Johnny Powers."

To Mihalik, Bruno was more than just an in-ring champion.

"Bruno was our Superman in the ring, but also outside it. He came across as real and a blue-collar hero, never pretentious. As champion, he conducted himself like a gentleman, and seemed classy yet approachable, very fan-friendly. He was that rare performer who, despite a busy schedule, would stay to chat and make certain all autograph requests were met."

There was a simple, yet effective, formula for booking Bruno.

Said Mihalik: "It was customary for both familiar and new challengers to show up on the local Saturday wrestling TV program and trash-talk Bruno, how what brought them to town was the goal of beating Bruno in his own backyard. Naturally, Bruno would take the high road on interviews and accept the match, which would turn into a series of battles over a few months if their styles clicked.

The feud would culminate in a brawl which Bruno inevitably won decisively with strongman tactics, sending the bad guy packing. Meanwhile, the next opponent would be featured in a prelim encounter, defeating a popular mid-card favorite, to set themselves up as Bruno's upcoming obstacle. This pretty successful booking formula sustained the Pittsburgh territory for over a decade.

"There was a clear ethnic flavor to many of the contests, with Bruno taking on, and overcoming, the likes of Professor Tanaka, Waldo Von Erich, Stan Stasiak, Ivan Koloff and assorted others. Not always, as there'd be repeated encounters against heels such as Blackjack Mulligan, Johnny Valentine and Bulldog Brower. Real heat would be generated when Bruno would face a former friend or protégé who 'betrayed' him, whether it was Bill Watts, Spiros Arion or, certainly, Larry Zbyszko. Big crowds showed up to see Bruno gain his revenge."

"It wasn't always about Bruno defending the WWWF belt," Mihalik added. "Tag-team matches were also pretty common main events, with Bruno joining pals Tony 'Battman' Marino or Dom DeNucci comprising the 'home team' versus a variety of tough duos. The Sicilians, The Mongols, George Steele and Baron Scicluna, the Fargo Brothers, to name a few."

While pro wrestling wasn't exactly the real deal, Bruno always was. Buoyed by his strength and charisma, he made the championship real in the eyes of the public and brought authenticity to the ring.

A young Zbyszko (Larry Whistler), who grew up watching Bruno in Pittsburgh and was billed as his personal protégé until he shockingly turned on him during a televised public workout, got a quick lesson on how much fans loved Bruno when he bloodied his teacher with a series of chair shots to the head.

"I was getting my car smashed, I had to hide in trunks," recalled Zbyszko, the traitorous student who quickly became the most reviled figure in the business. "I was going down the highway in a new Cadillac with the windows smashed, the mirrors hanging, the lights are out. It was a different time, a different day. My

God, the riots."

The two became engaged in a bitter feud that was capped by a steel cage match at Shea Stadium in 1980 in front of 36,000 people. Bruno escaped the cage a winner. The grudge bout broke box-office records for wrestling events, and it would be the final wrestling match to take place at Shea.

Bruno retired from the ring the following year.

"People hated me for 20 years after that match," said Zbyszko. "Everything I learned was from Bruno. He was my mentor."

Burying the hatchet

As the industry began to dramatically change in the late '80s and '90s, Bruno began to look on the profession he once loved with disdain. Leading a charge against the rampant use of steroids and drug abuse, he became a vocal and integral figure in focusing widespread media scrutiny on a burgeoning problem that would affect the entire business.

From famed performer to outspoken critic, he said the business sickened him and pointed to drug abuse, gratuitous violence, tawdry sexual overtones and growing vulgarity. The circus atmosphere and outlandish storylines that Vince McMahon turned to during the company's infamous Attitude Era were too much for Bruno to bear.

"Wrestling was my way of making a living," he said in a 2004 interview. "I did the very best I could. It was an even exchange. But it's a completely different world now, and it's one that I don't belong in anymore."

As Bruno continued to lambast McMahon's creative and business practices, his omission in the WWE Hall of Fame stuck out like a sore thumb. Without Bruno Sammartino as part of it, the WWE Hall would be like the Baseball Hall of Fame without Babe Ruth.

But after years of rebuffing WWE, things changed in 2013 when Bruno finally accepted an offer to be inducted. Ironically it was WWE executive Paul "Triple H" Levesque, McMahon's son-in-law and a central figure of the Attitude Era, who talked Bruno into coming on board.

Levesque assured Bruno that the company had instituted strict rules within their new wellness policy and had changed their platform to more family-friendly fare. Bruno's trepidations were assuaged, and the relationship began to mend.

"Nobody deserves to be recognized for being a big star and paving the way for the stars of today more than Bruno," said Levesque at the time of Bruno's induction. "Everything that we have today in the business, Bruno was a cornerstone of that foundation."

Not surprisingly, Bruno was inducted in the house that he helped build, Madison

Square Garden. At last, the journey had come full circle.

The bitter, two-decade split with Vince McMahon was finally over. The two had not spoken since a short phone call in 1988, when Bruno quit.

"One of the finest men I knew, in life and in business," the WWE chairman said after learning of Bruno's passing. "Bruno Sammartino proved that hard work can overcome even the most difficult of circumstances. He will be missed."

"Devastated to hear the passing of a true icon, legend, great, honest and wonderful man ... A true friend ... and one of the toughest people I've ever met," added Levesque.

Farewell to a hero

Bruno, who underwent heart surgery in 2011, died peacefully after battling health issues for the last two months. He passed away with his wife, Carol, and sons, Darryl and Dan, by his side, said family friend and former wrestling announcer Chris Cruise.

"Every day his high school sweetheart Carol was by his side," said Cruise. "She was his rock, and he was hers. They were married almost 60 years. Carol never wanted the limelight, never wanted to be known as the wife of a famous man. I always enjoyed talking with her and I always loved how much she loved Bruno. They were each other's best friends."

Cruise called Bruno the father he never had.

"I spoke with Bruno almost every day for the past 35 years, traveled with him to Italy and to Wrestlemanias and to other events," said Cruise. "We laughed and poked fun at each other; we talked about everything under the sun, we gossiped. He was the older brother and father I never had. I was thrilled to talk with him; it never got old."

As great a wrestler as Bruno was, he was an even greater man, said Cruise. He hated discrimination of any kind. He was strong, but also very gentle.

"He made you feel good, supported you through ups and downs. He felt your pain," said Cruise.

Athletes, politicians, movie stars, celebrities from all fields paid tribute to Bruno.

"Bruno Sammartino was a legend," said Arnold Schwarzenegger, who inducted Bruno in the WWE Hall of Fame in 2013. "He was the American Dream personified. From his childhood in Italy hiding from Nazis to selling out Madison Square Garden 188 times as the biggest star of professional wrestling, he was a hero in every stage of his life."

"I'm saddened to hear about the passing of Pittsburgh and WWE legend and my father's classmate Bruno Sammartino. My thoughts and prayers are with the entire Sammartino family," football great Dan Marino posted.

"Sending love and prayers to Bruno Sammartino's family. He was such a gentleman when I met him and really meant a lot to my father and I," tweeted pop star Bruno Mars, who famously added the "Bruno" name because Bruno was his father's favorite wrestler.

Hall of Fame wrestling manager J.J. Dillon (James Morrison) was among the hundreds who paid their final respects to Bruno. Admitting that he doesn't do well at funerals and viewings, it was a trip he had to make. It was Bruno who gave a young Jim Dillon his first big break in Pittsburgh nearly 50 years ago.

"There was only one Bruno Sammartino and I couldn't live with the thought of not making this trip which I would have regretted for the rest of my life. This was a trip I had to make to pay my respects to the greatest champion in our history."

"There are two things you didn't do, you didn't curse in front of the church, and you didn't bad-mouth Bruno Sammartino. That's the amount of respect we had for Bruno," said one mourner.

A household name all over the country, Bruno represented the best part of the profession. Even when the business changed in later years, Bruno went about his life with dignity. He was someone who commanded respect. He was a man of his convictions.

His charisma, strength, ethnicity and earnest persona made him a huge draw wherever he appeared. His fans were never turned away for a handshake or an autograph.

He embraced America and its people while maintaining ties to his native country. He was immortalized in Italy with a 10-foot statue, and his family home was transformed into a museum devoted to his career. A wing of a new medical center was named after his mother.

While Bruno's strict regimen of two-hour daily workouts probably added at least 10 years to his life, Cruise figures that the physical toll the business took on his body most likely took 10 years off of it. He paid a price for the sport he loved.

In 1976, Bruno broke his neck during a match with Stan Hansen in Madison Square Garden when the Texan brawler accidentally dropped him on his head. He came within one millimeter of being paralyzed from the neck down, but he returned less than two months later to defeat Hansen in a rematch at Shea Stadium.

At the end, the body that had made him one of the greatest wrestlers of all time began to fail him. His body had suffered decades of bumps, bruises, sprains and broken bones. Back and leg problems had made it difficult to walk, and he could no longer do his favorite exercises.

"I last spoke with him about a week ago," said Cruise. "He sounded weak but determined to get out of the hospital. In the end, the accumulation of injuries he suffered in the ring were too much. Bruno Sammartino gave his life for pro wrestling, literally."

Heart issues, which could have stemmed from rheumatic fever he suffered during his illness-ridden childhood, eventually led to multiple organ failures, according to Dave Meltzer of the Wrestling Observer Newsletter. Bruno had been in and out of the hospital in recent months, but wanted to keep details about his condition private.

Meltzer may have put it best when describing just what Bruno Sammartino meant to generations of fans.

"There's a saying about being careful to meet your heroes because you end up disappointed. Millions grew up with Bruno Sammartino, and the ones who got to know him, they were not disappointed."

A rarity in the modern generation of pro wrestling/sports entertainment, Bruno was a good guy his entire career. An honorable man in a less than honorable world, he represented the triumph of good over evil. He had the heart of a champion until the very end.

Wrestling has changed a lot since the glory days of Bruno Sammartino. When Bruno wrestled, it wasn't entertainment. It was serious business. And he never forgot how he got there.

"You look at success and thank God and the fans for the success. It's why I always feel indebted to the fans, I've had a pretty amazing life."

Randy Savage
'Macho Man' was true original

May 21, 2011

I was dining one evening with Ted DiBiase when I noticed that our waitress had a rather puzzled look on her face.

She approached DiBiase, the self-proclaimed "Million Dollar Man," and said rather sheepishly, "I know you from somewhere."

DiBiase just smiled, and before he could put down the tip, the waitress blurted out, "Now I remember! You're the famous wrestler Macho Man Randy Savage!"

It then became obvious that although she wasn't really a pro wrestling fan, the Macho Man was the one name she knew, although DiBiase had a pretty strong character of his own at the time.

And, like a typical wrestler, he worked the waitress.

"Oooh, yeah! Dig it!" he said, perfectly laying down the Macho Man's signature catchphrase and signing Savage's name on a paper napkin for the excited waitress.

That's how well known Randy Savage was.

The Macho Man was a true original, a member of a rare breed in not only the wrestling business, but in the broader entertainment industry.

Savage, who died Friday at the age of 58, transcended pro wrestling. He was a household name whose wrestling exploits, Slim Jim commercials and over-the-top character became a part of pop culture. In recent years, he starred in wrestling video games, appeared in movies including "Spider-Man" and produced a rap CD.

Ahead of his time

The son of former wrestling star Angelo Poffo, he came along at a time when territories were still in vogue, learning his craft the old-fashioned way and paying his dues every step of the journey. But by the mid-'80s, when the business exploded with the mainstream popularity of the World Wrestling Federation, Savage and his "Macho Man" gimmick was leading the charge along with frequent partner and opponent Hulk Hogan.

The two represented a new era of wrestling, and Savage's colorful and eccentric personality resonated with an audience that not only included traditional wrestling fans, but also a following that boasted pop culture celebrities who related to over-the-top characters like the Macho Man.

Savage had a swag and style that was ahead of its time.

"To me, he was one of the greatest ever," said Dutch Mantel, who broke into the business with Savage during the '70s. "He was a good friend ... I loved Randy. There'll never be another Randy 'Macho Man' Savage."

Mantel met Savage in Atlanta while working for Gunkel Promotions. At the time, Savage was working as "The Spider." The two met again in Nashville during the late '70s.

"We basically taught each other how to work," says Mantel.

Savage had an unmistakable presence that combined speed, power and charisma.

"If you walked by a TV in a department store and wrestling was on and he was doing an interview, I don't care who you were, you were going to stop," says Mantel. "If you didn't know better, you would have thought that this guy was messed up on drugs, and that he was nuts. And, in a lot of ways, he was nuts. But Randy was perfecting the Macho Man character."

That character, says Mantel, was a natural evolution of Randy Poffo aka Randy Savage.

"When you talked to Macho, you wouldn't be talking to Randy, and you would know that because Randy was hidden behind all those layers of Macho. And sometimes you'd have to ask yourself if there ever was a Randy there. Even his voice changed."

Savage, known for his raspy voice, sunglasses, bandanas and colorful outfits, would make the catch phrase "Oooh, yeah" part of pro wrestling vernacular.

"He did it so much that his voice changed naturally," says Mantel. "He trained his voice to do the Macho Man interviews. I used to say that Randy only had to do half an interview. He repeated everything twice. But he was very good."

Paranoia and jealousy

There was, however, another side to Savage. He was overly protective and notoriously frugal despite making millions in the business.

He constantly lived in paranoia, particularly regarding former wife Liz Hulette, who appeared with Savage as the lovely Miss Elizabeth.

For storyline purposes, he portrayed a jealous lover who assaulted anyone who came near Liz, his manager (and wife).

The role, though, was eerily similar to real life.

Billed as "The First Lady of Wrestling," the brown-haired beauty took part in one of televised wrestling's magical moments when she exchanged vows with Savage in a highly publicized ceremony at the 1991 SummerSlam pay-per-view. In reality, the two already had been married for several years, and by this time their real-life union was falling apart. The two subsequently ended their eight-year marriage in 1992.

"Randy thought everyone conspired against him," said Mantel. "He thought people were lurking behind every bush, every tree, just read to pounce on him. But he took it to another level. I think he may have suffered from a little hyperactivity."

Sixteen-time world heavyweight champion Ric Flair, who helped break Savage into the business, witnessed Savage's trials and tribulations firsthand.

"I was there when all of that stuff between Randy and Liz was going down. Randy spent many years being upset about Liz."

"I guess I'm not very surprised by the heart attack," added Flair. "We all deal with stress in different ways."

"He was jealous of Liz even when they first got together," says Mantel. "I remember them before they got married. I don't know that it was so much a matter of jealousy ... I think he was just very protective. Later on it might have morphed into jealousy, but he was overly protective of Liz at all times. And I consider that more of a virtue than anything else. I think it was his execution more than his intent that got misconstrued."

"If you can misconstrue barricading somebody else in the house," adds Mantel. "I don't know that you can misconstrue that."

There was also a very public split with Hogan.

Until a recent reconciliation, the two longtime partners and rivals hadn't spoken for much of the last decade.

"I feel horrible about the 10 years of having no communication. This was a tough one," Hogan tweeted. "He had so much life in his eyes and in his spirit. I just pray that he's happy and in a better place, and we miss him. I'm completely devastated, after over 10 years of not talking with Randy, we've finally started to talk and communicate."

His marriage last year to longtime friend Lynn Payne seemed to indicate a more peaceful and relaxed time of life for Savage. The two had first dated when Savage was playing baseball in Sarasota, Fla., and she was studying at the Ringling School of Art and Design.

"I was happy for Randy because it seems that he had finally found happiness again after all those years," says Flair.

Most in the business will remember the good times.

"Wrestling Randy at the first Wrestlemania I was ever at was huge for me," says Flair. "I have a lot of great memories of Randy. I loved being around him socially."

"I loved Randy," says Mantel. "Not only as a person, but he was tremendous in the ring. He was never lazy. If you couldn't hang on to him, he'd beat the crap out of you. When he went to that ring, he damn sure went to it for one reason. He was Macho Man, and he was going to entertain those fans. I never saw him have a bad match. To me, he was one of the best ever. I don't think there will ever be another Randy 'Macho Man' Savage. That came naturally to him, and I don't these today's creative teams could ever create another character like him. They'd be afraid of that type character today. Randy invented his gimmick. He knew what he wanted to do and he went and did it."

Multi-talented athlete

Savage also enjoyed a baseball career before turning to the wrestling game.

A two-time All-State catcher at Downers Grove North High School in Illinois, Savage played minor league baseball in the Florida State League in the early '70s for the St. Louis Cardinals organization at St. Petersburg where he was a teammate of future pro standout Keith Hernandez.

Savage was 18 years old when he was signed fresh out of high school by the Cards in 1971 and was sent to the Sarasota Cardinals of the Gulf Coast League. He hit .286 in the rookie league and was invited back the following year, when he proceeded to make the GCL All-Star team as an outfielder. But he was no defensive whiz, and though he hit .344 in 25 games in 1973 as one of the first minor-league designated hitters for another Cardinals GCL club, the Sarasota Red Birds, when he was given a promotion to Class A Orangeburg of the Western Carolinas League, he hit just .250 with little power.

But he did learn something valuable in Orangeburg under the tutelage of the legendary Jimmy Piersall. It was the brash, high-strung Piersall, Savage would later claim, who taught him "how to be aggressive and fight."

He played the 1974 season with the Cincinnati Reds-affiliated Tampa team in the Florida State League, batting .232 with nine home runs, 19 doubles, six triples and 66 RBI. The Reds released Savage after one season. He was prepared to pay his own expenses to an Arizona tryout for the San Francisco Giants when the Chicago

White Sox contacted him about earning a spot with one of their Class-A teams.

Savage converted to throwing left-handed because of arm injuries and moved to first base, but failed to make it with the White Sox.

Randy Poffo's career an as athlete, however, would be far from finished.

"He kept everybody (on the team) loose," said former Detroit Tigers star Larry Herndon, who played minor league ball with Savage. "He was always having fun."

"I have memories of him as a great teammate and a great man," Herndon told ESPN. "He was a pure-hearted individual. He really cared a lot about others ... He was a man who really loved life and loved people."

Savage was philosophical in a 2004 interview.

"Being a wrestler is like walking on the treadmill of life. You get off it and it just keeps going."

One thing's for sure," said Mantel. "Nobody's ever going to forget him, because his personality was so huge that he'll live forever."

Lou Thesz
The best there was …

May 5, 2002

"And the winner — and still heavyweight champion of the world — is..." Lou Thesz probably heard those words more times than any other champion in the history of professional wrestling. But early last Sunday, the man many regarded as the greatest wrestler of all time, passed away in Winter Garden, Fla., of complications from open heart surgery.

Thesz, a charming "gentleman's champion" who set the standard for a future generation of stars, graced us with his presence for 86 years. Martin Aloysius Thesz, however, wasn't your average octogenarian. He worked out every morning to maintain an incredible physical edge, traveled extensively and mentally was sharp as a tack. But he was unable to recover from a triple bypass and aortic valve replacement surgery he had undergone nearly three weeks earlier.

When Lou died, says wife Charlie, he left with no regrets. He lived every year, every day, to the fullest. What he did leave behind was a legacy the likes of which will never be duplicated.

Pure and simple, Lou Thesz was the best this profession has ever had to offer. From the night he won his first of six world heavyweight titles in 1937 to the moment he took his last breath, he embodied everything good about a business that too often has attracted its share of criticism.

To me, and many others, Lou Thesz was wrestling. He was the real deal. There was no other wrestler I looked up to or respected more. He was a national icon in post-World War II America and a major star during wrestling's first television boom, only later to become revered by a generation of fans in Japan where he was that country's first international champion and the first American champ to defend the title on Japanese soil.

The son of a middleweight amateur wrestling champion in Hungary, Lou Thesz was a one-man dynasty whose records will stand the test of time. He held the world title for more than 13 years, more than any other wrestler in history, with his eight-year reign from 1948 to 1956 ranking as the longest title run of all time. The youngest world champion ever, he won his first title at the age of 21 when he defeated Everett Marshall in his hometown of St. Louis. His sixth reign ended in 1966 at the age of 50, making him the oldest to hold the NWA championship belt. He also held the distinction of being the only male wrestler to have competed in seven different decades, having worked his last match in 1990 against Masahiro Chono, one of his students and a future NWA champion.

Some of my earliest memories of wrestling revolve around Lou Thesz, who graced covers of many grappling magazines during those days and, despite the fact that he was in the autumn of his illustrious career by the 1960s, remained one of the top workers in the business and enjoyed his last international title run late into the '70s.

Watching Lou perform in the ring was like watching poetry in motion. The 6-2, 225-pounder moved with catlike speed and quickness and could wrestle his way out of any situation. He was a legitimate tough guy, known in his day as a "hooker," a wrestler who could inflict serious punishment on his opponent, snapping bones and dislocating joints at will.

His reputation had left a big impression on this aspiring wrestling scribe, who more than 30 years ago consoled a tearful nephew with the calming reassurance that "Lou Thesz wouldn't cry!" The youngster, not even 10 at the time, had split his forehead on an errant dive into a swimming pool. But after hearing those four awe-inspiring words, his sobbing turned into a steel-grit determination, even though a trip to the hospital and a painful patch job. He still sports the scar, but no doubt learned something very important that day.

We all learned from the man affectionately referred to as "the master."

Before wrestling became sports entertainment, he taught us how to respect the business. The industry never had a better ambassador than Lou Thesz. He was the personification of professionalism, class and dignity.

Tim Woods, a former collegiate champ who enjoyed an equally successful pro career as the masked "Mr. Wrestling," was one of Thesz's closest friends in the wrestling business.

"As far as I'm concerned, Lou was the greatest professional wrestler of all time," said Woods, who estimates he wrestled Thesz at least 25 times during his career. "I had always admired him, even before I started wrestling professionally," added Woods, who began his pro career in 1962 and had his first match against the world champion in 1965 in Amarillo, Texas. "I was scared to death. Lou would test you. He'd decide if he was going to beat you like a dog or give you a little more respect. We weren't in the match five minutes when I think he realized I had some wrestling experience. We just had a great deal of respect for one another. Since that time we've been very, very close friends.

Woods recalled his conversation with Thesz the day before Lou went into surgery.

"He sounded so good. He told me after he got through this thing, that he was going to come back and beat the hell out me, just for fun," joked Woods. "He probably would have done it."

Thesz, who remained active in a number of charities, had served as president of the old-timers' Cauliflower Alley Club and had recently been inducted into the Missouri Sports Hall of Fame.

"We have all lost a dear friend," said wrestling historian Bill Murdock, executive director of the Eblen Charities, a nonprofit organization based in Asheville that helps families in western North Carolina deal with chronic illness and disabilities. "Lou and his wife, Charlie, were longtime friends and supporters of the Eblen Charities for many years. The joy, excitement, fun and love he brought to the (golf) tournament every year certainly was a highlight of our event.

"He was a true champion in every sense of the word, giving selflessly of his time to travel to Asheville to help raise money to assist families who were, in his words, wrestling against a much tougher, relentless opponent, illness and disabilities. Lou personified the word champion in every sense. The grace and class he showed throughout his world title reigns and his entire life set the standard for all the champions that followed and will continue to follow. From this day forward all will speak of him as a great wrestler, a great champion and a great man. He was much more than a great man … he was a good man. He has left a void in the sport of wrestling and in the lives of all who loved him that will never be filled. Lou was a true gentleman who will be forever missed."

Woods, who last year was inducted into the George Tragos-Lou Thesz Professional Wrestling Hall of Fame in Newton, Iowa, said Thesz visited him at his Charlotte home last year.

"We had a wonderful relationship," said Woods. "He came up a year ago and spent two weeks with me, which I treasure very much ... There has never been, nor do I think there ever will be, a man who symbolizes the entire industry like

Lou. He lived it, from the early days all the way through. He was it. He was the encyclopedia — not from hearsay, but because he was there. There will be a void there that nobody will ever be able to fill."

He's right. The wrestling world will not — cannot — ever be the same without Lou Thesz.

Several years ago Lou wrote an autobiography, "Hooker: An Authentic Wrestler's Adventures Inside the Bizarre World of Professional Wrestling," a definitive work on pro wrestling's history. "It's been a wild, exciting ride," he wrote in the opening chapter.

Thanks, Champ, for allowing us to be part of the journey.

Part II
ORIGINALS

Fred Blassie

Chyna

Killer Kowalski

Wahoo McDaniel

Sputnik Monroe

Roddy Piper

Johnny Valentine

Mae Young

Freddie Blassie
Classy Freddie Blassie:
Wrestling's 'fashion plate'

June 8, 2003

"Most any night you know where I can be found,
Yeah, stomping some geek's head into the ground.
So keep the faith 'cause in Blassie you can trust,
I won't give up 'til the last geek bites the dust."

— From "Pencil Neck Geek"

Classy Freddie Blassie may have been 85 years old when he took his final breath Monday night. But it's doubtful any wrestler ever packed as much punch in one lifetime as the man who made "pencil neck geek" part of the pro wrestling lexicon.

The self-proclaimed "Hollywood Fashion Plate" and "King of Men," who had been hospitalized in recent weeks with kidney and heart problems, will be remembered as one of the greatest — if not the greatest — heels in wrestling history. His string of 67 years in the business, dating back to the mid-'30s when he came up through the ranks with fellow St. Louisan Lou Thesz, is unparalleled in the business.

Blassie's passing represents a great loss not only to the pro wrestling community, but more intimately to World Wrestling Entertainment and the McMahon family. He claimed the distinction of working with four generations of McMahons — Shane and Stephanie McMahon, Vincent K. and Linda McMahon, Vincent J. McMahon and Jess McMahon. For his loyalty, Blassie held a lifetime position with the company, unofficially serving as its goodwill ambassador.

It was a far stretch, however, from the decades he spent as one of the game's most hated villains, boasting his superiority over other wrestlers he liked to call "pencil-neck geeks," and inciting riots and driving fans to violence. He was stabbed 21 times, doused with acid, lost vision in his right eye after being hit with a hard-boiled egg and had last rites administered to him twice. Once, after a judge fined an attacker $115, the defendant replied, "If I'd known it was gonna be that cheap, I would have cut him again."

His gift of gab and colorful interviews had helped make the sharp-dressed, silver-haired wrestler a celebrity in the newly expanding medium of television during the 1950s. A trend-setter and master showman, Blassie was a favorite among the Hollywood set, appearing in a number of films and TV talk shows while at the same time drawing sellout wrestling crowds from coast to coast. One of the first wrestlers to venture successfully into other media, Blassie made the hilarious cult movie "My Breakfast with Blassie" with the late Andy Kaufman, a parody of the popular art house movie "My Dinner with Andre." Blassie also released two albums, "King of Men" and "I Bite the Songs" in 1977, and his single, "Pencil Neck Geek," is considered one of the greatest novelty records of all time, making the top of the popular Dr. Demento Show playlist.

When Blassie was finally was forced to retire from in-ring competition due to a pair of shot knees, the McMahons enlisted his services as a manager and later as part of their front-office staff.

Even though confined to a wheelchair in his final years, the beloved Blassie, who was inducted into the WWF Hall of Fame in 1994, remained a larger-than-life figure in wrestling circles. And if anyone had ever doubted his devotion to the company and its owner, those doubts were surely erased as recently as three weeks prior to his passing.

In his final public television appearance May 11 on Raw, Blassie ordered The Dudleys to "get the tables," prompting the rowdies to slam their opponents through a slab of wood and garnering one final — and farewell — pop from the crowd.

"I was really happy that Freddie got to be in the ring one more time and hear that tremendous ovation," Bubba Ray Dudley told WWE's website. "I thought it was great as the icing on the cake of his career to be a part of something that was so live that night in Philly, out there with The Dudleys and Stone Cold Steve Austin. I'm just glad he got to hear that live crowd one more time."

Backstage, with the cameras off, Blassie verbally tore into Eric Bischoff after the former WCW boss introduced himself as a "new member of the (WWE) team." The 85-year-old ruffian "made mincemeat" out of Bischoff, an observer related, noting that the gravel-voiced Blassie colorfully and graphically expressed his distaste over Bischoff trying to run his boss (Vince McMahon) out of business during the heated Monday Night Wars.

But that was Freddie Blassie — brash, bold, blood and guts, take-no-prisoners. A veteran of thousands of wrestling wars, Blassie's career spanned the gamut from the days of the Depression through the Golden Era of wrestling, through his final major run as a wrestler during the '70s, and his role as a heel manager for such rising stars as Hulk Hogan and Jesse Ventura. Blassie also was there for the WWE's national expansion in the mid-1980s, managing the Russian and Iranian combo of Nikolai Volkoff and The Iron Sheik, who often would win their matches by using Blassie's ever-present cane.

Longtime fans still talk about Blassie's epic battles with the likes of The Destroyer, John Tolos, The Sheik, Bruno Sammartino, Bobo Brazil, Pedro Morales, and Dick The Bruiser. Blassie, who had a kidney removed in the mid-1960s, was still a main-eventer and one of the top draws in the business when he was forced to retire at the age of 55 due to a California athletic commission ruling. Vince McMahon Sr. offered him the opportunity to finish out his career as a manager in the old WWWF, where he would join an illustrious stable of managers that included Captain Lou Albano and The Grand Wizard.

Blassie always had impeccable timing. That he passed away during a Monday Night Raw segment when Ric Flair was cutting an old-style promo was surely coincidental, but there's little doubt that Blassie would have given the interview a thumbs up. Few were more effective at whipping crowds into a frenzy than Blassie, who once claimed to have caused a rash of fatal heart attacks among television viewers in Japan who were stricken by the sight of him sinking his teeth into the bloody foreheads of idols such as Rikidozan and The Great Togo. His penchant for biting his opponents and drawing blood had earned him the nickname "Vampire" in Japan, where he was one of the top foreign stars and horrified that sedate society with his heinous tactics. Blassie played the gimmick to the hilt, often sharpening his teeth with a nail file to promote his bloodthirsty gimmick.

"In my whole career 92 people dropped dead of heart attacks. My ambition was to kill 100, and I failed," Blassie once boasted.

Fortunately Blassie lived long enough to see the recent release of his autobiography, "Listen, You Pencil Neck Geeks," in which he details his seven decades in the business and candidly recounts his rise from a teenage tough guy working carnivals in his native St. Louis to the pinnacle of his profession as the man wrestling fans loved to hate.

Famed Los Angeles Times sports-writer Jim Murray once called Blassie "the worst villain since Hitler" and claimed that he "wrought something of a revolution in the unmanly art of exhibition wrestling."

Those who knew him, however, painted an entirely different picture of a man who was sometimes cantankerous, sometimes gruff, but always more affable and lovable than his gimmick would lead one to believe.

"He was a Rembrandt," noted WWE announcer Jim Ross. "He was an artist (who had) an amazing gift."

George "The Animal" Steele (Jim Myers), who spent several decades himself with the WWF, spoke fondly about Blassie in the book.

"Spending time with Blassie, I saw the effect he had on fans over a career of 50 or so years. After we both retired, we went out to California to do a radio show. We were walking back to the hotel, when some guy pulled up and said, 'You're Freddie Blassie.' He pointed at an old man in the passenger seat, and told us, 'My dad has Alzheimer's. He doesn't recognize anyone. But he just looked out the window and recognized you.' We went over to the car, and Freddie had a rational conversation with the guy. The son couldn't believe it. He said, 'I haven't heard him speak like that in 10 years.' It gives me chills just thinking about it."

Blassie was a contemporary of six-time NWA world champion Thesz, who died last year at the age of 86. The two spoke the same dialect of German, their parents had mutual friends, and Blassie was working in a butcher shop when Thesz first met the teen-ager. Like Thesz, Blassie was a child of immigrants who grew up in a working-class neighborhood in south St. Louis. Blassie had made his wrestling debut in a carnival at the age of 17; unhappy with his choice of occupation, his family persuaded him to keep his "real" job as a meat cutter. But after serving in the Navy in World War II (he wrestled under the name of Sailor Fred Blassie while stationed at Port Hueneme in California), Blassie returned to the world of wrestling, which was at the time still something of a carnival sideshow.

Blassie was a major star in every territory he appeared, but attained his greatest popularity in Southern California where his bloody feud with "The Golden Greek" John Tolos set box-office records. The man fans loved to hate would become an even bigger babyface when Tolos, in one of wrestling's most famous angles, "blinded" Blassie with a mysterious powder on May 8, 1971. Weeks after the angle, it was announced that Blassie's career was finished. When Blassie made his inevitable return, the Olympic Auditorium wasn't big enough for his revenge match against Tolos, so the show moved to the L.A. Coliseum. The Aug. 27, 1971, bout, which drew more than 25,000 fans, remains the largest live crowd in the history of pro wrestling in California and at the time was the largest money gate in U.S. wrestling history.

Blassie, now donning a sombrero and teaming with such fan favorites as Rey Mendoza and Mil Mascaras, had suddenly become a hero to Los Angeles' Latino crowd. Tolos and Blassie, whose feud spanned 27 years, would wrestle their final bout nearly a decade later.

Blassie held the NWA Southern heavyweight title a remarkable 14 times during the '50s and early '60s while wrestling in Georgia. More important during his time in Georgia, though, was a dramatic heel turn which unleashed unheard of villainy upon the unsuspecting babyfaces of the day, labeling his detractors "pencil neck grit-eaters."

"One of the first big matches I had after I got out of the Marine Corps was with Freddie," recalled veteran star Rip Hawk. "I wrestled him on Atlanta TV and had gone in there as a preliminary (wrestler). The match got over so big that I was main-eventing with him the next week at the City Auditorium. I was only about 25, and he was a great performer even back then. He was a nice guy and easy to get along with."

Blassie defeated Edouard Carpentier for the WWA world title on June 12, 1961, a month before scoring another major upset over Thesz in a two-out-of-three falls match.

The morning after Blassie's death, longtime friend Regis Philbin paid tribute to him on his show "Live with Regis & Kelly." Blassie had been one of his first guests when Philbin started out with his own late-night talk show decades earlier, Philbin recalled, noting the two had become friends during his frequent appearances.

Philbin showed several pictures from past Blassie appearances, including shots of himself with Ernie Ladd and (promoter) Jules Strongbow, a shot of Philbin's jacket after it had been torn up by Blassie, and a picture of Blassie and a team of wrestlers engaging in a tug of war with the San Diego Chargers.

After traveling became too difficult for his bruised and aging body, Blassie remained a lifelong WWE employee, working in the front office, making personal appearances and doing charity work.

"Freddie did a lot of things with the Veterans of Foreign Wars (VFW). Sometimes he was older than the guys he was visiting. The world was a better place because Freddie was here; my world was enhanced by meeting him," WWE performer Bradshaw (John Layfield) wrote last week on the WWE website.

Blassie is survived by his wife, Miyako, and three children. Funeral services were held Friday in Scarsdale, N.Y.

Chyna
Chyna was a force of nature

April 23, 2016

When will Chyna be inducted into the WWE Hall of Fame?

It has been an oft-asked question among wrestling fans over the past decade. And with good reason.

Billed as the "Ninth Wonder of the World," Chyna helped redefine women's wrestling during the '90s and was a major player during one of the hottest periods in WWE history.

With her death last week at the age of 46, that question now becomes much easier to answer. Tragically, and somewhat ironically, Chyna's passing undoubtedly will pave the way for her well-deserved enshrinement.

Whether or not she gets into the politically driven hall, though, is largely in-consequential in light of her massive accomplishments in the wrestling business. Born Joanie Marie Laurer in Rochester, N.Y., Chyna broke gender barriers and glass ceilings and proved that some women can more than hold their own with their male counterparts in, of all places, a wrestling ring.

The female powerhouse was a force of nature like no one had ever witnessed. She was Wonder Woman in black leather hot pants, boots and halter, a celebrity who not only entertained fans, but empowered women.

But she dealt with lifelong depression, insecurity issues and substance abuse. And in the end, sadly, they would prove too much to overcome.

Since unceremoniously parting ways with WWE in 2001, Chyna posed several times for Playboy magazine, appeared in a string of adult films, and was a reality star train wreck on series like "The Surreal Life" and "Celebrity Rehab with Dr. Drew." She also experienced a number of well-documented meltdowns along the way. To WWE, the centerfold and sex tape star became persona non grata.

Even former love interest and current company executive Paul "Triple H" Levesque was once quoted as saying there would be no way the sports entertainment pioneer would be inducted into the WWE Hall of Fame. At least while she was alive.

Since her death, there have been widespread calls for her to be inducted. But for many, Chyna was already there.

Haunting final video

Joanie Laurer was found dead on Wednesday at her home in Redondo Beach, Calif.

Unable to reach her by telephone for several days, a friend went to her apartment, found her not breathing and called the police, according to documents. Officers found her lying dead on her bed when they arrived. Police said there were no indications or signs that her death was a result of foul play.

TMZ reported that neighbors told investigators they suspected "overdose" as the cause of death since she'd seemed "under the influence" lately. A manager later said she had been taking medication for anxiety and sleep deprivation.

Days earlier Laurer, looking disheveled and disjointed as she wandered around her apartment wearing headphones and a feather in her hair, posted a rambling 13-minute video. She filmed herself making a smoothie and drinking it in its entirety from the blender in one long drink

At one point while surveying the view from her seaside apartment, she asked, "How lucky am I?"

"Love you all. Peace," were her final words.

The final results of the investigation could "take up to several months," the coroner's office said.

A friend told Daily Mail Online that Laurer was not suicidal and was planning for the future.

Erik Angra, who was working with her on making a documentary about her life, said she was trying to deal with the demons of her past, including her relationship with her late father, but had found the process upsetting. He said he and other friends were concerned about Laurer, but did not believe she was suicidal, and that her last message to him was a voice-mail in which she spoke about her plans for the coming week.

"She was going through a difficult time since she got back to the U.S. with the way she had to deal with media and fame again," said Angra.

Anthony Anzaldo, who worked as Chyna's manager and was involved in the documentary, told The New York Daily News that he was the one who found her body. In her bedroom, he said, were prescription pill bottles for Ambien and "one for an anti-anxiety medication similar to Xanax." Anzaldo said there was no alcohol or illegal drugs.

Anzaldo said Laurer would be cremated with some of her ashes spread in the Pacific Ocean and some in a location where fans can visit them if they wish.

"My only solace is that she obviously died in her sleep with no pain. She was alive one second and dead the next. It doesn't look like there was a struggle for air," Anzaldo said.

Dr. Drew Pinsky, who treated Chyna on Celebrity Rehab with Dr. Drew in 2008, told People magazine that he believes she succumbed to addiction.

"I am very sad for Joanie and her loved ones, but I am also terribly angry because I suspect addiction may have taken another life," he said.

Finding her niche

The story of Joanie "Chyna" Laurer is ultimately a sad and tragic one. Depression and substance abuse never seemed to be that far away. The signs were always there, even in her formative years.

In her 2001 autobiography, "If They Only Knew," Laurer tried to recall how many fathers she had growing up.

"I had three, possibly four, if you count the boyfriend in-between who never married my mom," she wrote. She would move several times (often depending on the man her mother was dating or married to), around New York and beyond. She battled bulimia, only stopping when the capillaries in her eyes burst from the force of vomiting and "stomach lining started showing up in the toilet," she wrote.

During her college years she claimed she was raped by two football players at party.

She would finally feel validated when she discovered professional wrestling. At 5-10 with a chiseled body and able to bench-press more than 350 pounds, she wasn't going to fit into the prototypical divas role. And unlike the other divas on the roster, she was neither pristine nor innocent. She was bigger, more athletically built and certainly more muscular than her counterparts, and she knew how to wrestle

Since she'd chucked a job as a singing telegram girl to train with legendary wrestler Walter "Killer" Kowalski in Massachusetts, she had no interest in the women's division and was thrilled to get a gig working as an Amazon bodyguard for fellow Kowalski product Hunter Hearst Helmsley (Paul "Triple H" Levesque), with whom she would develop a personal relationship outside the ring.

"I'd been rejected at everything," she told the Boston Herald in 1999, citing unsatisfying efforts as a bartender, saleswoman, and singer. But inside the ring, she found her success. "I could go out and be this big, huge female and entertain people. That'd be my niche."

"At its best, coming into WWF pro wrestling as a beginner is like suddenly having a private table at the best restaurant in town," said Laurer. "You have arrived, girl, and millions of people are gonna be shouting your name. Your scowling breasts will stare out at kids from the posters of you that they've pinned to their closet doors. It's movin' on up to the East Side, to a deluxe apartment in the sky. It's a dream come true in a dream come true."

But at its worst, she added, it was "a combination of walking the prison yard for the first time and Showgirls." She suffered abuse and humiliation from fans who spit on her and threw batteries at her, and from wrestlers who resented her being inserted into a man's world.

"I had to travel with these guys, be on the road with them 250 days out of the year, I had to dress with them, joke, cry, laugh, live with them, and try to make myself part of what was heretofore a man's world."

And she more than succeeded.

One of the top stars of WWE's wildly successful Attitude Era, Chyna helped found the ground-breaking faction D-Generation X, and earned the distinction of being the first and only female to hold the Intercontinental championship.

In the end though, "It's not about what she did. It's about who she was," said longtime friend and former WWE writer Vince Russo. But, he added, "It would be hard to come across someone that was more giving and more loving than she was. Joanie Laurer was the most loving, kind, giving individual I ever met in the wrestling business."

Tortured life

Considered smart and funny by many of her friends and colleagues, she lived a number of lives outside the wrestling business. She had graduated from the University of Tampa with a degree in Spanish literature, was a trainee with the Peace Corps in Costa Rica and Guatemala, and once contemplated a career in law enforcement.

Wanting to escape from the adult film world and the demons that had followed her for much of her life, he moved to Japan to teach English to Japanese children and center herself before returning to the U.S. last year.

"She ups and leaves and goes to Japan not knowing a soul ... not knowing anyone. So she's living in Japan on her own teaching English as a second language," said Russo.

After receiving a number of late-night calls from Chyna, Russo said he became convinced that one morning he would go online and read that she was found dead in her Tokyo apartment.

"She was so incoherent. There was no way she would have been able to get herself on a plane. That's how bad it was."

"I was taking a break, removing myself, regrouping, getting it together and I'm ready to come back. It was amazing, it was a really great, spiritual journey for me," she said upon her return.

Friends say she had been working out several times a week at a hot yoga studio near her home. Aside from her fitness workouts, she also was passionate about playing the cello.

And while her wrestling life was far behind her, she still, to the very end, wanted to reclaim a legacy that she felt was rightfully hers. Public pleas and even letters to WWE fell on deaf ears. Those in charge were well aware of her missteps after wrestling, and some felt they could not risk the possibility of further outbursts or behind-the-scenes intrigue on their watch.

And then, of course, was the bad blood that had existed since Levesque broke off his relationship with her in favor of one that eventually produced a marriage and three children with Stephanie McMahon, daughter of WWE owner Vince McMahon.

After discovering their affair, Chyna confronted the WWE boss, made demands for more money, and was eventually released from the company.

Her former beau and her romantic rival both responded to Chyna's passing.

"She was truly a pioneer in our industry, and she will be missed," tweeted Stephanie McMahon.

Chyna was "someone who wasn't afraid to blaze her own trail and create a path for those who would follow," Levesque posted on Twitter. "A pioneer whose star shined bright."

Outside of the wrestling realm, however, her tumultuous life began spinning out of control and her self-destruction began.

In 2005 she was arrested and charged with beating former boyfriend Sean "X-Pac" Waltman after returning from the Playboy Mansion in Los Angeles. The New York Post later reported that she had stripped naked and jumped into a fish tank at a New York nightclub. Later, during an appearance on the Howard Stern Show, she slurred her words and didn't deny wanting to do cocaine if it was placed in front of her.

Chyna told the Calgary Sun in 2005 that she was battling drug and alcohol-related issues as well as a mental illness, and confided on "The Surreal Life" she had once attempted suicide by taking pills. Waltman made a desperate plea to the show's producers.

"This is a crucial time for you and anyone else who has profited from doing business with her to step up and help save this woman's life," Waltman wrote on his website. "(She) is on the losing end of a life-or-death battle with drugs and alcohol, along with severe mental illness."

In 2008 she was hospitalized after mixing alcohol with prescription medication. Two years later she was hospitalized after overdosing on sleeping tablets.

As the demons of addiction closed in, her hopes of ever re-establishing a relationship with WWE evaporated. The company stayed clear of her until the end.

Seeking closure

In a podcast with Steve Austin last year, Levesque said that although her career warranted it, Chyna's involvement with the porn industry might keep her out of the WWE Hall of Fame.

"It's a bit difficult, though, and this is the flip side of the coin, and this is the side nobody looks at. I've got an 8-year-old kid, and my 8-year-old kid sees Hall of Fame, and my 8-year-old kid goes on the Internet to look at Chyna," Levesque told Austin. "What comes up? And I'm not criticizing anybody. I'm not criticizing lifestyle choices. Everybody has their reasons. I don't know what they were. I don't care to know. It's not a morality thing or anything else. It is just the fact of what it is. That's a difficult choice."

In an interview Thursday with The Daily Mirror, Levesque appeared to have softened his stance, calling Chyna "a great person, an amazing talent, a groundbreaking pioneer."

"You know it's not my decision, but I definitely think, as I have said before, that what she did in her life certainly warrants it. There was never anybody like her before her, and there will never be anybody like her after."

On a podcast with Russo, Chyna claimed Levesque had been abusive toward her during their relationship.

"I think Hunter's plan was to get me to leave the relationship first. That way he could start dating Stephanie and everything would be cool. We got into a heated argument. We were not getting along. I told him, 'I know something's going on; don't tell me something's not going on.' He swiped my hand, I swiped his hand, and then he hit me. And that's a deal-breaker for me."

She described the incident as a "Jerry Springer moment."

"I was just in shock ... it was very surreal. I just couldn't believe that he hit me."

It was a claim Levesque would vehemently deny.

Russo said he extended the invitation to Chyna because he felt Levesque had been taking "cheap shots" during his interview on the Austin podcast. "She's a human being struggling, fighting for her life, and you're going to take cheap shots. I'm glad that I did that, and I'm glad that interview still exists to this day."

Several years ago Russo managed to bring Chyna to TNA which she thought would be a "second life" for her, but the company released her due to her adult film. He would later help facilitate her move back to the states, and saw her at a convention last November.

"With all the heartache and the turbulence and the addiction and the pills and the alcohol and all she went through, she looked like a million bucks again."

Russo, though, said he was puzzled when he discovered that she was doing a documentary apologizing to WWE. "Her losing her fiancé wasn't enough. Her losing her job wasn't enough. Let's take her name now so she can't get work. That's where the problem began. The trouble didn't begin with two people falling in love. That's going to happen. Chyna herself recognized that. But what are you (Chyna) apologizing for? What do you have to be sorry for?"

She just wanted closure.

But there was none, said Russo. "To let a woman who has been suffering now for 15, 16 years over this incident that led to a downward spiral ... she's not asking for a job, she's not asking for money, she's not asking for help. She's simply asking for closure. How do they deny that?

"She wasn't validated by her own parents. She wasn't validated by her fiancé who went out and found somebody else. She was still looking for validation. That closure would have been validation."

Battling depression

Noted San Diego-based sports psychologist Dr. David Reiss says Laurer responded to a tweet he had posted on publicizing depression several months ago.

"Nothing personal, but she asked if she could help and I wrote back that I'd be glad to talk to her and I'd welcome her help."

Unfortunately she never did.

Without knowing the details of her particular case, Reiss says those suffering from depression have to want to be treated. Unfortunately, much of the treatment is superficial, and medication doesn't get to the root of underlying problems.

"Too many athletes are afraid to reach out for help or go for quick fix (often snake oil) rehabs," says Reiss. "Too many practitioners have trouble dealing with athletes in both directions — they get taken in by the celebrity and don't try to reach the real person and real issues, and they don't understand that athletes in general (and people in other professions where there is a tendency to enjoy the adrenaline rush and excitement) respond differently to both therapy and psychotropic medications typically used for treatment, and those issues need to be taken into account."

People who like to "live on the edge" are often put on anti-depressants, he says. In the case of ex-wrestlers and athletes, says Reiss, many are dealing with issues related to chronic pain and often with issues related to even low-level repetitive head trauma.

"At first, it numbs what they're feeling. But then they don't feel alive. They don't feel themselves. They don't feel normal. And then they become even more depressed. For some athletes it becomes the perfect storm. Even when they go for treatment a lot of times, they're not really getting sophisticated intervention."

Ultimately, says Reiss, those suffering from depression must deal with their underlying emotional issues.

"If you don't deal with the baggage you grew up with, all the rehab in the world won't help. You can go through the motions, say the right things, but it's not going to help," he says.

"Most of the programs out there focus on substance abuse, which is often a significant issue, but there must be attention to the unique individual using the drugs — who they are in 'real life,' their personal history, family, etc. — not just a general stereotype.   There needs to be more attention to the emotional needs of athletes — from the high school athlete who never goes any further to the retired professional."

Chyna reportedly had been regularly attending hot yoga classes near her home in recent months, with relationship strife behind her.

"At the end of the day, all she wanted was to be loved," Russo said on his podcast.

Russo, who has dealt with his own depression, said the breakup with Levesque was the unraveling of Chyna.

"It was an unravelling she never recovered from."

Russo said that while she was a full-blown addict "because of the circumstances that led to it," he believes acceptance from her former employer could have helped. "There is nobody that can tell me that that could not have possibly been the step in the direction of sobriety. All she wanted was acceptance and love ... which is free, which cost you nothing, and you could not give that to her?"

Russo concluded his emotional podcast by saying that God had gifted him with an angel.

"Am I heartbroken? Yes. Am I ripped apart? Yes. Am I thankful I had Joanie in my life for the best part of 20 years? Yes. That was an absolute gift from God."

"Joanie Laurer spent a good part of her life struggling for her life on this planet," he said. "But right now, as she looks down on all of us, she is the happiest person in the world. She has met her maker. Her maker has thanked her for everything she brought to us ... I know she's pain-free. I know she's sitting at the right hand of God with a huge smile on her face. I know they're pampering her and telling her how much they love her. They're giving her the affirmation that she never got."

From the heart

Tributes poured in by the hundreds following Chyna's death. Wrestlers and fans expressed an outpouring of support for the larger-than-life personality.

One of the most touching tributes came from WWE Hall of Famer Mick Foley, who bonded with Chyna shortly after she joined WWE.

Noting that his heart was aching and his eyes were swollen from crying, Foley posted the following:

"I will always be grateful for the friendship I shared with her, but particularly so for the kindness she showed my children, especially Noelle when she was younger. I will never forget those moments where Joanie would take Noelle by the hand at WWE events in the late 90's— off to have her makeup done, her fingernails painted; bonding time between big, strong Joanie, and her tiny sidekick. A father doesn't forget that type of kindness.

"I didn't know whether to post a classic photo of Chyna in her WWE prime or of Joanie from the last time I saw her — about 10 months ago at a convention on Long Island. I went with the photo from the convention because of the emotion; because it was taken at the exact moment I saw her for the first time in many years. I was told later that Joanie wasn't sure how I would react to her, and that it meant a great deal to her to be accepted. Like I said, a father doesn't forget. I called home on my way back from the convention — only about 40 minutes from my house. 'I'm bringing a friend over to watch the pay-per-view,' I said to my wife.

"Who's that?" my wife asked.

"Chyna."

"Chyna?"

"Yeah, Chyna!"

"And that was pretty much that. A mother, you see, doesn't forget the kindness shown to her child, either.

"I am so glad we had that night with Joanie. A night to let her know how much we cared about her, whether it was politically correct or not. A night to let her know we loved her — and always would. RIP my dear friend. I pray that somehow in death, you can find the peace that eluded you so frequently during the latter years of your remarkable life."

Killer Kowalski
Anatomy of a heel

Sept. 7, 2008

"Two roads diverged in a wood, and I took the one less traveled by, and that has made all the difference."

— Robert Frost

It takes a different breed to become a professional wrestler.

But one could hardly imagine Killer Kowalski as anything but.

Taking that road less traveled sums up the colorful life of Walter Kowalski, who recently passed away at the age of 81, leaving behind a legacy as one of pro wrestling's all-time great villains.

Kowalski was one of the sport's true originals, a character molded during the Golden Age of wrestling in the '50s when the business gained powerful media outlets through the advent of television.

The 6-7, 275-pound Kowalski gained worldwide acclaim as one of wrestling's most feared and despised "bad guys."

"There was a time not so long ago, in an America starved for larger-than-life heroes, when I was as close as anyone could become of being the ultimate public villain," Kowalski once said. "For almost 30 years, I was one of the most hated celebrities in America. They called me Killer Kowalski, and mine was not the gentlest of professions."

Outside the ring, though, was a different story. Kowalski was kind and charitable, a gentle giant with a gentle soul who spent the last three decades of his career training others the intricacies of the business.

He also raised funds for countless organizations and charities. Whether it was drug programs, YMCAs, charitable work for children with special needs, or helping a church build a new organ, Walter Kowalski was always there.

"You see the villain in the ring, you see the yelling and screaming during the promos, then you see a man who would go on religious retreats, a man who loved poetry, a man who read voraciously and would talk about philosophy," says Don Bravo, a Kowalski student and friend. "If you didn't have classical music in the car, he wouldn't ride with you."

The hated wrestler and consummate bad guy inside the ring was an image very much at odds with the one that emerged in his retirement, that of a beloved, elder statesman, a former Seminary student who studied theology and metaphysics, a lover of the arts who had a book of photography published in 2001.

America's anti-hero

Kowalski was born Edward Walter Spulnik on Oct. 13, 1926, but legally changed his name 37 years later. The son of Polish immigrants, he was raised in Windsor, Ontario, Canada. He majored in electrical engineering at Assumption College and worked part-time at a Ford automotive plant in Detroit to help pay his way, but pro wrestling would become his ticket to fame and fortune.

During a 30-year ring career that spanned from 1947-77, Kowalski wrestled everyone from Gorgeous George to Lou Thesz to Bruno Sammartino. A giant of a man with an impressive physique and unbelievable endurance, Kowalski was a major attraction throughout the world.

A handsome matinee idol early in his career, Kowalski started out as Tarzan Kowalski, an obvious nod to his chiseled frame.

The more infamous nickname was established after a match in Montreal during the '50s when he climbed to the top rope and delivered his signature knee drop to fan favorite Yukon Eric. His size-16 boot accidentally dislodged his opponent's cauliflower ear.

As the story goes, Kowalski later visited Eric in the hospital, and the two burst into laughter at the absurdity. When it was later reported in a newspaper that Kowalski visited the hospital to laugh at the sight of his unfortunate victim's missing appendage, his reputation soared to a new level.

Many of his matches ended in riots, and fans once tried to set the ring on fire, with Kowalski still in it. Some would wait with baseball bats and metal pipes in parking lots outside the arenas. Employing a ruthless and relentless style, he had the reputation of being the most hated man in professional wrestling.

"I was the man America loved to hate. I was, in fact, America's premier antihero. And I worked hard at being bad because it taught me the way to peace," Kowalski would boast.

"At the height of my career in the late 1950s and early 1960s, I received a thousand letters a week with the vilest of suggestions. Small riots would accompany my appearances. On several occasions, armed cops formed human walls to protect me. But I loved every minute of it ... I loved stalking the professional wrestling rings across America and the world. I absolutely reveled in twisting, smashing and pounding my opponents in brutal mayhem that made me one of the most loathed and feared men alive."

'Walter's boys'

Kowalski, who settled outside Boston in the '70s, made the transition from wrestler to trainer when he opened a wrestling school shortly after he retired from active competition. It was there a new chapter in his life would begin, and where many aspiring young wrestlers would receive an education of a lifetime.

One of those students, Don Bravo, met Kowalski in the spring of 1991 when he took his godson, a grappling fan, to a wrestling show that included an autograph signing by Kowalski. Bravo admits to being only a casual fan at the time, but he used the opportunity to ask Kowalski about vegetarianism, which the wrestler had adopted during his days in the ring.

"Kid, you sure you want to eat that rotting flesh," Bravo recalls Kowalski asking him about his eating regimen. The line at the signing was long, says Bravo, so Kowalski gave him a card and invited him to his wrestling studio.

A classical vocalist who was finishing up his study at the famed Julliard School of Music, Bravo took Kowalski up on his offer.

Before he knew it, Bravo was one of "Walter's boys," a close-knit fraternity who worked for the wrestler at his Killer Kowalski Institute of Professional Wrestling.

"Are you sure I know what I'm doing?" Bravo recalls asking Kowalski.

"Well, you stay around the circus long enough and I'll let you clean up after the animals," Kowalski quipped.

Bravo, who didn't know much about the wrestling business in the beginning, found himself in a colorful new world that had some striking similarities to the music business.

"I was doing 'Verdi's Requiem,' and it's the same business," he jokes. "It's just that now I got to wear a starched, white collar and a tuxedo. But other than that, it's the same business. Whether I am singing Beethoven's Ninth in a tux, or some guy's in wrestling trunks, you still need your technique, you still have to please an audience, you still have to know what you're doing. The best wrestlers are subservient to their opponent in that they need to make their opponent look good. You serve the music; it's not about your big high notes. It's about making Bach or Beethoven or Mozart sound beautiful. Plus you always worry about getting paid and a check clearing."

Bravo would perform a number of duties for Kowalski at the school, and was even prodded into wrestling once as part of a rib played by the veteran grappler. As a replacement for a worker who didn't show up, Bravo was inserted into a 16-man battle royal, and expected to be one of the first eliminated.

Only problem was that nobody wanted to throw him out.

"I blew up after three or four minutes," Bravo recalls. "I begged for everyone to get me out of there. I wasn't thrown out until we were down to the fourth man. The other three finally threw me over."

Bravo says he can laugh about it now.

"That was my baptism by fire. Walter pulled the most beautiful rib on me."

Bravo ended up being part of Kowalski's "wrestling carnival" for 8 1/2 years, and the two remained friends.

"Never a worker, but one of the boys" he says with pride.

School of hard knocks

Being around Walter Kowalski was an education unlike any other.

"You could identify your generation by where you trained," says Bravo. "His students can follow their lineage from Walter to Lou Thesz, and from Lou Thesz to Ed 'Strangler' Lewis. That's a pretty impressive pedigree. And to Walter's progeny, that's something to be proud of."

Kowalski, whose lifelong training regimen and healthy lifestyle helped enable him to wrestle into his 60s, taught his students to respect the history and tradition of the business.

"I enjoy not only the old school, but the school that burnt down before they built the old school," jokes Bravo.

It was special being a part of Walter Kowalski's fraternity. His school was a stepping stone to the next level, but it was always more about wrestling to Bravo and many of his colleagues.

"At the school, chin-locks, armbars, single leg takedowns, works and shoots are all part of the curriculum. That's what you paid for. But what we'd get without charge were the lessons outside of the ring — how to carry yourself as a champion, how to protect your opponent as well as yourself. If you love the business, it's not about you being the Macho Man, it's about making your opponent look good."

Kowalski, one of the most beloved men in the business, was a father figure for many of those students.

He was generous to a fault "if he knew that your love was honest ... that there wasn't a hidden agenda or a secondary motivation behind it," says Bravo. "He always saw the good in people."

"The ones who really loved the business of wrestling," says Bravo, were "his boys." They sported their nicks and bruises like red badges of courage.

"You had to achieve that to be in his fraternity of his boys. It wasn't just enough to pick up a thousand bucks and study and train with Walter. You had to be accepted through your own sweat and blood to get into that fraternity. The dignity that comes with honest sweat is a beautiful dignity. These were the ones who witnessed the real Walter."

Bravo says never failed to take care of his boys.

"This is a guy who, if you didn't have a place to sleep, would slip you the keys to the gym so you'd have someplace warm to sleep. He was that kind of guy."

"Gee, Boss, I'm desperate, can I just borrow maybe a hundred bucks till next month?" was heard more than once in the Kowalski camp.

"Where are you? I'll be there in an about an hour," Kowalski would say.

"Then he'd arrive and slip you an envelope with about seven times what you begged for. No lecture ... no guilt. Just 'I know you'll give it back to me when you have it. I trust you.'"

Kowalski, says Bravo, would always finish with those words: "I trust you."

"That 'I trust you' was more than my credit card or my mortgage loans, etc. That 'I trust you' was a bond ... that I had to pay back as a matter of my own dignity."

Bravo remembers the evening "Walter's boys" waited until after class before shutting down the lights and breaking into "Happy Birthday."

"What ... nobody baked me a cake?" Kowalski asked.

"Boss, you don't eat cake," they reminded him.

"Oh, that's right, OK, let's go to dinner," he replied.

"Walter led his band of merry men to one of his favorite restaurants," Bravo recalls of the birthday dinner. "Six or seven large, scarred men with broken noses and tattoos sat around a table, and we became 7- and 8-year-olds listening to our favorite uncle tell war stories. What we were were disciples, breaking bread, listening to our master. And his sermon would be "Love one another as I have loved you.'"

To Don Bravo, and countless others, he was "Walter" and he was their friend.

Trainer of champions

Kowalski was a world champion, but he also was a trainer of world champions. The most famous graduate of his school, Triple H (Paul Levesque), went on to become one of the premier performers in WWE history. Levesque made a rare appearance at a show in honor of Kowalski's 70th birthday. After working a match with Scotty Too Hotty, The Game grabbed the mic and shouted, "I want Kowalski! I want Kowalski in this ring!"

"Walter gets in there, and he doesn't know what to expect," relates Bravo. "I'm looking at his eyes, and he's looking to grab an appendage."

"You go around this country saying you trained me, and I would be nothing without you. You know something? You're right," said his former student, bowing to his knees in an "I'm not worthy" pose.

"Walter was really, really touched by that," says Bravo.

Levesque also had the honor of presenting his mentor when Kowalski was inducted into the WWE Hall of Fame in 1996.

His teacher, he says, passed down his wisdom so "guys could live the dream he lived."

"Live the dream, and you'll make it," Kowalski would always tell his young charges. And many did.

The list includes such names as Big John Studd, Chyna, Perry Saturn, John Kronus, Matt Bloom, Frankie Kazarian, Kenny Dykstra and Chris Nowinski.

To the boys who never made it to the big time, the consolation of working for Kowalski was reward enough.

"It's still one of the best times of your life ... telling war stories at three o'clock in the morning and having bad Chinese food with your buddies," says Bravo.

On the road with Killer

It was always an adventure traveling with Killer Kowalski.

"Those long car rides ... talking about life in general," reflects Bravo. "Those were times I'll never forget."

Many referred to him as "Uncle Walter," says Bravo, adding that was a term of endearment and respect. "Kind of like 'Godfather.'"

But Walter "Killer" Kowalski, the Polish giant, remained a formidable figure throughout his career, whether mauling good guys in the ring or training wrestlers when his ring days had come to an end. Just the name alone was one of the most recognizable in pro wrestling history.

Bravo says he will never forget Kowalski introducing him "as one of his boys" to the great Lou Thesz at a Cauliflower Alley event. Thesz, regarded as one of the greatest wrestlers in the history of the sport, had served as a mentor to Kowalski early in his career, and that alone earned Kowalski universal respect among his peers.

To be in the presence of two greats such as Thesz and Kowalski was a bit overwhelming for Bravo.

"I was ready to kiss Lou Thesz's ring," he jokes. "But the way he (Kowalski) described me as 'one of his boys' ... I was touched."

The enormity of Kowalski's reputation hit home again when Bravo was backstage at a wrestling show in New England where the promoter, the late Tony Rumble, was going over a finish with Abdullah The Butcher.

"He looked at me with that look that you don't want him to look at you with," says Bravo.

"You guys don't need me here," Bravo told them, quietly slipping outside the locker room.

About 10 minutes later, after Abdullah and the promoter had gone over the finish, the door opened.

"He (Abdullah) comes out, and it's like a scene out of 'The Godfather,'" recalls Bravo. "He comes over to me and says, 'You're one of Walter's boys? Hey, I didn't know who you were with, I'm sorry. Please give Walter my love. Next time you're in Atlanta, come to my restaurant, and I'll buy you dinner.'"

"Just the fact that being one of Walter's boys would have that much carriage," says Bravo. "And I truly was one of Walter's boys ... But Walter had hundreds of children. And they were all boys. Even the girls were his boys."

The final bell

Kowalski, who had been residing in recent months in a rehabilitation center recovering from a knee injury, suffered a massive heart attack on Aug. 8, never regained consciousness and was taken off life support 10 days later. But, like the character he portrayed in the ring, he battled until the very end.

The finish came at 12:45 a.m. on Aug. 30 when the Killer's heart finally gave out.

A number of his friends and former students had held vigil at the hospital. Bravo admits it was difficult to watch this giant of a man struggle as his hour of departure approached.

"He was such a towering physical specimen, and to see him go through this was hard. Looking at this shell in the bed struggling to breathe ... this was not the Walter I loved. This was basically the vessel that held that spirit I loved. The Walter I'll remember was so full of life. That's what I'll remember about Walter."

John Cena's father had spent the day and evening at the wrestler's bedside. "That's when we had last rites holding hands around the bed and praying for Walter," says Bravo.

A visit by former WWWF champion Bob Backlund nearly moved Bravo to tears.

"Mr. Kowalski, you've got to get your shoulders up. One, two, get your shoulders up," Backlund exhorted, hoping that the wrestler might kick out one final time.

"He (Backlund) looked at me, and I knew that he just couldn't bring himself to say three," says Bravo.

A confirmed bachelor for most of his life, Kowalski married for the first time at age 79. His twice-widowed wife was two years his junior at 77, but he would quip when asked, "I had to marry her. She told me she was pregnant."

"The more I found out about him, the more odd that nickname seemed," wife Theresa told the Boston Herald earlier this year. "He never smoked, never drank; in fact, he was a vegetarian. And he was serious about his religion. I found him to be a wonderful guy."

Bravo says his friend couldn't have found a better partner.

"She is the definition of 'love, honor and cherish, in sickness and in health, til death do we part,'" Bravo says. "She was there every day and took wonderful care of him. Her vigil ... just being with him. It was such a testament to her. It was sweet, and it was lovely."

"She would be the strong New England widow out of central casting," he adds. "You think of those cold, winter months in those port towns with their whaling ships, waiting for their men to come home."

"Walter was an easy guy to care for because he was such an easy guy to love," she would say.

Killer Kowalski, indeed, touched many lives.

"The pro wrestling world lost an irreplaceable figure with the passing of Killer Kowalski. No one will ever duplicate his career inside the ring," said longtime friend Jeff Archer, author of "Theater in a Squared Circle." "More important, the world lost a rare person: one who put the needs, desires and wishes of others far above those of himself. Altruism was Walter Kowalski's lifeblood."

"The world lost a great and kind human being in Walter Kowalski. I'll never forget him," said wrestler and former student Bryan Walsh.

"The people I have met, the relationships I have made, and my success in and out of the ring are a direct result of him," wrote Kowalski disciple Kazarian. "Walter loved angels. We had many conversations about them on our regular trips to church that we both enjoyed on Sundays. To me, and anyone who knew him, Walter was an angel. He was a gentleman, friend and honestly one of the best people to come into my life."

Pro wrestling great Cowboy Bill Watts credited Kowalski with putting him over and making him a success in the then WWWF (World Wide Wrestling Federation) when he was a newcomer to the business in the mid-'60s.

"Walter 'Killer' Kowalski came into my life for a moment and made a huge impact with who he was. He was a man of ethics. His word was good … his heart was huge."

Into that good night

Bravo thought of many spiritual things during his mentor's final days.

He remembers a statue depicting a pair of hands, with wrists touching and opening up, as if to pray, at the hospital chapel. He was struck by the sheer size of Walter's hands and how they resembled the beautiful statue.

"The hands are oversized because they're bigger than life. The hands are the size of Walter's hands. The hands are open as if, perhaps, to place our lives and trust in our creator. If we're lucky, we use our hands to build a good and meaningful life, and when it's over, we use them to offer it back to our master. And here was Walter, who used his powerful hands with the dexterity of a concert cellist to build an extraordinary career, yet could also use them lovingly, to guide students, always shake a fan's hand, write poetry, create masterful photos and expound on the power of love."

Those same famous hands were wrapped around a rosary and a statue of the Virgin Mary as he later lay in a casket. His hands had clutched it as they had in the hospital room.

"God would only let Killer Kowalski put a claw hold on the Blessed Virgin," says Bravo, "and I mean that in its most delicate and touching ways. Only he would have the delicacy to work it so that it would be so gentle."

"I felt like the squire Sancho Panza, standing at the water's edge, as his Don Quixote goes forward to perhaps his greatest adventure … praying for his gentle passage into the night to that mysterious and beautiful unknown island. And what will our friend find there? I'd like to believe his beloved Blessed Virgin, who will take him into the great house where, to quote Matthew 25, the master will say, "Welcome and well done, thou good and faithful servant.'"

Bravo also thought about the time he and his wife took Walter to the opera. Old-time fans would have been stunned to see the image of Killer Kowalski taking in such an event. Many had only known him as the ruthless Killer Kowalski.

"We also took him to Boston Pops, and we went to vocal recitals where they did classic Polish folk songs. He enjoyed the relaxation of classical music without having a true working knowledge of it. He couldn't identify the different Beethoven symphonies, but he loved to sit there and listen to it. He had a great appreciation of it."

It was the same Killer Kowalski who told Esquire magazine last year: "Someone once threw a pig's ear at me. A woman once came up to me after a match and said, 'I'm glad you didn't get hurt.' Then she stabbed me in the back with a knife. After a while, I got police escorts to and from the ring."

"Yet he could be as sweet and docile and shy as a lamb," says Bravo. "Out of his element, he was genuinely like a schoolboy, he was so shy. And there's a sweetness to that."

To Bravo, Kowaski was the avuncular, grandfatherly figure who would go to his favorite restaurant and order the same meal every time. He was someone with whom he shared a love of classical music and the arts, as well as headlocks and kneedrops.

Hundreds of people, many of them younger wrestlers, gathered Thursday at a Malden, Mass., church to pay their respects to the Killer. The Boston Globe reported the crowd at the church included young men with shaved heads, long ponytails and long feathered curls, who had been Kowalski's students. A few women were also among those in the crowd. Many had traveled from far away to attend.

In the final stanza, the man known as Killer was given a champion's send-off, with his boys paying their respects to a man they honored and respected. Among the boys was Paul Levesque, who left the Triple H moniker at home and served as a pallbearer for a man he loved and respected.

This was the Killer's final main event, and Levesque did everything he could to be anonymous, staying in the back of the room and out of the limelight. He was there not as a celebrity, just as one of "Walter's boys."

"He (Levesque) gave it a lot of dignity and class," said one attendee. "Walter would have been proud, because he really handled himself like the title suggests. He handled himself as a champion."

Bravo, who delivered a moving eulogy, says he will always cherish the time he spent with his mentor, and taking the time to go down that road less traveled.

"Sometimes you don't recognize the most significant moments of our lives while they're happening. There was always an adventure at the next exit with Walter. You go to a town, and there was always an adventure there for you waiting to happen."

Wahoo McDaniel
'There's only one Wahoo'

April 28, 2002

I first penned those words 20 years ago in a front-page piece I did on one of professional sports' most colorful and enduring characters. I repeated the same line 18 years later when I introduced him at a local wrestling show where he was making a special appearance.

Today, I can write with the same assuredness that I did two decades ago, that there will never be another Wahoo.

When Ed "Wahoo" McDaniel passed away on April 18 at the age of 63, it officially closed the chapter on an era of professional wrestling that longtime fans still talk about in reverent tones. It was an era of wrestling on which today's baby boomers were weaned, when grapplers were judged according to their grit and toughness as opposed to their catch phrases and Q ratings. To legions of fans in the Carolinas, Mid-Atlantic Wrestling was a religion, and Wahoo McDaniel was a high priest.

Wahoo, part Choctaw, part Chickasaw, and fiercely proud of his Native American heritage, was one of those characters that you'd never forget. He didn't even have to put his last name on the back of his pro football jersey. Just "Wahoo." A pioneer in the early days of the American Football League, he left the gridiron when he discovered the wrestling business was far more lucrative for a star of his caliber. His exploits off the football field and outside the wrestling ring only served to enhance his image as "that wild Indian," as his friends and even his own family affectionately knew him.

But Wahoo lived fast and lived hard, attacking each day like there was no tomorrow. That lifestyle, though, came with a receipt. Wahoo lost both of his kidneys more than four years ago, along with suffering from diabetes and other health problems that would ultimately keep him from enjoying his favorite diversions — golfing, hunting and fishing. In a conversation last year, he admitted that had he known he would have lived as long as he had, he might have taken better care of himself.

But that wasn't Wahoo McDaniel.

The Wahoo McDaniel fans and friends knew burned the candle at both ends, partying and brawling with the best of them. His well-deserved reputation dated back to his high school and college days, when Wahoo once drank half a quart of oil on a dare, right after jumping out of a car and running all the way from Midland to Odessa, Texas, a distance of more than 20 miles, on another bet.

Wahoo took his lumps the same way he accepted life's triumphs — with dignity and class. He admitted there were some regrets along the way, but that was the price one paid for packing as much punch into life as he did. He often wondered how things might have turned out had Johnny Valentine, whose name will forever be linked to Wahoo's in wrestling lore, not been on that ill-fated plane that crashed in 1975, ending Valentine's career and one of the most celebrated programs in mat history.

"John and I were always close," Wahoo said last year after his friend's death at the age of 72. Everywhere we went we had a big run. Just think how many more matches he and I could have had over the years ... We sure had some good matches, but he liked me. That was one good thing. There were some guys he didn't like, and he'd beat them silly."

"Their matches were legendary," recalled former WWWF champion Superstar Billy Graham, who enjoyed one of his greatest runs with Wahoo during the early '70s. "The building would rock when those guys pounded on one another, with Wahoo throwing those vicious chops and Valentine hitting him with those huge sledgehammer blows. I'm just thankful I wasn't around that area at that time, or I might have been tossed in with them."

But with all the success Wahoo enjoyed in the wrestling business over a 30-year career, the price of fame never came cheap. He was married five times to four women, and a normal family life was virtually non-existent.

"It's very hard on your home life," he once said. "You're constantly gone, and your wife has to stay home. You lose contact with your family. You come in one day, you leave for five, you never get to do anything together. You're always tired when you get there. You never have any nights off to go anywhere and do things together. It's very hard."

Wahoo, who was once featured on CBS' "60 Minutes" and was one of the biggest mainstream names in the business during the '70s, wrestled throughout the world, including more than a dozen tours of the Orient, along with trips to Canada, Australia, New Zealand, Hong Kong, Indonesia and Tasmania.

"When you wrestle for a living, you're never home, and that's hard on relationships, and, well, I never pretended to be an angel," he told Sports Illustrated last year.

Despite the fact that Wahoo was a star all over the world, he never was offered a run in the lucrative New York market, with the exception of an off-season stint there while playing with the Jets.

"He was always bothered by the fact that he could never get into New York," said Billy Graham. "That was because Chief Jay Strongbow was always there. (Strongbow was the resident "Indian" in the WWWF and later WWF, even though he was really an Italian named Joe Scarpa). That always bothered him. I didn't have any answers for him, but I knew that pained him. That would have been a crowning achievement for his career back then."

Wahoo's athletic prowess took shape early as an all-star catcher on a Pony League baseball team coached by former President George Bush who, in later years, would visit Wahoo at wrestling shows whenever he was in Houston. He became a prep football phenom at Midland High School in Texas, where he was a two-time consensus all-state selection who earned All-Southern and All-American honors, before being wooed to the University of Oklahoma to play collegiate ball for the legendary Bud Wilkinson.

A sports editor in Midland, in reporting Wahoo's football feats in the 1950s, wrote: "And fullback Wahoo McDaniel, winding up his career, acted as though he had the biggest grudge of them all, as he scored all four touchdowns, bruised, bulldozed and whirled his way to 281 yards on 35 terrifying rushes and tackled with primitive viciousness on defense to enjoy his greatest day — and in his two seasons as a Bulldog, the Indian has had some great ones, too."

The 5-11, 280-pound McDaniel was just impressive at Oklahoma, where he still holds the record for longest punt return, a 92-yarder against Iowa State in 1958. He also kicked a record 91-yard punt that still stands, and boasts one of the Sooners' longest touchdown receptions at 86 yards. The Sooners posted a 27-5 mark during Wahoo's three years as a letterman there. His pro football career would span from 1960-68, playing for a number of teams while wrestling in the off-season to supplement his gridiron income.

When he joined the New York Jets in 1964, he quickly became as colorful and controversial as his cocky teammate "Broadway" Joe Namath. A member of the original 1966 Dolphins, McDaniel, a linebacker, played three seasons at Miami and left an indelible mark on that team as well.

"Wahoo was a great practical joker who loved to laugh at himself as well as others," former Dolphins great Larry Csonka told the Miami Herald. "He was colorful, and he was especially hard on the rookies. Whether it was (heat rub) in the jockstraps or critters in your shoes, Wahoo did it all."

Wahoo's greatest fame, however, came in the wrestling business, where his contemporaries hailed him as one of the most unique characters in the history of the business.

"What a great guy," said former wrestling star and booker George Scott. "Wahoo was a helluva athlete, a helluva performer and a helluva guy. I had a lot of fun with him. There are so many stories about Wahoo, but most people would think they were fiction. Some of the things he did were unreal."

"One time coming home from Houston," recalled Scott, "Wahoo was doing 115 miles an hour on a four-lane highway. Instead of slowing down, he went around the right-hand side and passed all the other cars. He had a little bottle of Scotch sitting next to him. I picked it up instead and said, 'I need this more than you do.'"

Wahoo also was a big gambler on the golf course, said Scott, who remembers winning a $3,000 bet with Wahoo. "I later went to his apartment to make a long-distance call. I told him to knock $3,000 off what he owed me."

Sometimes Wahoo's ferocity and competitive spirit spilled over to the links, said Scott, who recalled a fight he had with Wahoo on the very first hole. "He hit me over the head with his golf club. I turned around and whacked him with mine. So we're standing there looking at each other. I put my hat on because I had this big bump on my head. But we went ahead and played nine holes after that."

(Among his favorite golfing partners were country singer Charley Pride and football coach Mike Ditka, but he also played with Arnold Palmer, Jack Nicklaus, Gary Player and Lee Trevino. When he lived in Dallas, he'd play regularly with Yankees great Mickey Mantle.)

Former WWWF champ and Mid-Atlantic great Ivan Koloff called Wahoo one of the best ever in the ring.

"I even remember hearing about Wahoo in my early days of wrestling when he was playing football," said Koloff. "(Fans cheering) 'Wahoo! Wahoo!' I never was a big football fan, but I remember that. He was a great athlete and a very tough man who had a good heart. He was always out there trying to help young guys in the business, and always had a word of advice about psychology and things like that. If he liked you, he liked you. If he didn't, you'd know it."

"Wahoo was very special to me," said Billy Graham. "It seems just like yesterday that we were in the ring together. After I left San Francisco in 1972 and after teaming with Pat Patterson and Ray Stevens, they really got me ready to go out and make a living. I went to Minnesota in late '72, and in early '73 I shot that big arm-wrestling angle with Wahoo. The angle did tremendous business, and we worked it to a blow-off Indian strap match. That broke all the attendance and gate records in the AWA in that era."

Wahoo was a perfect match for Graham: the American Indian babyface against the tie-dyed, California hippie. It was a unique clash of cultures.

"The arm-wrestling angle was Gagne's idea. It was going to be with either Wahoo or Billy Robinson. I really didn't want to go with Robinson because of his attitude, which everybody was aware of. I was in Calgary when he hurt some guys. He didn't like weightlifters or bodybuilders or football players, and I was all three. I said it had to be Wahoo. Our rough-and-tough, stomp-and-kick styles worked better anyway. We did tremendous business, which really launched me into the limelight and the magazine covers for the first time. Wahoo was my springboard."

"Out of all the major names I worked with — Bruno (Sammartino) and Dusty Rhodes included — Wahoo was the most giving wrestler during a match as far as letting you get heat on him before he would make a comeback," said Graham. "I remember him lying there for 10 minutes letting me beat on him. He'd say, 'Keep going, brother, we don't have it ready yet.' I have nothing but fond memories of him. We had a lot of fun together. I wasn't able to socialize with him much, because Gagne had that strong kayfabe deal up there. But I know I'll miss him. He was one of the best."

"We always had great relations," said Ernie Ladd who, along with Wahoo, blazed trails in the old AFC before joining McDaniel in the pro wrestling ranks. "He was very competitive and a very good linebacker. He played hard and he wrestled hard. He was a super guy."

"He always told a story that he blocked a field goal over me one day," joked Ladd who, at 6-9, was one of the tallest men in football. "He told it for years and years and years. Wahoo never blocked any field goal over me. I could block people to the moon, although I played defensive tackle. He blocked a field goal against the Chargers one time, and he said he blocked it over me. But he couldn't block a field goal over me. I was a rock in the line. But he loved to tell that story."

"Wahoo was a true sportsman and a true athlete who really believed in his profession," recalled longtime referee and booker Ron West. "He always stuck up for the business. There was one thing about Wahoo: If you didn't want to know the truth, don't ask him anything. He'd tell you in a minute."

"He hated for anybody to touch that (Indian) headdress," recalled Ole Anderson. "For a short period of time he and I were partners, and when he'd get into the ring, I'd tug on a feather. I'd turn around real quick like I was chewing somebody out.

Wahoo would come back over, and I'd have to calm him down."

"He was always living beyond anybody's reasonable lifestyle," added Anderson. "He was a hard-working guy and he did some incredible things."

One of those incredible things occurred while Anderson was running Georgia Championship Wrestling in the late '70s. Prior to a Saturday TV taping, Anderson was informed that Wahoo had gone through his windshield and skidded about 100 feet down I-85 in an automobile accident.

"I asked if anything was broken and was told that it wasn't, except that he had these tremendous abrasions on his head, his cheek, his back, his shoulders and his legs. The guy said Wahoo would be there if I wanted him to be there, so I said tell him to get down here. Wahoo showed up an hour later. I put him out there with Ernie Ladd, and when Wahoo came back in he was bleeding pretty good all over his body. I said, 'OK, take off tonight, go home, take care of yourself, and see you Sunday in Marietta.'

"When Wahoo arrived in Marietta on Sunday, all his cuts had started to heal over, and he could hardly walk. He struggled to get his pants over his leg. But when he got into that ring, you would have thought he was 20 years old again. Bang-bang, bang-bang, up and down and chopping like crazy. By the time he had gotten done, scabs had broken loose all over his body and he was just pouring blood. He was a sight to see. But he never took another day off. He just kept on going."

Anderson also recalled the wild tag-team matches involving he and "brother" Gene against Wahoo and Paul Jones. "This one match Wahoo hit Gene with a chop in the mouth, and knocked Gene from eyetooth to eyetooth. Gene had all his teeth removed the next morning."

Wahoo spent his last years hunting and golfing, when his health allowed, and raising his youngest son, Zack. In February, with his physical problems worsening, Wahoo moved from Charlotte to Houston to live with his daughter and son-in-law.

Wahoo was on the waiting list for a kidney transplant when he suffered a stroke and died 10 days later of complications from renal failure and diabetes. His body was cremated and his ashes were to be scattered over a lake near Del Rio, Texas, which had been the favorite fishing spot for Wahoo and his dad, a well-known West Texas welder and oil rigger.

And if you listen closely enough, somewhere in the distance, you're bound to still hear the echoes of those tomahawk chops and sledgehammer blows.

Few wrestlers knew Wahoo McDaniel better than 16-time world champion Ric Flair.

The two worked against each other more than 1,200 times, and Flair estimates that he took thousands of Wahoo's trademark tomahawk chops during the course of their classic rivalry, which spanned from 1974 until the late '80s. "I didn't give nearly as many as I got," Flair said Friday as he looked back on the career of his longtime friend, who died on April 18 in Houston at the age of 63.

"He and Harley Race were the toughest guys I ever met in my life," said Flair. "Wahoo was just an incredibly tough guy. Not just the way he wrestled, but the conditions he wrestled under. He wrestled hurt, he wrestled sick. I remember he had a vasectomy at four o'clock in the afternoon, then wrestled at 8 o'clock that night. Wahoo would wrestle under any conditions. He had an incredible work ethic. He wrestled long matches and was as tough as anybody in the ring."

Wahoo, however, was more than just a drawing card to Flair. He was a teacher and a friend who was instrumental in Flair's arrival in the Carolinas in 1974.

"To me, he was the one guy most responsible for me getting my career off to a good start. He was probably the most influential person in my career for the first 10 years," said Flair. "I respected him so much. If something was going down in the business, I'd always ask Wahoo's opinion. He was responsible for bringing me down to the Carolinas. I asked him all the time and learned an awful lot about working from him."

Flair first crossed paths with "The Chief" in Minneapolis in 1972 when Wahoo was headlining for AWA owner Verne Gagne. Flair, a Minneapolis native and a product of Gagne's wrestling school, was just getting his feet wet in the business.

"We became very good friends there. Even from the distance of our experience levels at that time, he always took me under his wing. We traveled together whenever I was lucky enough to be on the card. We lived close together and just became good friends. We got along great."

The Flair-Wahoo connection almost didn't make it off the ground, however, as Flair was involved in a 1975 plane crash near Wilmington, N.C., that killed the pilot of the twin-engine Cessna 310 and left Johnny Valentine paralyzed. Flair and Wahoo had been feuding over the Mid-Atlantic heavyweight title at the time of the crash. The angle was so strong that Wahoo, who was one of the first wrestlers to visit Flair in the hospital, startled attendants when they saw him arrive, believing the feud was real and that Wahoo was trying to get at Flair.

No one, with the possible exception of Johnny Valentine (and later, son Greg Valentine), enjoyed a more memorable program with Wahoo than the Nature Boy.

"Wahoo and Flair and (Johnny) Valentine were famous for throwing those chops and bruising each other's chests and causing the blood to flow," recalled Superstar Billy Graham. "They'd stand in that corner and chop each other like there was no tomorrow. When I took a chop, I'd only take one, and then I'd go down. I'd tell Wahoo: 'Now you can start working on me. Take over from down here, buddy. One's enough for this boy.' I wasn't about to stand there and trade chops with a buzz saw. He'd always laugh at me and tell me a few little chops weren't going to hurt me. I'd tell him, 'The way you throw them they do.' At least I knew I wasn't going to get chopped to death lying on the mat."

Flair, however, went at Wahoo full-throttle, resulting in some of the most legendary matches in wrestling history. One particularly grueling encounter in Charlotte resulted in Wahoo being taken out on a stretcher and rushed to the hospital for a patch job that required 42 stitches. During the course of that match, Flair crushed a ringside table and tore off one of its legs. He swung it at Wahoo, and a nail protruding from the table caught him in the head, busting Wahoo open over his eye.

"I'll never forget it," said Flair. "We had a lot of great matches, but that one got the most notoriety. He was in the hospital for about four hours getting his eye fixed. But he got me back."

Flair and Wahoo's exploits transcended the wrestling ring.

"We went up and down the road a lot, going a 100 miles an hour in my Cadillac chasing him or him chasing me," recalled Flair. "It was incredible. Of course, it was so kayfabe, and you couldn't ride with each other. You had to really be careful back then, because there was a big penalty."

Moncks Corner native Burrhead Jones recalled one such incident while traveling with Wahoo and a couple other workers after a show in Conway.

"We had stopped and got a six-pack of beer. I was neutral and got myself a little half pint of whiskey. We went from Conway to Charlotte on a little back road. Blackjack Mulligan and Ric Flair were riding together and after they passed us on a double lane, somebody threw a beer can. Wahoo got hot and told whoever was driving to catch them. A state trooper pulled us over 30 or 40 miles outside of Charlotte. So they swerve the game on the state trooper, but the game came back on Wahoo. Blackjack told the trooper that 'this crazy Indian' is trying to kill us back there. When the state trooper came back and saw it was Wahoo, they tried to work and stage a fight. The state trooper held them back and told Blackjack to go ahead, that they were going to hold Wahoo right there. They held him for more than 30 minutes. Nobody got a ticket, but Wahoo didn't get home until 2 or 3 in the morning. He was so mad. The next night we were in Raleigh for TV, and Wahoo was fit to be tied. Blackjack just laughed about the whole deal."

"There was no stop sign for Wahoo," added Jones. "But he was a heck of a nice guy. He really didn't mean any harm to anyone. He did more harm to himself than anybody else. He used to come over to the house quite a bit when Rufus (R. "Freight Train" Jones) would cook. We'd always have a wonderful time."

Wahoo and Flair also were involved in their share of barroom brawls, the most notable occurring in Charlotte, resulting in Flair and Wahoo going to court and paying $3,500 fines. The incident occurred when Wahoo was showing a friend his brand new diamond ring. The ring fell on the floor, and Wahoo bent over to pick it up.

"This female lawyer thought Wahoo was being fresh with her, and that's how it all started," said Flair. Three male friends, including another attorney, confronted Wahoo, who began putting the boots to the trio. "That's when she jumped on his back and Wahoo flying-mared her," said Flair. "That was it."

Flair regrets that Wahoo didn't take better care of himself, especially in his later years.

"You couldn't even tell him back then. He'd say, 'No, don't worry about it, I'm fine.' When he got diabetes, instead of quitting drinking, he'd double up on the insulin and drink just as much ... I'd say, 'Chief, let's go work out,' and he'd say, 'Boy, I've been working out 30 years, I don't need to work out any more. I'm tired of working out.'"

Flair last visited with Wahoo several months ago in a Charlotte hospital.

"He was an incredibly tough guy, but he was clearly aware that he some legitimate problems that needed to be addressed. It was probably the first time I ever heard him admit that he really needed help. It was really a sad day."

Even sadder, Flair says, is that many of today's fans will never realize just how important Wahoo McDaniel was to the business.

"I guess now I'm sad that not enough people knew enough about him or remember him. What bothers me is here we have probably the greatest athlete to ever be in our sport — the best athlete period to ever be a professional wrestler. Wahoo was such a legend to my generation. He'll always be that. That's what saddens me the most. It's called fleeting fame."

Flair says he cherishes the time he spent with Wahoo, but will never forget a night 10 years ago.

"Wahoo and Ray Stevens were at my house with my wife and my mother-in-law, drinking and laughing, talking about the old days. They were so drunk when they left, Wahoo ran over one of my wife's plants — just pulled the tree out of the ground and left it lying there. Some things never change. He just drove over the yard, drove over all the flowerbeds, just like he'd done a hundred times. No stopping for it — just put it in gear and took off. He was one of a kind."

"We had so many good times together," Flair continued. "The first time he took me to Mexico — Laredo. That's a whole other story."

Sputnik Monroe
One of a kind

Nov. 19, 2006

H e was the diamond ring and Cadillac man — "two hundred and thirty-five pounds of twisted steel and sex appeal with the body men fear and women love."

Long before "Stone Cold" Steve Austin became a national symbol for the anti-establishment movement, there was Sputnik Monroe, a salty-tongued, anti-authoritarian rebel who sported a trademark white streak down the middle of his hair along with a wild streak in the ring and a cocksure strut that just dared you to get in his way.

Monroe, who recently passed away at the age of 78 following a long battle with respiratory illness, was a character the likes of which professional wrestling will never see again.

"Sputnik was a force. He was a guy who made a difference. There just was never anyone exactly like him," said Lance Russell, the voice of Memphis wrestling for half a century. "There's the Jerry Lawlers, the Jackie Fargos, the Ric Flairs, and all these guys who are great in their own right, but Sputnik Monroe was an absolute one-of-a-kind-character."

"It's the end of an era, but Sputnik was a man who would want to be remembered the way he lived, full of fun and one who believed in rights for everyone," added longtime Memphis wrestling announcer Corey Maclin.

Monroe was one of the most colorful and controversial personalities in the super-charged world of professional wrestling. But his legacy transcends the wrestling ring.

A hero to fans black and white, Monroe will be forever remembered as a cultural icon who challenged and successfully broke down the color barrier in pro wrestling and helped exact change in the establishment.

Monroe's tremendous influence was given an entire chapter in cultural historian Robert Gordon's "It Came From Memphis," a book which looks at the town's rich musical heritage that nurtured Elvis Presley and the Stax soul sound, as well as its eccentric, larger-than-life characters like Monroe, who insisted on integrated crowds at his wrestling matches, laying the groundwork for rock shows to do the same.

Monroe captured the imagination of that segregated Southern town's avid wrestling following in the late '50s, building a strong rapport with black fans who were forced to sit in the nosebleed section of the old Ellis Auditorium, a section derisively referred to as the "crow's nest." He cultivated friendships within the town's black community, and even though he worked as a heel in the ring, he became a champion for the black cause.

Initially loathed by white audiences for his arrogant persona and detested outside the ring for his friendship with blacks, Monroe would merely turn to the small black audience in the building's segregated upper rafters, raise his fist in defiance and acknowledge thunderous cheers from those in the balcony who celebrated every performance of the one wrestler who treated them with respect and friendship.

"Sputnik wouldn't even look at the white people who were booing him when he came into the ring," longtime Memphis deejay and television personality Johnny Dark told the Memphis Commercial Appeal. "Then all of a sudden out of nowhere he'd look up and raise both arms in the air to the balcony. And every single black person in the balcony would stand up and raise their hands and cheer him."

And, not unlike another Memphis favorite, Elvis Presley, Monroe would become a hero to the rock-and-roll-loving white youth who related to his rebellious nature. His connection to African-Americans also was genuine.

"There was a group of wealthy white kids that dug me because I was a rebel," Sputnik once said. "I'm saying what they wanted to say, only they were just too young or inexperienced or afraid to say it. You have a black maid raising your kids and she's talking about me all of the time, so I may not be in the front living room, but I'm going in the back door of your house, feeding your kids on Monday morning and sending them to school. And meeting the bus when they come home. Pretty powerful thing."

Monroe, one of the town's top drawing cards, eventually was able to appeal to the promoters' sense of greed, convincing the local matchmakers that they were missing out on tremendous earnings by confining black patrons to the smaller "blacks only" section of the balcony. Finally, overlooking black and white in favor of the color green, promoters integrated seating and saw their profits climb.

"There used to be a couple of thousand blacks outside wanting in. So I would tell management I'd be cutting out if they don't let my black friends in," said Monroe. "I had the power because I'm selling out the place, the first guy that ever did, and they damn sure wanted the revenue."

Once wrestling's mixed audience became part of the status quo, the Memphis music scene followed and nightclubs became integrated.

Born to be wild

He was born Rocco Monroe DiGrazio on Dec. 18, 1928, in Dodge City, Kan. His father had been killed in an airplane crash shortly before his birth, and his formative years were spent living with his grandparents. His mother remarried, and at 17 years old, he became Rock Monroe Brumbaugh, taking the name of his stepfather.

He started his wrestling career in 1945. Monroe, wearing pink shoes and sequined robes, adopted the ring moniker Pretty Boy Rocque and spent his first several years working shows on the traveling carnival circuit where he would pick fights with local tough guys to sell more tickets. He claimed to have never been beaten in a "shoot" match during the five years he spent working the carnivals.

Monroe spent a few more years wrestling locals in small towns, but eventually moved to bigger shows and bigger markets and changed his name to Elvis Rock Monroe when a promoter in Louisville thought he looked like Elvis Presley.

"It sounded like rock and roll," Monroe once said. "I would carry a guitar into the ring. I think I could play one chord and then get the hell beat out of me with my own guitar."

Monroe got the Cold War-era nickname after he gave a black hitchhiker a ride to the arena one day. A fan saw Sputnik walking with his arm around his black friend and became irate when Sputnik pretended to kiss him on the lips. The racist fan made such a fuss that security threatened to throw her out if she didn't settle down and stop hurling obscenities.

Attempting to tone down her string of racial epithets, she screamed, "You're nothing but a damned Sputnik," a reference to the satellite the hated communist Russians had just launched into space. The name stuck with the wrestler the rest of his career.

Monroe was a master showman who walked the walk and talked the talk, combining mat ability with mic skills, but it was his electric personality that propelled him to the top.

"Win if you can, lose if you must, always cheat, and if they take you out, leave tearing down the ring," Sputnik would describe his life philosophy.

Dubbed "The Sweet Man," Monroe had bushy eyebrows, a whiskey voice that gave his promos a sharp edge and an impeccable sense of crowd psychology. And, like other originals from his era, he lived his gimmick.

Married six times, Sputnik carried a case of Scotch in the trunk of his Cadillac, driving from town to town in a life of one-night stands and baloney blowouts. He spawned a number of Sputnik look-alikes including a pair of Rocket Monroes (Bill Fletcher and Maury High), Flash Monroe (Gene Sanizzaro) and Jet Monroe (Sputnik's real-life brother Gary Brumbaugh).

Skirmishes with police weren't an unusual occurrence for Monroe, who liked to hang out around Beale Street, then the hub of the black community in Memphis, which made him a target of police who would charge him with violating the local vagrancy law. City leaders frowned at a popular local figure like Monroe spending his time socializing in black clubs on Beale Street.

"I got arrested once for vagrancy for hanging out on Beale Street," he once said. "I got a colored lawyer and went to court. I told them this was the United States of America, and I could go wherever I damned well pleased. They fined me $25, but after about a half-dozen arrests, they gave up."

But he loved the Beale Street lifestyle, and soon became a favorite of black wrestling fans at the Monday night wrestling shows at Ellis Auditorium, the site where Monroe made his strongest statements.

Years later he would be publicly honored with a display at the Rock 'N Soul Museum, located on that same street, for his role in the integration of public events. Along with exhibits of Elvis, B.B. King and Otis Redding, another display features a gold wrestling jacket, flowered trunks and wrestling shoes, with a plaque that reads, "Sputnik Monroe played a major part in destroying the color lines in Memphis."

Monroe also enjoyed hanging out at the legendary Sun Records studio with Elvis, Jerry Lee Lewis and other Memphis-based recording greats. His musical influence would be felt nearly a half-century later, with a current Los Angeles indie rock band naming itself "Sputnik Monroe" in his honor.

"He was as rock and roll as any of the artists and singers coming out of Sun," Jerry Phillips told the Commercial Appeal. Phillips, son of Sun Records founder Sam Phillips, was so enthralled with Monroe that he got into the ring as a teenager and wrestled under Monroe's tutelage as "The World's Most Perfectly Formed Midget."

Monroe further infuriated champions of racial purity when he teamed with a young black grappler named Norvell Austin for a stretch in the early '70s. It was one of the first interracial tag teams in the South and, to make things interesting,

Monroe talked Austin into placing a blond streak in his hair. Monroe put fuel on the fire when, after disposing of a pair of white opponents, he poured a bucket of black paint over the head of one of the defeated wrestlers.

"Black is beautiful," declared Monroe. "White is beautiful," proclaimed Austin. The two then hugged each other and proclaimed together, "Black and white is beautiful."

Longtime pro wrestler Burrhead Jones, another black wrestling pioneer, recalled traveling with Monroe and Austin during those early days.

"We had some rugged good times on the road," he said. "Neither one had a ride. I had to chauffeur them around everywhere they wanted to go. Sput just had that special way about him. He would always get in tight situations, but he could talk his way out of anything."

He recounts the time promoter Billy Golden had Jones and Austin, at that time the Alabama tag-team champs, and Monroe, who managed the pair, parade down the middle of a Selma, Ala., mall with their bulky belts in tow, plugging a local show later that night. "Here we are — two black men, one with a white streak in his hair, and Sputnik talking his (trash), in a crowded mall on a Saturday afternoon in Selma. It was a sight to see," said Jones.

Jones says Monroe wanted him to put a blond streak in his hair like Austin's so they could draw more money.

Jones, however, flatly refused.

"I had to turn heel on him," he jokes. "I told him that God didn't make any blond black men."

He did it his way

Sputnik didn't mellow with age.

He was an authentic tough guy who never caved in to being politically correct. He kept his arresting shock of white hair until it naturally disappeared.

"Sputnik made the most out of what was essentially a little guy," Russell said of Monroe, who won the world's junior heavyweight title from the heralded Danny Hodge in 1970. "He would have never made it in the WWE if he was the only heel that ever lived. But he sure was big in his mouth and his heart."

Monroe was two days shy of his 70th birthday when he wrestled his last match in a small Texas town. His knee gave out for good and, combined with four herniated discs in his lower back and two in his neck, it was time to say farewell.

Monroe spent his post-retirement years in Houston where he worked as a security guard and as a shuttle bus driver for a rental car company at the airport.

Monroe's last major public wrestling appearance was in July 2005 when he and Billy Wicks reprised their Memphis feud at a legends show. The two had set an attendance record for a match in 1959 at an outdoor stadium in Memphis in front of more than 17,000 fans and guest referee Rocky Marciano. (Marciano collected $1,500 for his ref duties, while Monroe and Wicks both got $750). The mark lasted all the way until the Monday night wrestling wars of the late '90s.

"He was my 'Sweet Man,'" Wicks, 75, said Thursday night from his home in Waynesville, N.C. "In the last five years, we became very close. We'd call each other regularly, and we'd talk about guys in the business and things in the past."

"I was influenced a lot by listening to him and the stories he told off the camera as much as I was on the camera," said Russell. "He was a special guy like that. He'd do a lot of things that would irritate the fool out of you. But he was just being Sputnik. He did everything with a splash."

Folks down South, particularly in Memphis, also still talk about Sputnik Monroe.

"Just last year, we were in downtown (Memphis), and he wanted to go to Beale Street," recalled Dark. "And we parked at Peabody Place and walked, and on the way down there at least four young black kids walked up to him and hugged him and told him their parents had his picture on their wall of their house growing up, that they knew who he was and what he had done."

Sputnik died in his sleep at a nursing home in Florida, but not before battling the loss of half a lung, prostate cancer, gall bladder surgery and gangrene. Down to 145 pounds and given 72 hours to live, he was brought out of his drug-induced coma long enough to say goodbye to his son, Bubba.

Wicks, whom Monroe jokingly referred to as "Granite Hands," had a bet that Sputnik would read Wicks' obituary first.

"I called Sputnik up that Friday morning," said Wicks, who had last talked to Monroe about two weeks before he went into the hospital for the last time. "I'd always call him late in the morning because he would sleep late, but he always seemed to be glad to hear from me. I talked to his wife, Joanne, and asked her how my Sweet Man was doing. She then informed me that he had passed away during the night. I told her he was a double-crosser because we had a deal that he was going to read my obituary before I had to read his."

"He was a very big-hearted guy, but he was a con man at the same time," laughed Wicks. "But I loved the guy. I really cried at first and got very emotional, but now I'm celebrating. Like I told him, he was a hero to me but certainly not a role model."

The unlikely pioneer lived life on his own terms. But he single-handedly and uncompromisingly bettered the lives of many. He made a bold statement when he refused to perform unless fans, regardless of their race, were allowed to sit anywhere they liked. He demanded equal treatment for his black fans and used his craft to literally fight for social change.

"Like Sputnik used to say, "Often imitated but never duplicated,'" said Wicks.

He just may have been the most improbable civil rights hero the South has ever seen.

Roddy Piper

Roddy always knew how to make an exit

Aug. 9, 2015

Henry Marcus was pacing nervously through the dressing room at County Hall.

"Anyone seen Roddy Piper yet?" the veteran promoter asked a group of wrestlers huddled in the corner.

Glen Lane of Charleston was one of those grapplers on the show that night in 1983. He vividly recalls the sense of desperation that was mounting as bell time neared and one of his two main-event combatants was nowhere to be found.

Although Marcus was simply displaying the angst of a promoter who dreaded finding a last-minute replacement for his star attraction, the other wrestlers in the dressing room were confident that Piper would never let down a promoter or his audience.

But time was nearing for his "New York Street Fight" with Greg Valentine, recalls Lane, and the 15-minute intermission between semifinal and main event had already begun.

"Henry was walking from dressing room to dressing room, asking if anyone had seen or heard from Piper," said Lane, who had already showered after working the third match on the show. "He was a nervous wreck."

Mere minutes before bell time, Lane heard someone walking up the stairs toward the locker room. The back door suddenly opened. It was Roddy Piper.

"He had pulled up in the back of the building and left his Cadillac running," said Lane. "He was in his street clothes, pulled out a link of chain and took his jacket off."

"I'll be back in just a minute ... watch that for me," Piper instructed Lane.

Piper walked to the ring, whipped the crowd into a frenzy and left Valentine lying in a bloody heap in the middle of the ring in less than 10 minutes.

Without missing a beat, Piper briskly returned to the dressing room, grabbed his coat, and told Lane, "I appreciate that. I've got to go."

"And he was gone," said Lane. "Never saw Henry, never said a word to nobody, he just came and did his thing and was gone. By the time Valentine got to the back, Roddy was probably already down I-26. That's a professional right there. He was old school. He was supposed to be there and he was going to be there and put on a show."

Just as quickly as he exited that old building more than 30 years ago, Rowdy Roddy Piper left a loving family, countless friends and millions of fans when he passed away suddenly, in his sleep, on July 31.

Never forgot fans

Roddy Piper, born Roderick George Toombs in Saskatoon, Saskatchewan, left a lasting impression throughout the world during his 61 years.

His exploits in and out of the ring, his film accomplishments and his influence on pop culture have all been well documented.

But what many never got the chance to see was what I found most impressive about Hot Rod. He loved the fans, and never forget his hardscrabble beginnings.

He was kicked out of junior high school and left home at an early age. An outcast of society, the teenage runaway played his bagpipes on the streets for quarters to get into youth hostels. Inexperienced and undersized, he broke into the rugged mat business while still a teenager.

And, in his words, "They didn't want me in the business. It was simple as that."

The fact that Piper wore a kilt and played bagpipes as part of his ring act made it all the worse.

The saving grace, he said, was that the wrestling business had given him something to cling to. It gave him a shot at being somebody.

When he made the "big time," Roddy made it a point to remember his fans. When cameras weren't running and no one was looking, he could be found signing that last autograph, honoring that last photo request. And when he spoke to fans, it wasn't an abbreviated, obligatory nod. He would make face contact and engage in conversation.

"He was top of the line," said Lane. "He was real old school. He was a true classic."

And, ultimately, Roddy Piper was as big as they got in the sports entertainment genre.

"Do you think they would've loved you so much if they hadn't hated me?" he once asked Hulk Hogan.

No truer words were ever spoken, says Piper doppelganger Ric Flair. "He made Hogan."

Final exit plan

It was as though Piper knew his ultimate fate long before it befell him.

The fact that he was one of the wild boys of the business was not lost to anyone in the profession. He settled down in later years, but the scars remained.

The wrestling business, with its fame and corresponding adulation, had a great entrance plan, he told Bryant Gumbel in a 2003 interview, but "it's got no exit plan." Piper was still working because he couldn't get anything from his pension until he turned 65, and "I'm not going to make 65," he said.

It was a cruel twist of fate, to be sure, but nobody will ever say Piper didn't live life to the fullest.

One of my lasting memories of Roddy was more than three decades ago and early in his run as a top heel in the Carolinas. He had used some nefarious tactics to get the win over a beloved babyface, and while making his way to the dressing room, an irate fan armed with a full cup of beer decided to target the Rowdy One.

Piper ducked, the flying projectile missed its mark, and its foamy contents instead splattered in the face of my future wife, who had made the dubious decision to attend her first live wrestling show with me.

Roddy looked back, flashed one of his devilish winks, and successfully made it to the back.

The kid always did know how to make an exit.

Johnny Valentine
The passing of a champ

April 28, 2001

There were wrestlers, and there were wrestlers.

Johnny Valentine was a wrestler.

Over four decades covering the business, I've seen my share of legitimately tough customers who made their living putting their bodies on the line every night and living out of a suitcase. There was none tougher than the man we all respectfully called "The Champ."

So when word began to filter Tuesday afternoon that the final three count had tolled for this true wrestling icon, a sense of sadness and deep loss filled the wrestling community. Not just among the older fraternity of fans and wrestlers, but also among the current generation who had heard remarkable tales about this legendary performer.

The incredible sledgehammer blows that could be heard throughout an arena. A simple stare with those piercing blue eyes that could work a crowd into a frenzy. A seemingly never-ending feud with Wahoo McDaniel with matches brutal beyond description that gave new meaning to the words "chopped meat." A man of deep intellect whose creativity extended beyond the wrestling mat to the painter's canvas, opera and gourmet cooking. A bizarre sense of humor that earned him the reputation as the sport's greatest ribber. They were all Johnny Valentine.

He was 72 when he died, but it had been more than 25 years since Valentine last worked inside a wrestling ring.

Cut down at the height of his career, at the age of 47 years and already a 27-year veteran, he forever will be linked with the 1975 plane crash outside Wilmington, N.C., that ended his career and nearly ended the career of a young Ric Flair, and left a gaping hole in the wrestling business that has never been filled.

The accident left him paralyzed, forcing him to maneuver for the rest of his days with the assistance of crutches, wheelchairs and a permanent brace on his right leg. None of it, however, stopped him from working out almost daily and displaying the toughness that made him a legend in the wrestling business.

Valentine, who once admitted he never threw an easy punch, earned his respect the hard way — with blood, sweat and tears. And he always insisted that promoters call him "The Champ."

Valentine, who stood 6-3 and weighed 245 in his prime, was the biggest box-office attraction in the Carolinas during the early '70s as he successfully defended his thousand silver dollars against the best the area had to offer. With his trademark sledgehammer blow, he never was defeated for that bowl of silver.

Johnny Valentine was extreme decades before anyone ever thought of ECW. He was doing Texas death matches, cage matches and ladder matches before they were in vogue. He was box office wherever he went, and wherever he went nobody would ever forget him. The words icon and legend are overused and often misused, but Valentine was both.

Valentine had been in and out of intensive care since August when he fell off his porch in a freak accident, fracturing his back and twisting his colon. Both of his lungs eventually collapsed due to a staph infection, he had ongoing problems with his respiratory system, his kidneys had stopped operating and his bowels had completely shut down.

Making matters even worse were the financial and bureaucratic battles Valentine's wife, Sharon, was forced to wage with HMOs, insurance companies and doctors in the fight to keep her husband alive.

Even more unsettling was the fact that professional wrestling, an industry that for years considered its workers as independent contractors with no unions or little health insurance support, had basically neglected not only one of its own, but one of its finest.

Valentine had been given only hours to live after contracting pneumonia four days after back surgery upon arriving at a hospital near his home in River Oaks, Texas. But, true to form, Valentine survived for eight months, continuing to overcome insurmountable obstacles and fighting bravely until he drew his last breath at 3:07 a.m. April 23. It was how he lived, though, that has left an indelible impression on a generation of wrestling fans.

Tough as nails

McDaniel, Valentine's most famous ring rival, said no one was tougher than JV.

"We sure had some good matches, but he liked me," Wahoo said last week. "That was one good thing. There were some guys he didn't like, and he'd beat them silly."

Valentine, who was born Jonathan Wisniski near Seattle, Wash., had his first pro match in 1949 in Buenos Aires, Argentina, and was a top drawing card throughout the world. It was his raw strength and stiff style that captivated audiences, and often put fear in the hearts of his opponents.

"He was tough, he was strong, and I'm telling you, if you didn't get your hands up and fight him, he'd beat you to death with his own hands," said McDaniel. "I'd hit him as hard as I could. I'd beat him with that strap, and goose pimples would come on him. But I think he liked it. John was as tough as any man I ever crawled in the ring against. He was a great wrestler, he had a lot of talent and he was a very smart individual."

Sandy Scott, whose brother George brought Valentine into the Carolinas in the early '70s, recalled some of the brutal matches between Wahoo and Valentine.

"I refereed one their matches over in Winston-Salem or Greensboro. All I would hear is Valentine saying 'Harder! Harder! Harder!' Wahoo would say, 'My hand's about busted!' John would say 'Harder!'

"If he were around today, half of these guys wouldn't be here. They'd have bruised ribs and bruised chests. We lost a good one."

"He was the hottest thing I had in the territory," said George Scott. "He was unreal. We did ungodly business with him."

"John and I were always pretty close," said McDaniel, who had his first match with Valentine more than three decades ago in Fort Worth shortly after Valentine had dethroned Fritz Von Erich for the Texas heavyweight championship. "I beat him that night when I came in. We pounded one another. Everywhere we went we had a big run. Just think how many more matches he and I could have had over the years."

Flair, who teamed and feuded with Valentine several years before doing the same with Johnny's son, Greg, called JV "a master psychologist with a distinct style that nobody could copy."

Flair said he still flinches when recalling those torrid Valentine-Wahoo blood-baths.

"They made believers out of everybody. It was just unbelievable. That blow to the back of the neck was brutal."

Plane crash tragedy

Valentine was, indeed, the hottest star in the Carolinas-Virginia territory until tragedy struck in 1975 when a twin-engine Cessna 310 plane carrying David Crockett and four wrestlers took off from Charlotte for Wilmington for a Saturday evening show at Legion Stadium. Also on the plane were Valentine, Flair, Tim "Mr. Wrestling" Woods and Bob Bruggers.

The overloaded plane ran out of gas and the engine started to fail as it crossed the Cape Fear River and approached the runway. The plane, however, never made the landing, cutting across several treetops and a utility pole before crashing.

The pilot was critically injured and died two months later. Bruggers, whose back was shattered, never wrestled again but was able to make a full recovery. Valentine broke his back in three places, as did the 26-year-old Flair, but the latter returned to the ring within six months. The others suffered an assortment of injuries, including head trauma, bruises and broken bones.

But the landscape of Crockett Promotions - and the entire wrestling business - was changed forever.

As fate would have it, Valentine initially had taken a seat in the back of the plane, but moved to the front next to the pilot at the request of Flair.

"I was in the back playing chess with Tim Woods," recalled Valentine in a 1998 interview. "Ric Flair talked me into the front seat. Flair absolutely didn't want to sit up front with the pilot. Something must have told him. I said, 'What the hell, we'll play later.' Otherwise he could have been in my condition."

"I remember it well when Flair switched seats with him," Woods confirmed. "I was there, and that was true."

Valentine claimed the crash was caused by pilot error. The pilot, a Vietnam veteran, had trouble getting the plane off the ground in Charlotte and had poorly distributed the weight of his passengers on board. At that point he made the fatal decision to dump fuel from the gas tank to lighten the load.

"We were almost there ... just a few minutes away," said Valentine. "I remember looking at this big gas gauge right in front of me showing empty. I asked the pilot about it, and he said we had a main wing tank full. Ric Flair started looking at that gauge, too, and he began hollering like a banshee. I sort of built it up and said, 'We're out of gas, we're out of gas,' but I was just joking, or so I thought.

"The pilot changed over to the wing tank, and both engines started. One quit, and then the other quit. He had forgotten, though, that one of the engines was still running on the main tank. Had he switched back, we would have made it in on one engine, because we were not very far. But it was a mistake that ruined us.

He was a military pilot, but he panicked."

The plane leveled off at several thousand feet, began to plunge and landed on top of a tree before nose-diving into a railroad embankment, about 100 yards from the runway.

"Just before we hit the ground, our tail hit a wire and that kind of straightened us out. Otherwise we would have gone nose in. That saved most of us."

After spending 10 days in a North Carolina hospital, a plane was chartered to take Valentine and Bruggers to a hospital in Houston, where the two underwent back operations in which their spines were attached with clamps.

Bruggers, walking out of the hospital in only three weeks, was the more fortunate of the two. A piece of bone lodged itself into Valentine's spinal column and caused major damage.

Valentine might have died then had he had not been transferred from the North Carolina hospital to a facility in Houston. He always maintained that a lack of care and expertise contributed to his paralysis.

"They didn't know what to do with us at that hospital in North Carolina. They were constantly rolling me around, because they were worried about my skin. They were turning me and rolling me around with my broken back. They used a cleanup crew to turn me clear over on my stomach. It was crazy. It was like a story out of the past. I'm just fortunate that I found out about Houston, or I might have died."

"They were moving him every six hours, and then they'd get a guard from out in the parking lot to turn him over," said McDaniel. "They finally flew him and Bruggers out to Houston and put those rods in their back. I went out and saw them, and they were hurting but in a lot better shape than they were down here. They were coming around. Bruggers played golf with me the day he got out of the hospital, but John never recovered. Bruggers had a broken back worse than John's. They said he'd never walk, but he was young and he came back. John was coming back well, but then his nerves just quit growing."

Ironically, Wahoo could have been on that same plane, but backed out at the last minute.

"I was lucky I wasn't," said McDaniel. "I was wrestling in Richmond that Friday night, and the next night we were going to be in Wilmington. I called the airport and asked them if there were any flights going to Wilmington. He said there was a flight leaving at 11:15, and that if I could be there by 11, they could get me on the flight. I drove that rental car right to the front door and left it. I called Bruggers, who was a buddy of mine, and said, 'Bruggers, don't get on that damn plane, they're overloaded. You've got five guys on a Cessna 310. Don't get on there. He said he would get a ride."

Wahoo went on to Wilmington for the show, but he still had an uneasy feeling about the plane.

"We were sitting there getting ready for the matches and an ambulance driver walked up and asked if those boys were flying on a plane. I said they were, and he said he thought they crashed. He got on the radio and told me they just got Valentine and Flair out of the plane. They weren't cut up real bad, so they didn't say much. They were hurt - they had broken backs - but you couldn't immediately tell it by looking at them. I went straight to the hospital. When I got there, everyone was sort of in shock. John was stitched up a little. I called George (Scott), and he told me to get the show over the best I could. I put it together and went back out there. They had kind of settled back, but you could tell they were in shock."

George Scott also had been booked to be on that flight.

"I was supposed to be on that plane, but I canceled out the day before. Had it not been for John, I think the other guys (in the back of the plane) would have been dead because he held them there. He was in the front, and his arms went right through the dash."

David Crockett had been a last-minute substitute on the plane, filling in for brother Jim, who was forced to stay home because of the flu.

Valentine, who was the U.S. heavyweight champion at the time of the crash, said he probably could have wrestled for another 10 or 15 years had it not been for the career-ending injury. He said his greatest triumphs in life were his first small steps after the accident.

"John was as tough as they come," said Thunderbolt Patterson, who enjoyed several successful runs with Valentine. "I'm just glad the pain's finally over."

George Scott, who was booking the Carolinas when he brought Valentine into the territory, earlier this year attended a Cauliflower Alley banquet that honored the legend.

"I guess rather than going through all the pain the son of a gun was going through, he is probably better off. We took up a collection for him. He wouldn't give up."

"He was one of the great ones," said Sandy Scott. "He didn't budge, and you didn't get anything. He was a hard worker and he expected you to be the same way. He mellowed a little with his ribs when he came into the Carolinas. We were up in Calgary with him years before that. He had got into some problems up there, but always got his way out of them with the guys. The Carolinas was dead at the time. He told everybody, 'Hey, this is the way we're going to do it, and if you don't want it, there's the door, goodbye. That's the way I work,' and that's the way it was. It took about seven months, but boy did he get over."

Wahoo remembers George Scott telling him that Valentine would never get over in the Carolinas with his slow, methodical style.

"I told him that if he didn't, George was going to lose his whole thing because nobody will be over. I told him to take my word for it, that he works a style, but when he gets over, nobody else will ever be able to get over. It was that slow, rugged, brutal style. He was a brilliant man with the best timing in the world. He could wrestle a guy who looked like he should be in the hospital, and make him look good."

Woods was the last person to wrestle Valentine.

"He had a very strong constitution," said the former masked Mr. Wrestling. "He may not have been the most popular guy there ever was, but he sure as hell had everyone's respect. He earned it. He had some incredible matches with Flair and Wahoo. You could hear the chops a block away."

Woods also remembers hearing his leg snap while Valentine had him in the figure four leglock during a televised match for Valentine's thousand silver dollars.

"I was out for several months after that," said Woods. "I even moved to California just to get away from things. Things were going hot and heavy when I came back. And then we had the plane wreck. I had just bought a house here and had been in it only two weeks when the plane wrecked. I was making more money than I ever made in my life just before that wreck. I had made the statement to my wife: 'This is too good to last.' I'll never say that again. But we were all very lucky we didn't die."

McDaniel said he last saw Valentine at a WCW Slamboree reunion show nearly 10 years ago.

"I tried to talk to him, but it was hard because people were all around. I tried to get a hold of him two or three weeks ago in the hospital, but they told me it was hard to get through. They said he was having a hard time talking, and I left a message. I didn't want to bother him.

"It's a shame he's gone. He was a blessing to this business. Everywhere he went he drew money."

Valentine captivated audiences around the world, but he was revered by his contemporaries.

"Johnny Valentine was my idol," said Swede Hanson. "He was my kind of wrestler. He took a liking to me when I first got into wrestling. He said he liked the way I wrestled and he gave me a lot of advice that really helped me. When you go in there and you hit somebody, don't keep pounding on them. Just stand over them and laugh, and the people will get hot at you. I've seen him come into an arena, walk out to the ring, and somebody would start booing, and that's all he'd have to do. He'd just stand there, not say a word or point or nothing. He'd pick out a spot and pick out one guy and just stare at him. That whole place was in an uproar. They were going crazy."

MAE YOUNG···LADY WRESTLER

Mae Young
Remembering the Amazing Mae Young

Jan. 19, 2014

S he was a trailblazer, a pioneer and a role model for generations of women wrestlers and divas who would follow her into the profession.

But above all, Johnnie Mae Young was a force of nature.

Several years ago she made a deal with WWE exec Stephanie McMahon that, on her 100th birthday, she would wrestle Stephanie's oldest daughter, who by then would be approaching 18 years of age.

Until she drew her very last breath Tuesday evening, with 90 years notched on her belt, no one ever doubted that she would reach that goal.

Mae Young, quite simply, was one of the most incredible characters to ever step inside a pro wrestling ring.

And she did it — for a remarkable nine decades — with force and fury, and with grace and guts.

Plenty of guts.

Know of any other 77-year-old woman who would tell a hulking behemoth half a century her junior that he didn't hit hard enough? Especially when she was on the receiving end?

Mae did just that when she got power-bombed through a table on a 2000 episode of Monday Night Raw.

When Bubba Ray Dudley expressed reservations about doing the high-risk spot, Mae grabbed his wrist and demanded that he treat her like a regular opponent.

"Hey hot shot, if you're gonna slam me, you slam me like one of the boys," Dudley later recalled being told. "I was like, 'Holy crap, yes ma'am, no problem, whatever you need.'"

Bubba Ray apparently got the message — loud and clear — and the next week power-bombed her off the stage and through another table.

"By far, that was the toughest person, pound for pound, we've ever been in the ring with," Dudley later said.

Truth be known, in her prime, Mae was tougher than many of her grizzled male counterparts on the circuit. The late Fred Blassie, one of the greatest heels ever, once opined that Mae was tougher than probably 60 percent of the men in the business. And that, by most accounts, was a conservative estimate.

"Hands of Stone" Ronnie Garvin, a mere neophyte out of Montreal when he broke into the pro ranks in the early 1960s, found out the hard way.

Making an advance toward Young, whose natural beauty predated WWE's pinup-model divas by decades, Garvin quickly found himself on the business end of a haymaker.

"I've never been hit so hard in my whole life," Garvin later joked.

It would be a painful lesson many would learn over the years.

You didn't mess around with the Amazing Mae Young.

Colorful career

Young's longevity in the wrestling business is unparalleled. It's highly doubtful — and likely impossible — that any future mat performer will ever be able to match her nine decades of active participation in the profession.

She began her career in 1939 and was in a Memphis locker room two years later when news of the Japanese attack on Pearl Harbor broke. Nearly 60 years later she would win WWE's title of Miss Royal Rumble. And, on Nov. 15, 2010, she won a "falls count anywhere" contest against the team of LayCool,

Her last appearance with the company was on March 3, 2013, during an old-school episode of Raw. The roster celebrated her 90th birthday, and after the show WWE owner Vince McMahon presented her with a replica of the WWE divas championship, naming Young "the greatest divas champion of all time."

Those many years in between her debut as a 15-year-old rookie and a nonagenarian on the WWE roster saw the tenacious spitfire tackle a variety of jobs ranging from auto mechanic to evangelist, in addition to being a top-flight lady grappler and trainer.

Life, though, wasn't always easy for Young, who grew up in the post-Depression Dust Bowl in Sand Springs, Okla., a small town eight miles west of Tulsa. The youngest of eight children, Mae never knew her father, who left the family before she was born and never returned.

But Mae was an exceptional athlete who knew she would one day cash in on her physical talents.

When she wasn't beating boys on the high school wrestling team, starring on a nationally recognized softball squad or kicking field goals for the football team, she was working at a cotton mill to help ends meet at home.

"She had such great admiration for her mother," recalls Ruth Ellen Henry, one of Young's closest friends over the past 25 years and a fellow native of Sand Springs. "She absolutely idolized her mother. Her mother took care of Mae's grandmother and an invalid sister. Mae would walk back and forth to school for lunch, and she would work before she was (legally) old enough at our cotton mill to help support her family."

Ed Dubie, a beloved local high school football coach who had played collegiately at the University of Tulsa, was the first to recognize the superior athletic potential in Mae.

"He always said she could kick the football further than any boy he had ever seen," said Henry.

It's only fitting that a bronze statue of Young, recognizing her place in the Sand Springs Hall of Fame, occupies a prominent spot today in the Ed Dubie Fieldhouse.

"She loved every award she ever got, but that's the one she would ask me about the most," said Henry, 70, whose mother attended school with Young. "She loved Sand Springs."

Mae and Moolah

No name is more closely associated with Mae Young than perennial women's champion The Fabulous Moolah (Lillian Ellison). Young trained Moolah, hooked up the South Carolina native and her troupe of girl wrestlers with the late Vince McMahon Sr.'s Northeastern-based organization, and shared a special friendship with Moolah until her death at age 84 in 2007.

Their strong bond and relationship with the McMahon family endured.

"Vince (Jr.) is a great man. He loved Lil," Young once said in interview. "I was one of the first girls to work for Vince Sr. when he opened up Joe Turner Arena in Washington, D.C. At that time, Lil (Moolah) had never worked for Vince Sr. She had been calling me and writing me to use some of her girls.

"Mildred (Burke) and Billy (Wolfe) had split up at that time, and Vince asked me what I thought about getting Lil and his girls. I told Vince that would be the greatest thing that ever happened."

Moolah, in fact, sold the rights to her championship to Vincent K. McMahon in 1983.

"There will never be another Mae Young," McMahon in a statement last week. "Her longevity in sports entertainment may never be matched, and I will forever be grateful for all of her contributions to the industry."

The relationship between Mae and Moolah extended beyond the boundaries of the squared circle.

For nearly 20 years Mae, Moolah and Katie Glass (former women's midget star Diamond Lil, who Moolah adopted many years ago when the 17-year-old knocked on her door looking for work in the wrestling business) lived on separate floors of Ellison's 42-acre estate in the back of a tranquil neighborhood in the suburbs of Columbia — appropriately dubbed "Camp Moolah" — that included a 13-room home, eight- and 12-acre lakes, a row of lake houses and a gym equipped with a wrestling ring where hundreds of men and women came to train over the years.

"Johnnie Mae was in California and had lost all of her family, and I told her this big place was just sitting here and she could have the whole upstairs," Moolah once explained.

The two golden girls, both members of the Pro Wrestling Hall of Fame, were delightful hosts and reservoirs of grappling history.

A couple of ordinary senior citizens and matronly grandmothers these queens of the canvas weren't.

And if proof was needed, one only had to venture a few hundred feet from the sprawling house to watch the grand ladies of wrestling in action, training (and sometimes stretching) aspiring mat hopefuls with ease at their official training facility, which in reality was a cramped building that resembled a little red barn.

'Tough broad'

The professional wrestling community — past and present — would collectively agree that Mae Young, dubbed "The Great" and "The Amazing" throughout her career, was as fearless as they had ever witnessed. She boldly proclaimed that she was one of the dirtiest fighters alive, and tried to prove it every night by pulling hair, gouging eyes and taking cheap shots.

"She was a rough, tough broad," said one of her old opponents.

The late Penny Banner recalled feelings of utter fear upon meeting Young.

"She had men's shoes on, men's pants on, with the zipper up the front, a cigar hanging out of her mouth," said Banner. "Back in 1954, you didn't do that."

"I don't like women's wrestling, but if ever there was one born to be a wrestler, you're it," the legendary Ed "Strangler" Lewis once told Young.

Young was a villain, and she played the role to the hilt.

"Anybody can be a babyface, what we call a clean wrestler," Young said in "Lipstick & Dynamite: The First Ladies of Wrestling," a 2005 documentary film about the early pioneers of women's wrestling. "They don't have to do nothing. It's the heel that carries the whole show. I've always been a heel, and I wouldn't be anything else but."

But there was another side to this remarkable lady. A spiritual one.

"She was a fine Christian woman. She taught me so much," said Henry, who escorted Young to many of her wrestling functions in recent years, an arrangement facilitated by the McMahon family.

It's that side of the many faces of Johnnie Mae Young that Henry feels is important for her fans to know.

"It's how she loved the Lord with all her heart. And she led a lot of people to the Lord."

Ellis said she was overwhelmed by the love and support shown by her friend's fans and colleagues.

"We were able to share some wonderful, wonderful times. And I got to meet so many of her wonderful friends. It was amazing how many people loved Mae … especially the women (divas). They all loved just being around her and listening to her stories. They loved her because she had set the path for them. It was really something to see."

Ellis fondly recalled the night in 2008 when Mae was inducted into WWE's Hall of Fame.

"She was so happy that night. When we walked in there that night and the crowd went crazy, she was just on cloud nine. She loved her fans."

Bridging generations

Pro wrestling, now more commonly known as sports entertainment, has changed dramatically over the years. It's a different business since the days Young and her contemporaries traveled, often piled up in cars, on rural back roads, on endless journeys of one-night stands. Women's wrestling has long evolved from its roots as a sideshow attraction that was banned in several states and even considered taboo for young ladies to join.

But Young's love for the business never wavered.

"This is a business that you have to love, and if you love it, you live it," she said in "Lipstick & Dynamite." "You move along with it. You grow along with the entertainment as it grows."

And Mae never stopped growing and evolving despite her longevity.

She had even worked the past 30 years with just one kidney that was only partially functioning. Her strict physical regimen of doing crunches and leg-lifts before going to bed at night and upon getting up in the morning most likely allowed her to outlive her failing kidney.

But she never used it as a crutch or an excuse. The show must go on, and there was no greater practitioner of that old adage than Young, whose sense of humor allowed WWE colleagues to sometimes respectfully poke on-air fun at her advanced age,

"When God said let there be light, Mae Young flipped the switch," WWE commentator Jerry "The King" Lawler would often crack during WWE telecasts.

"There's been only one Mae Young, and there will only be one ever," said WWE Hall of Famer Pat Patterson, who inducted her into the WWE Hall.

Shooting star

Tributes poured in following Mae's death last week.

From world-famous celebrities like The Rock to the many independent performers who had been fortunate enough to train with Mae and Moolah.

"She's a wrestling pioneer. I truly had deep affection and respect for 'Aunty Mae' Young, tweeted Dwayne "The Rock" Johnson.

"I have so much respect for Mae Young. Incredible person and pioneer of the wrestling business. An honor to sit in the WWE Hall of Fame with her," 16-time world champion Ric Flair chimed in on his Twitter page.

"You lived the life that most could only dream of. You touched so many lives. You certainly touched mine. You, despite aging, were forever young," posted Johnny Cook of Columbia, who wrestles under the name Johnny Flex.

Henry said her friend would be "beside herself" to see the outpouring of love from all corners of the world.

"If you think she danced on that WWE stage, just think what kind of dance she'd be doing now."

And no doubt Moolah would be ribbing her.

"Moolah's voice is still on her answering machine. She never took it off."

Henry said she expects Glass to continue to live in the Columbia home she shared with Young.

"Katie was her angel. She's a rough and tough little gal, but I'll tell you what. She would have killed for Johnnie Mae. She really loved Johnnie Mae and would have given her heart to her.

"And I do think Katie was there at the right time. There a scripture my mother used to tell me about 'in His time, all things are perfect.' I think that was one of the reasons Katie was put there ... to be special for Johnnie Mae. I know Moolah loved her greatly too."

Henry said her friendship with Young was special.

"She was amazing, but she was the great Mae Young," says Henry. "She touched my heart in such a way that few people will ever understand. When we would say goodbye and she told me she loved me, it was from the heart. And there was no doubt. We loved each other … we were best friends."

While Young's passing leaves a tremendous void in her life, Henry said she can only be encouraged because she knows where her friend is today. There is no more sorrow and pain in Young's new home, said Henry, but a renewed body in a happier world.

"I loved her with all my heart. It's very sad, but she is free. Those eyes that couldn't see well … they're now seeing colors and things that we can't dream imaginable. I know where she is because I know her soul. She's fine. I will see her again."

When the time grew near for that final bell, the old warrior was ready, said Henry. There would be no kickouts this time.

"It's not good," Mae confided in her friend shortly before her passing.

"But," she added, "I know where I'm going. And I'll be there waiting."

Mae Young, indeed, was the last of an old guard that will never be forgotten. Few have lived a life such as hers.

"She lived to the hilt," said Henry. "If you could write your own story and go out on a comet, she did. She did it all. Next time I see a beautiful shooting star, I'm going to know who it is. That's the way she left this earth … and went right straight to heaven. There is no doubt in my mind."

Part III
UNDERRATED

Penny Banner

Eddie Guerrero

Buddy Landel

Danny Miller

El Mongol

Penny Banner
The original wrestling diva

July 25, 2004

I t's never easy writing about the passing of a pro wrestling legend. It's even harder when the legend happens to be a close friend.

Penny Banner, who I've always known and will forever know as "Pretty Penny," left us early Tuesday, peacefully at home and in the arms of her beloved daughter, Wendi.

The records may list her chronological age as 73, but to those who knew Penny, she was ageless, timeless and forever young.

"When I think of my dear friend Penny, I think of '57 Chevys, poodle skirts and rock and roll. God bless her. She was the eternal teenager right up until she left this earth," Les Thatcher said last week.

Amen to that.

Penny Banner's accomplishments in the wrestling business could fill a book, as they did a few years ago in her autobiography "Banner Days." She was the first AWA world women's champion during the early '60s and was perennially ranked among the top two or three female performers in the business during a career that spanned from 1954-77.

The St. Louis native also was a diva long before the wrestling world even considered such a term. The focus of women's wrestling back then was skill, ability and toughness, not sports entertainment, titillation and eye candy, all staples of today's product. Penny, though, combined wrestling skill, raw athletic ability and glamorous looks to produce the total package. A drop-dead gorgeous blonde bombshell, she easily could have been the queen of the divas in the current incarnation of the profession.

But an amazing 50 years ago she was a queen of the mat. It was a golden era for the profession, and she was a pioneer who helped usher in the Golden Age of Women's Wrestling.

Beautiful and classy

Dick Beyer, who achieved worldwide acclaim as The Masked Destroyer, broke into the business around the same time as Penny. Twenty-four years old and just out of college, he started pro wrestling at Al Haft's gym in Columbus, Ohio.

"There was a very good-looking blonde by the name of Penny Banner training in the same gym," he recalled. "Needless to say, I had a difficult time trying to concentrate on my training when I just wanted to put my favorite wrestling hold on Penny, 'the double lip lock.' I never saw much of Penny during my 39 years of wrestling, but for the last several years we had plenty of time at the CAC (Cauliflower Alley Club) reunions to visit and tell stories about our separate careers."

"She was beautiful, well-tanned, strong, very sexy, yet wholesome with class," is how former mat great Cowboy Bill Watts described Penny.

Jody Hamilton, who formed half of one of wrestling's most successful tag teams of the '60s and '70s, The Masked Assassins, said Penny's striking beauty was even greater on the inside. She was, he said, one of the very few people in the business he loved and trusted implicitly.

"Penny was beautiful not only on the outside, but on the inside," Hamilton said Friday. "I measure beauty more by inner beauty than outer beauty. She was a knockout on the inside as well."

Many folks share his sentiments. Penny had a unique style that was endearing. One of her suitors in the early years was Elvis Presley, whom she dated several times over a three-year period. The king of rock 'n roll become a regular for Penny's matches in Memphis and would invite her to his Graceland home after the shows.

"We'd kiss all night long while the guys (the 'Memphis Mafia') played pool," Penny would recall.

Penny, indeed, was captivating. Graceful, beautiful and talented, she was as athletic as most of her male counterparts. She also married the territory's top star, Johnny Weaver, and that fact made her even more of a fan favorite.

But Penny, who had a six-year run as a heel before marrying Weaver, whom she had met in 1959 in the St. Joseph, Mo., area, lamented that she had to play the role of a babyface when the Weavers moved to Charlotte in the mid-'60s. It was fairly common knowledge among fans that the two were married, and promoters demanded that she work as a crowd favorite.

"I could have been the Buddy Rogers of women's wrestling," she once said. "I'm the first girl who started wearing two-piece bathing suits in the ring. I always tried to do something to be memorable and different — something more than just flying mares and dropkicks."

She and Weaver, who was one of promoter Jim Crockett Sr.'s most popular stars during the '60s, also made a pact that she wouldn't work a territory that he didn't. With Weaver firmly entrenched in the Mid-Atlantic wrestling office, Penny's career became limited to dates in the Carolinas and Virginia, working with a select number of women.

Surprisingly enough, Penny never fully knew just how good she was. She once confided that she wished she had realized it years ago while still in the business. But it was tough being a woman in the sport then, and she admitted being scared and nervous at times.

"If I had known I was that good, I would have really put on a show," she joked. "I would have been like Buddy Rogers. I would have gotten confidence. I never thought of me as being good. I guess I always wanted to be a perfectionist."

"She was so well respected by her peers — not only as a person, but for her tremendous physical ability in the ring," said Hamilton. "It was well known among her peers that she was a tremendous icon in our profession, but she never let that go to her head. She was always Penny. What you saw was what you got."

Life after wrestling

Penny's wrestling days ended more than 30 years ago, following an illustrious 23-year career, but she found joy in many other facets of life. She began working in real estate in 1977 and made a comfortable living at it. She joined the Senior Olympic Games at age 56 and captured a shelf full of medals and trophies to show for her efforts. She loved to dance and sing karaoke with friends.

And while their marriage for years had been portrayed as a picture-perfect relationship in magazines and in front of the camera, the reality of the situation was far from it. Penny tried her best to make things work, often immersing herself in things to get her mind off her troubled marriage. She took guitar and clogging lessons. She even put a wig on and went out dancing with the wives of other wrestlers when her husband was on the road. She was petrified of horses, but she learned to train them and to rodeo. She was president of all the 4-H clubs in Charlotte. She became a top competitive swimmer in the Senior Olympics. She was a board member of the Cauliflower Alley Club and regularly attended its annual convention in Las Vegas as well as the Gulf Coast wrestling reunion in Mobile.

The marriage ended, in 1994, after 35 years.

Penny continued to champion the cause of serious women performers, and she never broke kayfabe. She always maintained the purity of the sport and her own image, paving the way for all the girls who followed.

She would joke when recalling how she and other lady wrestlers from her generation had to sew elastic around the legs of their suits to be sure their cheeks didn't hang out. "Now, anything can hang out," she'd laugh.

Penny, who was born Mary Ann Kostecki in St. Louis on Aug. 11, 1934, was inducted into the Professional Wrestling Hall of Fame in 2005 and the St. Louis Wrestling Hall of Fame in 2007. She was to receive the Frank Gotch Award at the George Tragos/Lou Thesz Professional Wrestling Hall of Fame in Waterloo, Iowa, the first woman to be so honored.

Always upbeat and positive with a youthful exuberance, Penny was never anything but the life of the party who would brighten up a room when she was in it. "The pleasure of her company was not an experience to be forgotten," one acquaintance said of her outgoing personality. There was no pretense about Penny. She never failed to offer words of encouragement.

"She was always eager to do something new and always eager to be helpful to everybody," said her daughter. "That's what teenagers want to do. They want to go out and explore the world. They have a zest for life, and she's always had that."

"Penny was a dear, dear friend," said Hamilton, who had known her since 1954. "Her passing has left a void in my life that won't be filled. She was not only a great person, but to me she was one of the greatest of all the female wrestlers. I loved her dearly.

"It was a close relationship that had grown and matured over the years. We were friends through good times and bad times. She was always there if I needed anything, and she knew that if she needed anything I was always there for her. She was such a tremendously loyal friend."

Valiant battle

Penny's passing has been especially hard on daughter Wendi, who is still grieving over the loss of her father, stricken at the age of 72 less than three months ago with a fatal heart attack. Weaver, just months away from retiring from the Mecklenburg County Sheriff's Department, had gotten a clean bill of health from the doctor two days earlier. He had suffered from a heart arrhythmia a year and a half ago, but had been fine ever since, says his daughter. Three trips to the doctor this year also had checked out fine.

"It was just his time," says Wendi. "I know he died in a manner behooving him, because he could not have gone through what my mom did."

Wendi and her mother were like bookends. "She was the loving, caring, supportive mother. She definitely was somebody to look up to."

Penny had been diagnosed with peritoneal cancer in late 2005. Like every other obstacle in her life — numerous family hardships which resulted from an absentee father, a tumultuous marriage and working in a man's sport — she faced the disease with remarkable courage and resilience. Through the surgeries and chemotherapy treatments, this regal lady would greet friends with cheerful phone calls and e-mails, never allowing herself to get down over her own condition.

Penny had valiantly battled the disease, but suffered a relapse in January. Wendi had been by her side since then, and spent a week with her in the hospital when Penny lost her appetite after getting laryngitis and an infection in her vocal chords. Penny's condition worsened in April. Her muscles began to shut down and she lost 50 pounds.

Still, Wendi says, her mom would have an occasional good day, and she would start talking about the two of them going to Waterloo for Penny's award and a real estate class she was going to take. Wendi would bring her protein drinks and do whatever it took to lift her spirits. The two had been going back and forth to the doctor every week, and Wendi took her mom to her home in Mint Hill, N.C., where she learned to administer some of the medical procedures necessary to care for her mom.

At the same time, she says, she was going to her dad's house once a week just to "get her grief out and talk to him."

Now there are two homes to consider. "I can barely step foot in my mom's house, because now there's just so many recent memories," she says.

The two had spent Mother's Day together, but Penny took a turn for the worse later that day. Wendi had been warned by doctors about the normal end-life process that could be expected, although she never gave up hope. She held her mom's hand and rubbed her feet. "It was so natural and peaceful. We just sat and talked."

A couple of hours before she passed, says Wendi, the bedroom door popped open without explanation.

"I thought, oh my God, either her sister's coming with the Lord to get her or Betty Jo's (Hawkins) coming to get her, or she's walked out of the door. I remember a slight whisper, and I think I know now what she was trying to say. I think she told me that she loved me. They know you're there. That's what's important."

With Wendi by her side, holding her hand, Penny peacefully drew her last breath at 1:30 a.m. Tuesday.

Penny, preparing her daughter for the inevitable, had told Wendi a week earlier that "she was ready to go and be with her Lord and her friends in heaven." From a daughter's point of view, says Wendi, it was unnerving and "something you don't really want to hear."

But Penny, a ring general who knew a three count when she saw one, assured Wendi that it would be OK.

"I've got just as many friends in heaven as I have down here," she told her daughter. "I'll be talking to them for a long time."

Penny had lost a number of friends and loved ones over the past year. One old mat rival, Judy Grable, had passed away only a week earlier. Her son called Penny from the hospital.

Up until the end, though, Penny's friends remained optimistic that she would win her final battle.

"If there was any possible way this thing could be beaten, she was going to do it, because things like that (cancer) don't run into people like her very often," said Hamilton. "People who won't give in and won't give up. She fought it until the bitter end."

Penny's remains were placed close to her best friend, Betty Jo Hawkins, who she teamed with in the ring and loved like a sister.

"So many good things have happened to me that I didn't ask for. I'm so green about so many things, but I've been so blessed," she once said. One of those good things was her friendship with Betty Jo. The two shared each other's deepest secrets.

"They were partners and they were just little angels together," says Wendi. "They drove across country together, and were just so close." Hawkins, who had been married to wrestler Brute Bernard, died in 1987 at the age of 57 after suffering for years from rheumatoid arthritis.

Wendi is now "going through a whole lifetime" of photographs and memories as she prepares to say goodbye to another parent. It's all overwhelming, she says, but she knows both of them would want her to live life to the fullest.

"She was my angel. She protected me all my life ... and now she's going to be my real angel."

Eddie Guerrero
Wrestling's wake-up call

Nov. 27, 2005

I t's now been two weeks since pro wrestling lost one of its favorite performers. The outpouring of emotion and personal sentiment for Eddie Guerrero from friends, fans and colleagues has been overwhelming to say the least.

Eddie was the complete package in many ways. He had the pedigree, the skill and, most of all, the love and the passion for the business that the greats of the game always seem to possess.

But Eddie may have been guilty of loving the business too much. I'm sure many diehard fans and even some in the business will scoff at that remark and its implication, but it's true. One of the things Eddie truly loved and lived for, wrestling, may have been what killed him.

Eddie was only 38 years old when he left this world. That's too young by anyone's standards. But it happens over and over and over in the business of professional wrestling.

I certainly don't want to diminish the touching tribute shows WWE presented in honor of Eddie, along with the heart-wrenching expressions of love from many of his friends in the company. I just wonder when someone will step up to the plate and take notice that too many of wrestling's offspring are dying long before their autumn years.

Some call it a culture of death. Roddy Piper labels it "The Sickness." But until this problem is dealt with, wrestlers will continue to drop dead in motel rooms, families will be left behind, friends will mourn and wrestling companies will toll the bell 10 times.

Another broken heart

Like many others had before him and many others undoubtedly will after him, Eddie Guerrero considered professional wrestling the be-all and end-all. Only four months out of his life did he ever consider anything but wrestling as a livelihood, and even then it wasn't all that serious.

And, like many of his colleagues in the business, Eddie had an addictive personality. Whatever he did, he went all out. And that included an affinity for drugs and alcohol.

The autopsy attributed Eddie's death to heart failure. His wife, Vickie, said that his enlarged heart showed signs of damage. Blood vessels had been worn from years of abuse. "It was from his past — the drinking and drug abuse," she stated. By all accounts he had been sober for four years. But the damage had already been done, and the grueling ring schedule only served to speed up the process.

"Eddie just worked out like crazy all the time. It made his heart grow bigger and work harder and the vessels were getting smaller, and that's what caused the heart failure. He went into a deep sleep."

It may take weeks before the official cause of his death is determined. Toxicology tests will be conducted, and blood will be sampled.

Eddie left behind a wife and three daughters. Just weeks earlier he had moved his family from central Florida to Phoenix, Ariz., into a new home where bags and boxes still lie unpacked. Like Martha Hart a few years earlier, another wrestling widow will unpack in a brand new home, and will raise children without their father.

Concern for Eddie

I had a nagging, uneasy feeling in the early Sunday morning hours of Nov. 13. Not one prone to premonition, I thought about Eddie Guerrero and went through a couple of my old interviews with him. Like a number of his co-workers, I had expressed concern about Eddie over the past year. His short-lived title run in early 2004 had placed a heavy burden on his shoulders, and some feared he might be cracking under the pressure.

Eddie was a perfectionist, and he always wanted to have the best match on the card. On the rare occasion he didn't, he would spiral into an emotional abyss, fretting over a botched move or a missed spot. But that was just Eddie.

Fitting the image that the company places a premium on, Eddie had bulked up considerably over the past couple of years in WWE, looking nothing like his cruiserweight version in WCW or his even lighter days in Mexico. It wasn't a secret that he was carrying far too much muscle mass for his 5-7 frame. He constantly worked in pain and pushed himself beyond his physical limits, but he rarely complained.

A lot of the pain, of course, stemmed from a serious car accident seven years ago that nearly claimed his life. He gradually got hooked on painkillers, and combined with alcohol, the deadly mixture got him fired from WWE four years ago and also cost him his family. But WWE owner Vince McMahon got him help, funded his rehab and brought him back a seemingly new and better man who was poised to live out the balance of his life clean and sober.

The pain, however, never stopped. And apparently without painkillers, the pain from the constant bumps grew worse.

So when I got a call later that morning that Eddie had been found dead in a motel room just hours earlier, I was stunned but not shocked. And as devastating a blow as Eddie's death was to the entire roster who loved and respected him, I don't think his passing came out of left field to them either.

Solving the problem

Eddie's passing has shed light on a serious situation the wrestling business faces today. Wrestlers self-medicate to deal with the pain. Death has become an all-too-frequent occurrence.

The industry, specifically World Wrestling Entertainment since it is by far the largest and most profitable wrestling organization in the world, is in dire need of safeguards and reforms, and must take steps in order to prevent performers like Eddie Guerrero from dying on their watch.

There are no easy answers, but there are moves that can — and must — be made to clean up the business.

Wrestlers should be given extended time off each year in order to recharge their batteries and reconnect with their families. Mandatory routine physicals should be instituted with full-time physicians on staff. Medical insurance should be offered to wrestlers who put their bodies on the line every time they step into the ring.

McMahon already has taken a first major step in combatting the problem. Last week he announced a new drug policy that includes performance-enhancing drugs, recreational drugs as well as abuse of prescription drugs. In addition, the company is going to mandate more comprehensive cardiovascular examinations for its athletes. All performers under full-time contract will be subject to frequent, unannounced and random testing.

There are many others besides Eddie Guerrero who have dealt with or are currently dealing with issues in a less-than-conducive atmosphere for personal healing. Less than a week after Eddie's death, Nick "Eugene" Dinsmore was rushed to a hospital during WWE's European tour after he was found passed out in a hotel lobby. After regaining consciousness, Dinsmore admitted to taking somas, a popular prescription pill among wrestlers that is often abused, and other prescription medication. As a result of the incident, he was sent home from the tour and suspended indefinitely. He currently is being evaluated at a drug rehabilitation facility.

It's imperative that the company continues to make changes to prevent future tragedies and to ensure the long-term health of the industry.

A heavy burden

I've listened to many of his fans over the past two weeks express sadness that one of their favorite wrestlers would no longer grace their TV screens. Eddie was more than just a wrestler. He was an international superstar who was a role model to a growing Hispanic audience.

Winning the world title last year was the pinnacle of his career, but it proved to be a very stressful and trying time for Eddie as well. He blamed himself for the poor ratings and house show business that plagued the company during his title reign. Some argued that he was too small to carry the world title, but his outstanding mat work, ring psychology and interview abilities were unquestioned even though his body was breaking down.

He expressed his own concerns in an interview earlier this year with the London Sun. "It's a great responsibility being champion, as you're the one carrying the ball, and I found it very difficult. It was the first time I'd held the title and I don't think I was ready. I was ready to win the belt, but not for what lay ahead of me. I wasn't prepared mentally for what happens outside the ring — because I think that's where the real challenges lie. I was taking things like attendance and ratings very personally."

Eddie knew what his limitations were and fought hard to overcome them.

"I'm an extremist and that's one thing I'd like to change in my life. It's good to be hard on myself but not to the point where I beat myself up about things. If I'm honest and look back at my mistakes, then I was too hard on myself when I was carrying the title. I let things eat me up inside and I questioned myself when I shouldn't have, but it's a lesson learned and I won't make that mistake again."

A humble soul

Edouardo Gory Guerrero wasn't a saint, and he'd be the first to tell you so. His life literally was an open book. A DVD and UPN special last year, "Cheating Death, Stealing Life," was the basis for a book on Eddie's life that had been scheduled to be released next month. He was a recovering alcoholic who battled his demons each and every day of his life. He admittedly had a fiery temper that he fought hard to quell.

But unlike many who talk the talk but don't walk the walk, Eddie was a humble, caring family man with a compassionate heart. He counseled a number of the younger workers on the WWE roster, often with a Bible in his hand and a wealth of real-life experience to draw from. He lived out his faith in front of his fellow performers. WWE champion Batista spoke recently about how Eddie would quote him Scripture when he felt discouraged. Shawn Michaels talked not about their wrestling connection, but rather how they shared and encouraged each other in their faith. Chris Jericho called him the most humble man he had ever known and a true warrior for God.

While other wrestlers would share off-color road stories in the locker room, Eddie would pull out his Bible and go into the zone. He was the voice of reason other wrestlers turned to when their own lives went spiraling out of control.

"When we were on an overseas tour, he was really explaining a lot of his faith to me in a way that I could understand it as I hadn't understood it before," WWE performer Rob Van Dam said. "Straight up, asking him serious questions about Christianity that I didn't understand. He obviously wasn't going around preaching because he thought it was the right thing to do, because he wasn't a Bible thumper at all, but you could tell that he was so into it and it's great to hear anyone talking about something that they are so into, that you can tell they are speaking from the heart."

Eddie struggled, but he never gave up. He dealt with his addiction, and he turned to God.

"The Lord is merciful, and if you really accept Him in your heart, what you're doing you're going to have to answer to Him for eventually," he once told me. "It doesn't give us the license to sin. But once you're saved, you're always saved, and that's the grace and the love that the Lord has for us."

I have no doubt that Eddie believed every word.

A greater purpose

I re-read an interview I had done with Eddie (who used the spelling of Eddy outside the ring) not long after his favorite tag-team partner, Art Barr (formerly Beatlejuice and later The Juicer), died suddenly at the age of 28.

Barr, one of pro wrestling's fastest-rising stars at the time, was struck down in the prime of his career and the prime of his life on Nov. 23, 1994. The second-generation wrestler lived hard and fast, but he died peacefully in his sleep as he held his 5-year-old son during a visit home over a Thanksgiving holiday. Although his death initially was attributed to heart failure, it was later revealed that he had a mixture of alcohol and drugs in his bloodstream.

In ensuing years Eddie would tell me that a day didn't go by that he didn't think of Barr. "He was like a brother to me."

What made it easier for Eddie was knowing that he might have had an impact on his friend's life. He admitted, though, that there were aspects that he wished he could have changed.

"I wish I hadn't been doing the same thing as far as the prescription pills were concerned. I wish I had been a better influence on him as far as that's concerned. But I'm glad I was able to talk to him about the Lord, and that's the only consolation that I really have. I witnessed to him a lot, but I was doing the same thing with him. But we're nobody to judge. It's still a sin no matter what it was."

Eddie also was convinced that there was a greater purpose for their association.

"I think God put us together for a reason," he said. "One of the reasons was to help me get out of the rut I was in. Art taught me so much about the business. Art was always real good with me, my wife and the kids. He was a great friend and a great father."

There may, however, be an even greater purpose for the man affectionately known as "Latino Heat." If his untimely death serves as a wake-up call to effect a change in how the wrestling industry goes about its business, then perhaps this fallen hero will be remembered for more than his classic smile and contagious laugh, his ability to capture the hearts and imaginations of wrestling fans, and even his inspirational battle against addiction.

Buddy Landel

'Nature Boy' Buddy Landel battled his demons, but found redemption

June 28, 2015

"If ever there was such a talented rascal who would always be unconventional, it was Buddy Landel."

— Cowboy Bill Watts

Buddy Landel, who passed away last week at the age of 53, never had a problem admitting to anyone that he — far too often — had been his own worst enemy.

In a lengthy 2011 piece titled "The Redemption of Buddy Landel," he readily acknowledged a litany of mistakes and missteps that not only derailed his promising wrestling career, but also wreaked havoc on his personal life.

"The bottom line is that I was just selfish and it was all about me," he lamented.

"Nature Boy" Buddy Landel was one of the hottest young stars in the business during a brief period in the mid-1980s.

"I was 23, cocky and had a hundred grand in the bank. I didn't see that I had any problems," he said.

After all, Landel was making money hand over fist and headlining shows with the likes of NWA world champion Ric Flair, whom he emulated, and was rocketing to the top of his profession.

"He had everything you could have to be a superstar," recalled one promoter.

But Landel had one thing that would ultimately spell his downfall, and that was an addictive personality. Undependable and unreliable, prompting many bookers to label him "No Show Budro," his star extinguished just as it was ready to shine, and his career flamed out in a long-running battle with drug addiction.

"I always wanted to be great in everything I did. Whether it was to be great in sports or whether it was to be a great drug-taker," said Landel.

A group of WWE performers once lost money betting on the wrestler in a macabre dead-pool.

"A few of them walked up to me and said, 'Man, I just lost a lot of money on you.' I asked them how was that. They said, 'You were on deck,'" Landel recalled.

On the eve of what Landel claimed was to be the beginning of a coveted world title run with a high-profile match against Flair, Landel went on a cocaine bender. He arrived late the next day at a TV taping that had been designed to set up an angle leading to the title change.

Missing what could have been the opportunity of a lifetime, Landel was fired on the spot by booker Dusty Rhodes.

When he dried up and returned several years later, the wrestling landscape had changed and he was dropped down on the card.

"I got busted by the IRS. I was making four or five thousand dollars a week, and (Jim) Crockett paid my IRS tab. He then dropped my check down to $300."

"I was just too young to handle it," Landel admitted. "It was too much too soon."

The rest of Landel's career and life was marked by a series of ups and downs.

North Carolina-based wrestling journalist Bruce Mitchell summed him up thusly: "An enormous character, an enormous talent, and an enormous mess."

Fighting spirit

In recent years Landel had made it his mission to try and right wrongs and restore his legacy.

"Our choices affect so many lives," he said, happy to offer advice and counsel to colleagues in the business, while even encouraging others at one point as a practicing minister.

But there always seemed to be a black cloud hovering in the distance, including one that unfortunately would befall him for the final time.

Landel was involved in a serious automobile accident in Johnson City, Tenn.

Instead of going to the hospital by way of ambulance, he is said to have gotten there on his own. Against doctor's orders, he reportedly discharged himself from the hospital and returned to his home in Chilhowie, Va. Less than 24 hours later, he was dead.

Talk to anyone who knew him, and they'll tell you that was typical Buddy. He could never stay down for long.

Former Mid-South Wrestling promoter Bill Watts saw that fighting spirit in Landel early on.

"He'd give you his all in the ring," said Watts. "First and foremost, he never had a bad match. And second, he made the match come first."

Those qualities carried a lot of weight in Watts's book. Known as a taskmaster quick to fine his crew when rules were violated, Watts saw great potential in Landel, although sometimes "he could really push my buttons," said the promoter.

"I thought the world of Buddy. But Buddy was always his own worst enemy. I used to fine the heck out of him, and then I'd generally bonus him back because he worked so hard."

"Buddy was a free spirit," recalled J.J. Dillon (Jim Morrison), who managed Landel during his Mid-Atlantic heyday in 1985. "Watts ran a really, really tight ship. Buddy would screw up and get fined heavily, and Bill basically applauded the fact that after Buddy screwed up, he'd turn around and work twice as hard to redeem himself."

Passion for business

Dropping out of high school his junior year following football season, Landel made his pro debut at the age of 17 in 1979. In the process he left behind a slew of potential college scholarships to pursue a career he had fallen in love with.

While he regretted that he didn't finish school and get an education, he never regretted moving into a career field that made him, for a time, both rich and famous.

Six years into the business, Landel would find his niche working the talent-rich Mid-Atlantic area for Crockett Promotions.

With flowing blond hair and glittering robes, "Nature Boy" Buddy Landel found himself headlining cards throughout the circuit, challenging "Nature Boy" Ric Flair for the world heavyweight title.

The pressure, he would later admit, was too much to handle.

"They had put the whole weight of the world on my shoulders," he said. "I was breaking Elvis' attendance record, selling out with the world champion every night, doing 60-minute Broadways. It was very tough and the pressure was unbelievable. I just stayed self-medicated."

Despite his out-of-the-ring issues, Landel was a great performer inside the squared circle, and when he was on, few were better.

"The Nature Boy vs. the Nature Boy was a natural," said Dillon, who managed Landel at the time. "I got to be around Buddy a lot and got to know him. He really was a good guy, but sometimes made some bad decisions and sadly at times could be his own worst enemy.

"But Buddy had a passion for this business and had a lot of talent. When he applied himself and wanted to, there weren't a whole lot of guys better than him."

Dillon, who guided Landel to the National heavyweight title in 1985, said Landel's potential was unlimited.

"There were a few things that happened, had Buddy made other decisions, God only knows what a great career he could have had. But we'll never know."

Faith and family

Even in recent years, Landel would admit that he still had to walk a fine line, that those demons the old Buddy Landel fought were never more than a step or two behind. This time around, though, with a new grandson and another he was helping raise, he discovered a new purpose. Accountability had taken on a greater meaning.

"I feel like I've had another opportunity at life. Except this time to actually participate instead of watch it go by," he said.

Those who knew Buddy Landel best didn't see the cocky, unpredictable, unreliable heel that drew heat everywhere he went. What they saw was a caring, compassionate soul who deeply loved his family, with faith at the center of his universe. They saw someone who never failed to give credit to his wife of 34 years for not only staying the course, but also for holding him accountable when he strayed.

"Whatever I've got or whatever I'm worth is because of my wife," he'd say.

"To this day my wife will watch me when I get up to go the bathroom at a truck stop or anywhere else. But that's a good thing. You can make it a good thing because you have to be in agreement with each other.

"The Bible asks in Amos 3:3 how can two walk together if they're not in agreement. I agree with my wife that she has to watch my back. I don't trust me. I might have to live the rest of my life like that, but that's OK."

"I've watched my friends die, divorce, rehab, alimony, child support and lose everything they have," he said. "I myself have been spared those things. Maybe one day they will have an award for not hanging around too long and doing the right thing."

While Landel faced a tremendous amount of adversity in his life, some of it admittedly self-inflicted, he never stopped trying to do the right thing. He and wife had secured custody of a grandson some years ago while their then teenage daughter battled a drug problem of her own.

Landel says it turned his life around. "All it took for me was opening my heart and loving this little boy and raising him. The next thing I know, two or three years had gone by, and I was drug free. I could think. I could sleep. My grandson is what saved my life and, of course, the prayers of my family."

Buddy lost his daughter several months earlier, and friends say her passing gutted him. While his daughter spent time in a coma, he devoted himself to taking care of her.

Dillon, among other contemporaries, will remember Buddy as a friend who could brighten up the locker room with his big smile and gift of gab. Longtime fans will hearken back to when Buddy Landel and Ric Flair waged bloody battles over the 10 pounds of gold and the Nature Boy name in front of packed houses.

Buddy, who finally found solace and personal redemption, never forgot either.

"I just thank God that He allowed me to live through that era."

Danny Miller

Danny Miller had giant heart

June 12, 2016

"I'm just not sure anybody would remember me."

That's what Danny Miller told me shortly after he was invited to the Mid-Atlantic Wrestling Legends Fanfest in Charlotte back in 2013.

Miller had been selected as member of that year's Hall of Heroes class, a high distinction that honors some of the greatest stars to ever appear in the old Mid-Atlantic territory.

Even though I assured him that certainly wasn't the case, he still expressed reservations.

"It's been a long time," he said, pointing to the fact that 40 years had transpired since his last major run on the circuit.

What the veteran star would come to discover, however, was that nobody had forgotten Danny Miller, a fact borne out by the large, receptive crowd that turned out to meet and honor him during the weekend gathering.

WWE Hall of Famer Jerry Brisco was on hand that night to present Danny at the awards ceremony. Calling him "one of the honest guys and one of the good guys in this business," Brisco credited Miller with helping elevate the image of wrestling by advancing charitable causes through the Mid-Atlantic territory.

"I've known Danny for years and worked with him throughout my career. I did some research on him and I was stunned at his accomplishments and titles. The guy was a stud. He was a star."

Miller was visibly touched by the love and respect shown that night. And any doubts about not being remembered were quickly erased as the capacity ballroom crowd rose to its feet and gave Danny a standing ovation as he strode to the stage to deliver his acceptance speech.

"I'm sure that the wrestling fans who came to this great event feel the same way I do ... It's worth being here," he told the audience.

At that point, said Mid-Atlantic historian Dick Bourne, "he must have known his legacy was intact and he was far from forgotten. On top of that, his speech was one of the most sincere and heartfelt in the history of the annual event. Any young fan who might not have been familiar with him before that banquet certainly knew then they were in the presence of a legend. I'm so happy Danny got to experience that."

"I knew Danny had reservations about coming to Fanfest," added Bourne. "So many years had passed and so many young fans are at these conventions. I believe he really had started to believe that he might have been forgotten after such a long period of time. His induction into the Hall of Heroes certainly showed him that wasn't the case."

"You could tell the kindness that Danny had for everybody," said Brisco. "And everybody gave that kindness back in return. It was genuine kindness. That's what was so amazing about the guy. Here's this big guy in the ring, but outside the ring anybody could walk up to him and he'd make them feel comfortable and relaxed around him."

That was just Danny Miller. Humble to a fault, a true gentleman in a rough and tumble business, and someone who put family first but never forgot his fans.

Danny, who passed away last week at the age of 84, leaves behind a treasure trove of lasting memories that began with his first pro match on Nov. 15, 1955, in Springfield, Ohio, 100 miles from the farm in Fremont where his four brothers and two sisters grew up.

The younger brother of the late Dr. Big Bill Miller, one of the greatest athletes in Ohio State history, Danny recalled in a 2013 interview that he "was scared to death" when he stepped into the ring that night.

"Evidently they had someone was who hurt, sick or couldn't make the show. I was shaking all over."

At the time he broke in, recalled Miller, there was no shortage of seasoned, grizzled veterans based in the territory. He knew very well what they could do to a young upstart. He plotted his strategy accordingly.

"The only way I could get away from them was to get to the ropes so the referee would make them break. I had mat burns on my cheeks, my shoulders, my chins, my elbows, my knees. I told my brother Bill that I didn't know if this was the right business for me."

As it turned out, though, it was the perfect business for Miller, who enjoyed a successful 34-year career.

"As time goes on, you get smartened up. You learn to go with the program. But at first I got put in with those older guys, and they didn't want to see the younger guys get that chance. Those were the days when you wrestled at the county fairs up in Maine and Vermont where it was colder than a well-digger. You took your shower out in the pens with the cows and the horses. It was a lot different than it is today."

Miller Brothers

While Danny was sometimes overshadowed by the phenomenal collegiate and professional success of his older brother, he achieved greatness in his own right.

Like his brother, Danny attended Ohio State University, where Bill had been a nine-time letterman. But Danny stayed in school for only a year before joining the military.

Stationed in Fort Jackson, S.C., it was a brand new experience for Miller.

"It was very good. I got to see a lot of things I would have never seen in Ohio," said Miller, who served from 1953-55, following the end of the Korean War. "When I got out of the military, Bill trained me to come into pro wrestling."

Miller, who stood 6-foot-1 and weighed 245 pounds, couldn't have had a more qualified trainer teaching him the ropes.

Brother Bill, at a towering 6-5 and tipping the scales at nearly 300 pounds, had been an All-American heavyweight wrestler, a two-time Big Ten heavyweight champion and conference MVP his senior year. He also was an All-American shot-put and discus track star who would be voted into the Ohio State University Athletic Hall of Fame in 1997 for both wrestling and track.

"I had the good fortune of working with Dr. Bill," recalled Brisco. "You talk about intimidating. He was a giant of a man. And when Danny was young, he was a beast too. He was up there at 275, 280. But those two guys were so kind. Both of them were very educated and both of them were so kind. They could sit you down and talk to you and make you feel comfortable and not be intimidated by them. They worked like normal guys, though, and didn't try to go beast mode on you."

Danny and Bill would team sporadically throughout the years, with one of their biggest wins coming in 1965 at Madison Square Garden where they defeated Gorilla Monsoon and Cowboy Bill Watts for the WWWF tag-team title.

The Miller Brothers usually worked as heels, but it didn't matter to Danny.

"The fantasy of wrestling is: What can I do to give these fans their dollars' worth? I always contended that the first match on the card was very important. If you put the people in the palm of your hand, then you can manipulate them and do anything you want to with them. But you have to gain their confidence first before you get their response. Once you have a million dollars, it's not too hard making the second."

Mid-Atlantic champ

Miller's career took him to many parts of the globe, including most of the 50 states, Japan, Mexico, South America, Canada and Australia.

"Wrestling is what I did all my life," he said. "I often sit back and wonder to myself had I been in another business for 34 years, where would I be? At my age now, it's a good memory. I'm glad I did it. I got to see a lot of the world I would never had been able to afford to go and see myself."

One of his most prominent runs was in Jim Crockett Sr.'s Mid-Atlantic territory where he and Les Thatcher were an incredibly popular tag team but were never pushed as the top team, something that was later attributed to locker-room politics.

Miller won the Eastern States championship, the forerunner of the prestigious Mid-Atlantic title, in 1974 with a win over The Missouri Mauler (Larry "Rocky" Hamilton) in Greensboro, N.C. Three years later he toppled Ole Anderson to win the Mid-Atlantic TV title.

In the interim he formed a top team with Thatcher. "Les was very talented, and we had a great time together," said Miller. "He was like a brother to me."

He recalled a 1971 match the two had with The Masked Marvels (Billy Garrett and Jim Starr) in Norfolk, Va.

"We won the match, and the fans went over the barriers. The TV crew was there. We had sold the place out. The fans put us on their shoulders and carried us out of the ring. The place was electrified."

Despite their popularity and their wins over such top teams as The Marvels, Rip Hawk and Swede Hanson, The Mauler and Brute Bernard, and Art Nelson and Gene Anderson, there were signs that politics in the booking office may have prevented them from going further.

"The people in Charlotte didn't see that. It would have been to their good advantage to have Les and me as tag-team partners (champions). We were enthusiastic. We didn't walk to the ring — we ran to the ring. We had red, white and blue outfits, and we were quite popular."

Miller, though, has nothing but fond memories of Jim Crockett Sr., who passed away in 1973.

"Jim Crockett Sr. was a big guy. What a man he was. He would sit and observe. He was honest as the day was long."

Miller always remembered going into Crockett's modest office in Charlotte, and talked about the standards which Crockett demanded.

"If somebody came in his office with their shirt outside of their pants, they got sent away without their check," said Miller. "When you walked into his office, you presented yourself as a professional person. He was really a straight-laced guy. He was good to work for because you knew where you stood with him. He had his rules, and he ran a great business."

Respected by his peers and promoters, Miller was called on to help Crockett Promotions run towns throughout the Carolinas following his retirement from the ring in 1976. He initially worked under George Scott, the booker at the time, and helped promote several of the markets in the territory. It was the same George Scott with whom he had waged classic tag-team battles nearly two decades earlier in Calgary, Canada, with Danny and brother Bill locking horns with George and brother Sandy in the Stu Hart-run promotion.

"George taught me the business and television end of the game, which I didn't participate in before, but being there physically as a wrestler. Knowing the business end of it was a lot different. I enjoyed what I did."

Respected by peers and promoters, "Dandy Dan" was as well-liked as anyone in the business. Whether it was helping Sandy Scott run weekly shows at the Greenville Memorial Auditorium, or working with Henry Marcus at the ticket office at Charleston's County Hall, Miller remained a familiar face in the territory before returning to Florida in 1985.

'Gentle giant'

Miller's final move was to Tampa where he worked for several years in the wrestling office as an event coordinator for Florida Championship Wrestling. He later spent nearly 12 years working for the Tampa Electric power company. "It was pretty interesting for me because I had been in wrestling for 34 years and didn't know anything else. It was a smart move on my part."

The job also offered something that wrestling never did: health care benefits and life insurance. "In wrestling, being self-employed, you don't have those privileges," he said.

After retiring from the wrestling profession, Miller lived a relatively quiet life, residing at the same home for 30 years with wife Karin.

While he kept up with some his old colleagues and occasionally reunited with other wrestlers every few months at an Irish pub called O'Briens, the business was a thing of the past.

It was a dramatic change from all those years traveling the roads, but the jovial Ohioan seemed to find solace in settling down and putting down solid roots.

Eldest daughter Corinna Miller, speaking on behalf of her three sisters, called her father "a gentle giant."

"He loved God, country and his family. He had so much love and care in his life. He was a friend to everyone in need. He always had a smile on his face and a wonderful sense of humor."

"He was very active in the church," she added. "He did a lot of volunteering and spent a lot of time with church activities. He also was the handyman of the neighborhood for all the ladies. We have some widows and divorcees on our street, and my dad was their handyman until he just couldn't get up on the ladder anymore."

Miller also was a member of the church's ROMEOs (Retired Old Men Eating Out) group. "They went to lunch every week," said his daughter. "The women, who went once a month, were the RODEOs (Retired Old Dames Eating Out). We used to laugh that the men went to the cheap places, and the women went to the fancy places."

"It's wrestling's loss of one of the greatest from the Golden Age of Wrestling," posted Dotty Curtis, widow of Don Curtis, a longtime friend of Miller's who also was a top Florida heavyweight and promoter in Jacksonville. "Wrestling lost a great man."

Fellow Buckeye Thatcher called his former partner one of the finest men he had ever known.

"Danny Miller was my brother, partner, mentor and voice of reason," Thatcher posted on his Facebook page. "I was so honored to travel the highways with him and share wrestling rings, more importantly honored to call him friend and share a mutual respect.

All of us touched by knowing Dan are better for it."

The last few months were difficult ones for Miller. He went into the hospital in January experiencing breathing problems, said his daughter. He had suffered from bladder cancer 15 years ago and laryngeal cancer nearly five years ago, but had since been clear from both. But a cancerous tumor was recently discovered on his bronchial tube, and his condition had only worsened after chemotherapy. He entered hospice several days before his passing.

Like the great warrior he had always been inside the ring, Danny knew when the fight was over.

"His strength had started to wane," said Corinna Miller. "He never wanted to just linger."

Danny died June 6, mere hours after his 84th birthday, at the Melech Hospice House in Tampa. Among his survivors were his wife of 55 years, Karin; daughters Corinna, Ursula, Erika and Christa; and grandson Gianni.

"I guess he didn't want us to associate his birthday with his death," said his daughter.

Again, it was just like Danny Miller, thinking of others and calling his own shots.

"He was a really great dad and a really great man. He was one of a kind. But he's in a much better place now," said Corinna Miller. "The ladies at hospice were so wonderful. He was in no pain. My dad was dancing with Jesus, and it was time to go to the dance."

Les Thatcher, his old tag-team partner, said the wrestling world hasn't heard the last of Danny Miller.

"Dan will be hooking up once again with his brother Dr. Bill Miller, and tag teams in heaven had better look out."

El Mongol
Beloved Georgia favorite

Oct. 15, 2016

Few pro wrestlers made as big an impact in the talent-laden Georgia territory during the late '60s and early '70s as Raul Molina.

While that name probably wouldn't ring a bell with most longtime fans, his mat alter ego, El Mongol, was one of the biggest stars on the Atlanta circuit during an era in which wrestling was held on a weekly basis in towns such as Savannah, Augusta, Columbus and Macon.

Molina, 86, passed away last Sunday at his home in Lawrenceville, Ga. His oldest son, Raul Molina Jr., said his father had been hospitalized for several days after breaking four ribs and puncturing his lung due to a fall inside his home. Molina, who was in the beginning stages of dementia, also suffered a seizure. With two blocked arteries, his weakened condition and advanced age dictated that open heart surgery would not be a viable option.

He returned home on Friday where family gathered to honor the man many affectionately referred to as "Papa Mongol." While doctors told the family that he might have six months to live, it was only three days before Raul Molina took his final breath.

But up until his final day, said his son, the man known during his entire career as "Mongol" was smiling and laughing with his family.

His eyes lit up, says Molina Jr., when his 6-year-old great-granddaughter informed "Papa Mongol" that she had a boyfriend.

"My dad did his thumbs up and said, 'Muy bueno (very good).'"

Hated heel

Raul Molina's easygoing, gentle demeanor certainly belied his days as one of the most feared and intimidating competitors on the Georgia wrestling scene.

From hated heel to fan favorite, El Mongol rode a wave of popularity no matter what side of the ring he was on. Alternately billed from either Mongolia or Lima, Peru, Molina began his career in his native Mexico in 1951 where Lucha Libre legend Gory Guerrero bestowed him with the name "El Mongol."

Nearly 10 years later Guerrero, patriarch of the famous Guerrero clan, provided the papers for Molina to cross the border to El Paso.

At first Molina was reluctant. "Not without my family," he told Guerrero.

But Guerrero, who owned part of the Texas promotion and saw Molina as a potential drawing card, convinced Molina to make the move.

"Gory had watched my dad for years before he approached him about coming to the United States," says Molina Jr. "He told my dad that he would fix his papers for his whole family to come over and get the necessary permits. He told my dad that they could make some money together."

After several years working the Texas, Arizona and New Mexico circuits, Molina ventured to California in 1965 where he captured the vacant World Wrestling Association tag-team title with "Manchurian Giant" Gorilla Monsoon (Ithaca College wrestling standout Bob "Gino" Marella). It was a title he would later hold with Killer Buddy Austin (Austin Rogers).

By late 1966, Molina had begun his most successful run in the business when, as the mysterious and feared El Mongol, he invaded Georgia with a fury.

Behind the scenes, veteran Enrique Torres had convinced Atlanta booker Leo Garibaldi that there was money to be made with El Mongol, who had cut quite a swath through the Los Angeles circuit.

"My dad sent him pictures and a tape of some of his matches up in California, and they told him to come on down. So we left for Atlanta," says Molina.

Wrestling in bare feet and sporting a Fu Manchu mustache, shaved head and pigtail, the 5-9, 235-pound El Mongol was a rule-breaker trained in martial arts. Seconded to the ring by dastardly mouthpiece Dandy Jack Crawford, Mongol chopped his way through some of the top names in Georgia before later turning babyface after being attacked by manager Crawford and tag partner Tarzan Tyler.

Fan favorite

El Mongol would begin a new run as one of Georgia's favorite performers. He held the Georgia heavyweight championship a total of eight times over a five-year stretch, with title wins over such performers as Buddy Fuller, Mr. Wrestling (Tim Woods), Bobby Shane, Nick Bockwinkel, Buddy Colt and Dale Lewis. In all, Mongol held the Georgia tag-team title twice with The Pro (Doug Gilbert), the Southern tag-team title with Hans Schmidt, the All-South tag-team title with Ray Candy, and the Georgia TV title.

He also became the Los Angeles-based WWA's last heavyweight champion before the territory merged with the NWA.

In late 1970 El Mongol and Bobo Brazil defeated Mr. Ito and The Great Ota in the first racially mixed match in Atlanta history.

Classic TV historian and former wrestling newsletter editor Steve Beverly remembers Mongol well.

"I sold pictures for him when I was 13. He was one of the nicest of the group wrestling in Georgia at the time. He also was one of the best ever at drawing heat from a crowd, yet he never did a verbal interview. His manager, Dandy Jack Crawford, handled that end of it quite well. His matches with Paul DeMarco drew huge crowds all over the state."

At the peak of his popularity, Molina and wife Maria opened a restaurant aptly named Maria's Mexican Restaurant in 1970 in the Georgia Motel near Chamblee. Naturally, many of the area's wrestlers would frequent the establishment, which became a meeting place for fans and grapplers alike.

The Molinas expanded the operation to a larger site in downtown Atlanta six years later when business picked up due to his dad's popularity and the great food served there. A second business was opened in nearby Griffin two years later. Mongol operated the Griffin eatery, while Maria ran the Atlanta restaurant. Both did all the cooking.

"They were excellent cooks. Dad was a very strict owner. That's why we worked for our mom instead of our dad," laughs Molina. Molina, who accompanied his dad to many of his matches, said traveling to different cities and watching his father perform was the experience of a lifetime.

"My mom would get mad at him sometimes because we'd go to towns like Columbus and wouldn't be home until 4 in the morning, and I'd have to go to school that day. She really hated that. But my dad told her that he couldn't take that away from me. I wanted to be with him and his profession. Of course my mom didn't win."

Father and son

Molina, who was the oldest of five children, even considered trying his hand at wrestling, but never got far.

"Wrestling was not for me. I love wrestling, but I tried getting in the ring when I used to travel with my dad. I'd work out in the ring with guys like The Samoans and Dickie Steinborn. One time my dad and one of the Samoans flipped me up in the air, and I fell on my shoulder. I had it in a shoulder strap for three or four months."

While that effectively deterred Molina from pursuing a ring career, he nonetheless enjoyed many years of traveling with his dad and meeting hundreds of wrestlers along the way. It was an education one couldn't get in school. At a young age Molina had a ringside seat to a colorful but secretive world, one of great joy and successes, but also one of many trials and tribulations.

"They were all good people," he reflects. "It was a hard life for many. But everyone has problems. To me it was really awesome being a part of that. I enjoyed all of it."

Even when El Mongol was one of the most hated grapplers in the territory.

"They were booing up a storm during that time," laughs Molina. "But it really didn't matter to me. I'd go everywhere with my dad."

Just as Gory Guerrero had helped bring Mongol into the United States, and Enrique Torres had helped bring Mongol to Georgia, Mongol helped facilitate bringing in other Hispanic performers to the Atlanta area.

"A lot of times, I'd travel with some of the younger generation wrestlers that my dad helped get here," says Molina. "Guys like Sabu Singh and Roberto Soto from Puerto Rico. I'd travel with them when they went to the smaller towns (on the circuit). I was good friends with all those guys. When I couldn't go with my dad, I'd go with them. That's how much I loved wrestling."

Molina says his father was a disciplinarian who expected his children to toe the line.

"He was an awesome dad," says Molina, who is now 62. "He was very funny. He was a good person all the way around with everybody. If he liked you, that was it. He was with you all the way and wouldn't let you go. But if he didn't like you, stay away. There was no in between. He was very strict and didn't play around. When he told you something, he meant it. When he told us once and he'd give us that look, we knew we better straighten up real quick."

One of those patented Mongol chops wasn't out of the question for those who didn't walk the straight and narrow. Once when Molina Jr.'s future brother-in-law defied a rule, he found himself the surprised recipient of a smack from Mongol.

"We still laugh about it. He chopped my brother-in-law right across his chest. I guess he thought he was in the ring with another wrestler. It was so funny the way he did it. He had that handprint on his chest for a while.

"As the years went on, you respect somebody like that more and more even though at first you don't realize it. He instilled a lot of good values in us. I respected him so much."

Family man

More than anything, Raul Molina Sr. was a dedicated family man. Unlike many of his colleagues who uprooted families while bouncing from territory to territory, Molina never veered far from his home base of Atlanta.

"He always was a family man. Once we got to Atlanta, he became an all-around Georgian. He wasn't like many who traveled and went outside the state. He never did. He had many opportunities to do so, but he always told them he was fine making his money here."

Even when he left the main office in Atlanta to work for Ann Gunkel's All-South promotion, he remained steadfast in his loyalty to his family, choosing not to pull up stakes.

Mongol, the Georgia heavyweight champion at the time, knew his days with the NWA-affiliated Atlanta office were nearing an end when Tony Atlas approached him in an Athens dressing room prior to a two-out-of-three falls title defense against Crazy Luke Graham. Atlas relayed the message that the office wanted him to drop two straight falls to Graham.

Mongol, though, would have none of that. When Atlas returned later with the same message, Mongol gave him the same answer.

"Tell Luke Graham if he can beat me two straight falls, then go for it," he told Atlas. Graham's response was straight to the point: "No way." Graham, who had teamed with Mongol several years earlier in California, knew full well that Mongol was more than capable of handling himself in the ring.

To add insult to injury, the office further demanded that Mongol cut off his trademark pigtail. The pigtail had been an important ingredient of Mongol's overall ring presentation, something he had worn since Guerrero came up with the idea back in Mexico.

With his restaurant doing well and job security not an issue, Mongol told the office what to do with their demands. He took his name and skills to the rival Gunkel promotion, and would wind down his wrestling career in 1980.

"After Ray Gunkel passed away, it wasn't the same," says Molina Jr. "My dad never liked it like he had before. Ann Gunkel did things pretty much her way, and it just wasn't working out. She took a lot of the smaller venues. But she did try to take care of my dad. Ray had told his wife before he died that if you don't do nothing else and stay in the business, then I want you to take care of Mongol. Those were his exact words."

Molina says his dad watched bits and pieces of the current wrestling product, but it was a far cry from the wrestling he remembered. He would take his father to make occasional special appearances for promoters who would advertise the legendary wrestler. But unlike others, Mongol refused to charge for autographs or even photographs, often taking hundreds of signed 8x10s and giving them away to fans. He was old school all the way, thanking the fans who remembered him and supported him all those years.

"He wasn't going to those places to make money," says Molina. "That's what kind of dad I had. He appreciated what the people did for him. Now that he was retired, he didn't just want to sit down and sell stuff and make money off of it. The fans put money in his pocket when he was wrestling. Now it was his turn to repay them. That's just what kind of person he was."

Bits and pieces of those glory days can be found in memorabilia and souvenirs that Molina has collected over the years. There are images of his dad gracing the front page of Atlanta City Auditorium wrestling programs, photographs of his dad wrestling Gene Kiniski for the NWA world title and other mementos from an illustrious career.

Mongol had a number of tag partners over the years, but he really liked teaming with Doug "The Pro" Gilbert, says Molina. His matches against the likes of Paul DeMarco, Rock Hunter and The Assassins stand out.

"Probably one of the bloodiest battles that fans talked about for a long time was his matches with Louie Tillet," says Molina. "They had some big matches here and some big brass knuckles matches down in Tampa. They'd sometimes wrestle for an hour at a time. They were something else."

It was, he says, a special time to be a fan and a wrestler.

"It was really nice while it lasted. Those were times I'll never forget."

Part IV

MID-ATLANTIC
MAINSTAYS & STARS

Swede Hanson

Rip Hawk

Burrhead Jones

Bronko Lubich

Nelson Royal

George Scott

Sandy Scott

Johnny Weaver

Tim Woods

Jay Youngblood

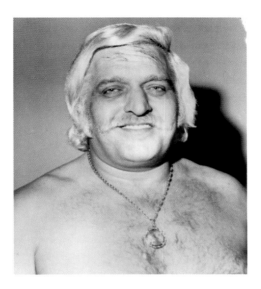

Swede Hanson
A part of wrestling died with Swede Hanson

Feb. 24, 2002

Today's column is not about the return of the NWO. Nor is it about the ratings, The Rock or Wrestlemania. Many younger readers may have never even heard of the man to whom this article is devoted. But without him, there's a chance I might not have ever written my first line on the subject of professional wrestling.

This generation's fans can look to icons like Hulk Hogan, Ric Flair and Steve Austin. When my fascination with pro wrestling took hold in the early '60s, at the top of this fan's list was a main-event star by the name of Big Swede Hanson.

Wrestling, of course, was an entirely different business back then. There were no paid leaves of absence, time off for injuries or guaranteed contracts. The only thing guaranteed was working and traveling at least 300 days a year and the satisfaction that you were part of one of the most unique professions in the world. It was a business especially designed for real men who often lived their gimmicks and their lives to the fullest. It was tailor-made for men like Robert "Swede" Hanson.

When Big Swede passed away at the age of 68 in a Columbia hospital, a part of the wrestling business died with him. I know a part of mine did.

I'd like to share a few things about Swede. First, it's almost impossible to talk about Swede Hanson without mentioning Rip Hawk in the same sentence. As far as teams go, they rank right up there with Martin and Lewis, and Batman and Robin. They were, in fact, so good that it wasn't long before I was hooked on the business after watching these two larger-than-life stars wreak havoc on their opponents week after week.

Rip "The Profile" Hawk was a cocky, trash-talking early version of "Nature Boy" Ric Flair, who Rip would later introduced to this area as his "nephew" in 1974 shortly after Swede suffered a heart attack and was forced to sit on the sidelines. A stocky 5-9, 240-pound ex-Marine, Hawk appeared to be a peculiar match for the 6-4, 280-pound Swede "Big Foot" Hanson, whose massive mitts and size-17 boots made him one of the most powerful men in this or any other business, as he proved as a two-time Golden Gloves champion in New Jersey with a 64-3 record (he lost to the same fighter all three times; as Swede would admit, "the guy just had my number").

But the partnership clicked to the tune of an unbelievable 16-year run. Their act was simple: Rip did the talking. Swede was the enforcer. Both were talented workers inside the ring, since actual mat ability was an absolute prerequisite in those days. But they were first-class "bad guys," and their job was to make the fans hate them. Nobody did it better. They were headliners from Charlotte to Tokyo, from Singapore to the Australian Outback. More importantly, "we were closer than any brothers could ever be," Rip would say. Both would readily admit that they burned the candle at both ends, but neither would have done it one bit differently.

"It was the hard life we lived, but we had outstanding times," said Rip. "We lived it all the way. We lived it like we were supposed to. Sixteen years of fun."

Their out-of-ring exploits would easily fill the pages of a hefty novel, but one of their most interesting adventures occurred while touring the Far East when Swede, after consuming a large quantity of sake, dove into a small pool in the lobby of a swank Japanese hotel and started chasing the goldfish. "Swede didn't know that goldfish are sacred over there, and the people went nuts ... It seemed like we were always in a beef," said Rip, adding that they were as formidable in bar fights and scuffles outside the ring as they were in actual wrestling matches.

Like the time in Lynchburg, Va., when rowdy fans sliced Swede down the side of his leg and later tried to overturn the ambulance that was transporting him to the hospital. The shaken ambulance driver quickly regained his composure when Swede warned that he would commandeer the vehicle if the driver thought twice about slowing down for the unruly crowd. Swede was back in the ring the next night.

Or the time at the Township Auditorium in Columbia when fans rioted prior to Hawk and Hanson's grudge match with Nelson Royal and Paul Jones. The bout never started and the show was stopped.

Swede began his pro mat career in October 1957 and wrestled in four different decades. A native of East Orange, N.J., he was a prep football star who passed up a scholarship to Wake Forest when he quit his last year of school to become an aviation mechanic in order to help his struggling mother pay the bills.

He sparred with the likes of Archie Moore and Rocky Marciano, and counted Sugar Ray Robinson and Joe Louis among his friends. Former basketball great "Dr. J" Julius Erving would attend Swede's matches in Philadelphia, and once gave Swede a pair of his favorite basketball shoes, only to give him a replacement pair when Swede wore out the old ones. He was also a Duke sports fanatic who adorned his Fort Mill trailer with Blue Devil memorabilia.

"We lost a great Duke fan," Bob Harris, the voice of the Blue Devils for the past 25 seasons, said Friday. "He was not an Iron Duke, he was not a season ticketholder. As a matter of fact, he never stepped foot inside Cameron Indoor Stadium, although I invited him several times. But he was what a Duke fan was all about. He pulled for Duke, he admired (coach) Mike Krzyzewski tremendously. I once got Mike to autograph one of those mini-balls for Swede. When I gave it to him, he looked at the ball and he looked at me and looked at the ball again. When he looked back up, there were tears rolling down his cheeks. It thrilled him to death. It was better than looking at a kid at Christmas."

Swede had been married and divorced twice during his wrestling years, but the light of his life was a lady named Patsy Hughes who had booed and jeered Hanson as a fan, but in later years discovered that the big guy was actually just a big teddy bear who wouldn't harm a fly.

It was hard not to chuckle when Swede once recounted the story about going to the movies with his fiancée of nine years and seeing "Snow White and the Seven Dwarfs" for the first time in 50 years. "I was singing 'Heigh-ho, heigh-ho' with the Dwarfs, and my girl was sliding down in her chair," the big guy admitted.

Swede also loved the five acres on which his doublewide rested, a good stone's throw from the South Carolina-North Carolina border, and where his ashes will be spread.

As for myself, I'll remember when I first became a fan, waiting outside the old County Hall every Friday night for that big white Cadillac to pull up, just to get a glimpse of the coolest heels I'd ever seen. I'll remember the "Blond Bombers" waging bloody battle with babyface duos like George and Sandy Scott, George Becker and Johnny Weaver, and Nelson Royal and Paul Jones, as well as fellow "bullies" like Skull Murphy and Brute Bernard, Aldo Bogni and Bronko Lubich, and Gene and Ole Anderson. More than that, however, I'll remember Swede Hanson my friend, a hero of my youthful past who helped introduce me to what would become a lifelong passion.

Declining health (diabetes, high blood pressure, heart problems and Alzheimer's) in recent years had frustrated Swede, who, like any good fighter, dreamed of that one last comeback. As recently as a year ago, Swede had called his longtime buddy, Rip Hawk, and talked about "one more match." Rip politely told him that, at the age of 70, he didn't think that would be the wisest of ideas. But it didn't stop the big man from dreaming.

"Nobody will ever know how much that guy meant to me," wept Rip when learning the news on Wednesday.

I know the feeling.

Rip Hawk
'The Profile' left lasting legacy

Dec. 29, 2012

I t's a tough pill to swallow when one of your childhood heroes passes away. It's even tougher when that hero is one of your best friends.

Rip Hawk, who was born Harvey Maurice Evers, died Dec. 22 in Hereford, Texas. He had been in and out of hospitals for much of the past year, and had spent the last several weeks in a rehabilitation center.

Rip was 82 years old when the final bell tolled. I can only imagine what those doctors, nurses and caregivers must have thought as Rip passed through the final stages of his life.

If only they could have known the Rip Hawk I knew.

Rip's obituary noted that he was a former professional wrestler and a personal trainer at the local YMCA.

But Rip Hawk was more than that. So much more.

The Rip Hawk I knew was one of the toughest guys to ever compete in one of the toughest sports in the world.

As the late Gordon Solie might have pontificated, Rip was the kind of guy who could fight a buzzsaw and give it the first two rounds.

He was just a child when the Great Depression struck, but he vividly remembered what it was like when people had to stand in line for food. He lived on a farm in the country with an outhouse in the back and no electricity or running water in the house.

Rip's path to the wrestling game nearly took a detour since he was raised in a baseball family. He was the son of a baseball star who played in the old Texas League. Related to Johnny Evers of the immortal Tinker-to-Evers-to-Chance trio, his father became a scout and trainer for the New York Yankees when his elbow gave out and cut short his pitching career.

"They pulled me into baseball all the time, but I couldn't take it," said Rip. "It wasn't my thing. I loved wrestling."

He broke into the sport in the late '40s, learning the ropes from the "freaks" of the rough-and-tumble business, whose barbaric methods made today's training look like a cotillion.

"Those guys would come in and beat the hell out of us," Rip would recall. "They walked on our faces and arms. They were tough men who didn't care about anything."

But Rip was more than up to the task. Toughness was part of his DNA, and he embraced every painful lesson he had to learn.

Rip was one of the few who persevered. He had the ability and the desire, but his mat persona was not complete until a promoter came up with a catchy ring name.

"My sister started calling me Rip when I was about 10 years old," he said. "It was a good wrestling name. The Chicago promoter asked me my name, and I told him it was Rip Evers. He said that I had a sharp nose and I moved like a hawk. 'We're going to call you Rip Hawk,' he said."

The name stuck.

A five-year stint in the Marine Corps and the Korean War interrupted his ring career in the early '50s. But nothing else would for the next three decades while Rip was doing what he loved the most.

Rip and Swede

I first crossed paths with Rip "The Profile" Hawk nearly 50 years ago. Rip was a cocky, brash performer who played his role to perfection. I was a young wrestling fan who was mesmerized by his bombast and bluster and his ability to back it up in the ring. Sharp-dressed and always driving big cars, he had swag, and it was cool.

Rip was a heel, for sure, but one who would have been wildly cheered had he come along in today's wrestling business. Back in the glory days of the profession, when the line between good and evil was sharply delineated, he was a villain of the first order.

Rip, though, was just part of the equation. The other half was Swede Hanson

Wrestling back then was a business especially designed for real men who lived their gimmicks and their lives to the fullest. It was tailor-made for guys like Rip Hawk and Swede Hanson.

Known as "The Blond Bombers" for their platinum blond flattop haircuts and rugged ring style, the duo became one of the most feared and hated teams in the business during the '60s and '70s.

They were physical opposites, but their partnership was a match made in heaven. They were a unique combination of brains and brawn.

Swede was the enforcer and the silent member of the team who, at 6-4 and nearly 300 pounds, towered over his 5-9, 240-pound partner. But it was Rip who was the unquestioned leader. He did all the talking, and he was mighty good at it.

As the silent partner, Swede would usually just nod in agreement during interviews while Rip enraged fans with his controversial rhetoric.

Outside the squared circle, the two were closer than most brothers. Spending 15 years on the road together can create that kind of bond.

Their travels took them around the world — Japan, Australia, Hong Kong, Singapore and all points in between.

"When you travel all over the world and you're with someone 24 hours a day, you get to know a guy pretty well," Rip said.

They had great fun along the way. Sometimes too much fun.

"I guess we liked to burn the candle at both ends ... a little too much," Rip would admit.

There was the time when Big Swede, after consuming a large quantity of sake, dove into a small pool in the lobby of a swank Japanese hotel and started chasing the goldfish.

"Swede didn't know that goldfish are sacred over there, and the people went nuts ... It seemed like we were always in a beef," said Rip.

The two were as formidable in bar fights and scrapes outside the ring as they were in actual wrestling matches.

"We lived it all the way. We lived it like we were supposed to. Sixteen years of fun."

Big Swede, a former Golden Gloves boxer from New Jersey, played the perfect foil for Rip's constant ribbing.

"I always had him on a rib," said Rip. "I loved it, and he loved it too. But he always knew I was going to get him."

When Swede died in 2002, a little bit of Rip died with him.

"Nobody will ever know how much that guy meant to me."

New generation

While Rip was instrumental in Swede's success in the business, having introduced him to Jim Crockett Sr. and convincing the longtime promoter to team them up in the early '60s, he would play a major role in the development of a number of stars from the next generation.

It didn't come as a surprise when Rip, 44 years old at the time, took a 25-year-old up-and-comer named Ric Flair under his wing, groomed him as his storyline nephew and helped him win his first major title in 1974.

Rip Hawk was Ric Flair before there was Ric Flair. The Nature Boy was the logical extension of The Profile.

"I learned a lot from Rip," said Flair. "He was a real ring general."

The respect colleagues had for Rip stood as a testament to the many lives he touched in the business.

"I loved the man ... he got me my first break in the business and taught me how to be a complete pro," said WWE Hall of Famer Jerry Brisco.

"Rip Hawk was a brilliant mind," said trainer and former mat star Les Thatcher. "We got spoiled because as a babyface, when you went up against Rip, all you had to do was shut your mouth, open your ears and go along for the ride. You'd have to be an idiot to not get better in the ring with someone like Rip.

"That's why they gave him Flair when Ric first came into the territory. Ric had been in the business a little over a year when he came to the Carolinas, and they put Rip with him as a teacher. They couldn't have picked a better guy."

Even the late Johnny Weaver, who became one of the biggest stars ever in Mid-Atlantic wrestling, owed a big debt of gratitude to Rip.

Rip had Weaver while working main events in St. Louis for promoter Sam Muchnick, and was instrumental in bringing him into the Carolinas to work for Crockett Promotions. Although Weaver was working on the bottom of the card, Rip recognized star potential and knew he had the perfect candidate when Jim Crockett Sr. asked him where he could get a good babyface to pair with aging veteran George Becker.

"I know of a young guy who's out in St. Louis," Rip told the promoter. "I'd be glad to give him a call." "Is he good?" Crockett asked. "Hell, yeah," Rip replied, "and he's getting better every day."

And the rest was history.

Leading by example

Like most old-school performers, Rip sported his scars like badges of honor.

But when the business and age began taking a toll, Rip was wise enough to sense it, hung up his boots and never looked back.

Rip spent the last 30 years of his life in what he called his little slice of heaven — the cattle town of Hereford, Texas. It was a vast departure from the big-city lights he enjoyed during his wrestling career, but he loved it with a passion.

His love of the Texas Panhandle was only surpassed by his love for his wife, daughters and grandchildren.

"I'm just a happy man. I enjoy life and I love life. That's why I think I'm still here," he said earlier this year.

Rip also loved teaching youngsters how to wrestle. He had started an amateur wrestling program at Charlotte Catholic High School in 1969 with David Crockett while he was wrestling in the Carolinas. For the past two decades, he had served as a wrestling coach in Hereford and had sent several young wrestlers to the Junior Olympics and to college on athletic scholarships.

"I loved it," said Rip. "Seeing the kids progress made it worthwhile. I've had kids come out of this program with scholarships from Ohio, Oklahoma and Arizona State."

Some are now doctors, some are youth ministers and some even went into the Marine Corps since they knew Rip had served in that branch.

"To know that you helped kids ... it means a lot to me."

A life well lived

Rip knew he had packed more into one lifetime than most folks could even dream of.

Over the years he had survived scores of close calls in and outside the ring.

Early in his career an unruly crowd in St. Joseph, Mo., came close to hanging him after he had disposed of a local favorite. He also has been stabbed by fans who took things a little too seriously. He's had more than his share of near misses flying the friendly skies.

His laundry list of injuries included eight broken noses, a split sternum, broken ribs, elbows and kneecap, along with hundreds of stitches. He sported a cauliflower ear for good measure.

"Other than that, it was pretty good," he'd joke.

Rip and I would talk often over the years, but I never saw him as anything less than the unique character that left me in awe as a youngster.

He'd have to forgive me when I couldn't help but utter those words that "fans" would shower him with every week: "Squawk, Squawk, Chicken Hawk!"

If they had only known that it was music to his ears.

I still pass by the old County Hall on occasion, and it never fails to bring back memories of the old marquee with the familiar bold letters: "Wrestling ... Friday night ... Hawk and Hanson."

Before I know it, I'm back in time, waiting for The Blond Bombers to roll into the parking lot in that big Caddy, primed and ready to punish another set of opponents.

Neither of us ever forgot those days, and Rip never tired of talking about them. I'll always remember some of the very last words Rip spoke to me.

"The good Lord has been very good to me in my lifetime. If it ended today I'd die a happy man."

I'm quite sure Big Swede is closer than ever in getting that hot tag from The Profile.

The Blond Bombers, says daughter Angela Van Wyk, are finally reunited.

"You just know that they're there tearing it up up there."

Burrhead Jones
'There'll never be a cotton-pickin' nuther'

Oct. 29, 2017

I've written my share of pro wrestling obituaries over the years. Some are tougher than others. That comes with the territory when you've been around the business as long as I have.

This one just might be the toughest.

I got the news late Sunday night. Melvin Nelson had passed away at 8:45 that evening in a New York City hospital. He had taken ill 24 hours earlier, and his condition rapidly deteriorated. Life support was tried temporarily, but it would be in vain.

Burrhead Jones, Melvin Nelson's more well-known alter ego, always knew when it was time to "go home."

The past two years had been challenging. Two bad knee replacements had left Jones immobile and in a nursing home, while glaucoma eventually took its toll and rendered him blind. His spirit and love of life, though, never waned. His only complaint was that his facility didn't have cable and he was unable to follow his favorite wrestling shows.

He was in great spirits the Friday before his passing. His wife, Viola, had delivered one of his favorites, a shrimp dinner with potatoes, okra and broccoli, topped off with a lollipop for dessert. "He absolutely loved it," said youngest daughter Jiquetta Nelson.

Twenty-four hours later, though, he suffered a setback that would lead to pneumonia. He was taken to the hospital and died the following night. He had just turned 80 last month.

Those who knew Burrhead Jones will never forget him. He had overcome obstacles in his life not by being bitter and resentful, but instead with a unique, good-natured humor that made everyone want to be his friend. And he had many. I was lucky enough to be one of them.

A special character

It had been a wonderful journey for the man thousands of fans over the years knew as the inimitable Burrhead Jones, "the one and only and there'll never be a cotton-pickin' nuther," as he would often proclaim. While many might have faltered, he was a survivor and overcomer, a black man battling the odds in a business that mirrored a segregated society.

A generation before pay-per-views, high-dollar contracts and "sports entertainment," pro wrestling was a life of one-night stands, going up and down the road, making six bucks and spending four, a life of spilling blood on canvases and breaking bones in smoke-filled arenas and dingy union halls.

It was more than just a wrestling life for Jones. It was an odyssey through a tumultuous period of American history, an experience that gave him the chance to bask in the spotlight of a profession that seemed tailor-made for him.

The world of professional wrestling is full of colorful figures. They come in all shapes and sizes, and their stage is a ring in which their personalities often reach larger-than-life dimensions.

Many, if not most, of today's characters are carefully crafted, molded and tweaked by a creative team that builds personas from scratch. It's a far cry from the old days when most wrestlers were their gimmick.

Burrhead Jones was one of those special characters.

He never won a world title, nor did he ever command the six- and seven-figure salaries commonplace in the industry today.

What he did do was much more noble and inspiring. He worked his way out of Berkeley County cotton fields, survived the rampant racial discrimination of the time, and achieved his dream of becoming a professional wrestler.

'Hero from the past'

We all loved Burrhead. To many of us inside and outside the wrestling circle, he was like a breath of fresh air. While the business can easily sour relations and friendships, it's highly unlikely that anyone ever had an unkind thing to say about Burrhead. With a down-home sense of humor that made him easy to like, the fact that he had many friends was not a surprise.

Veteran wrestling star and trainer Les Thatcher was one of them.

"Melvin Nelson was one of the kindest, sweetest human beings I have ever been honored to call my friend," said Thatcher. 'Burr' was never world champ, he never headlined a PPV, he never owned a BMW … hell, he may have never owned a car, but he was more the embodiment of our industry than Ric Flair, Bret Hart or John Cena.

"Why? Because six or seven nights a week, he ground it out in tank towns in front of a hundred fans and to big crowds in major arenas making the current and future stars of wrestling look not good, but great, and he did it with love and passion and because that was his job. He always met you in the back after making you look good with a handshake and a smile on his face."

"Nothing but fond memories of a fine gentleman," echoed WWE Hall of Fame announcer Gene Okerlund.

"Burrhead so often liked to joke that 'there's only one Burrhead Jones, and there'll never be another cotton-pickin' nuther.' There is no question about that," said friend and longtime fan Andy McDaniel, who helped organize a 1998 reunion in Charleston that honored Jones and other former wrestling stars. "He's a hero from the past, a true legend who didn't just portray a role. He was that character."

While tributes poured in from friends and colleagues in the wrestling business, it was the response from fans that truly exemplified the connection Jones had made with those who had cheered him on over the years.

Many expressed how he graciously took time with them, offering advice on the wrestling business or life in general. He was never too busy to share special moments.

"I have never forgotten his kindness to me as a kid when I met him a few times," recounted Dylan Hales. "He was actually a big part of me becoming more involved in the business because of the time he took to speak to me with kindness during an era where very few did."

Lowcountry roots

He performed in front of thousands and traveled around the world, but it was his rural Berkeley County roots that helped prepare Melvin Nelson, the future Burrhead Jones, for a career in professional wrestling more than 50 years ago. His humble beginnings provided a sturdy work ethic that would serve him well in later years.

He grew up in a small clapboard home built in the early 1900s on land that his ancestors owned, near what would become Carolina Nurseries Inc., off U.S. Highway 52 in Moncks Corner. In those days, the 600-acre horticultural smorgasbord was endless rows of tobacco, corn and cotton fields where Jones spent his afternoons and evenings picking cotton for two cents a pound when he wasn't busy plowing his own family's fields with the help of his grandfather's ox.

"My grandfather used to cut the plow handle off so I could reach it, so I figure I was only about 7 years old at the time," Jones recalled.

His grandparents lacked formal education, but they were honest, family-oriented, hard-working people concerned about raising their children and trying to do their best. "They had a good sense of humor and knowledge," Jones said. "They had what they needed to get them through that time. You didn't need a high school education to pick cotton. You didn't need an education to plow."

"I've had every patch in my clothes except an okra patch," he'd laugh. "That cover we had on us was about two feet thick. We had everything on that bed to keep us warm ... Life was beautiful. We never had any money, but we had happiness."

The Golden Rule

Unlike others who garnered big incomes during their prime only to pull into their senior years with little to show for it, Jones saved his money wisely and found steady employment long after his wrestling days were over.

He never forgot his work ethic, and what it took for him to have a better life.

"I just wanted to get out of the cotton fields. Farming and logging wood was about the only things to do when I was young. I was picking cotton for 25 cents a day. I went to New York and was making 40 dollars a week. You couldn't tell me nothing. I was making good money."

Although he always looked back at his early days with fond memories, life had been far from easy for Jones.

His father skipped out six months before Jones was born. His mother moved to Charleston when he was only 2 to "better her conditions," although he would spend time with her and his future five siblings whenever he could find transportation to the city. The arrangement left Jones in the primary care of his grandparents, along with a number of aunts and uncles who lived in the area.

"We didn't have electric lights," said Jones. "There were no modern-day luxuries. The bathroom was about a block away from the house. We started out with a one-seater and moved up to a two-seater."

What Jones did have was love and support from a family that abided by one standard: the Golden Rule.

"The priorities back then were church, work and school. We used to go to church three times on Sunday - Sunday school, the morning service and the evening service. Church played a very important role in our lives." Church was a place they could tap their feet, clap their hands and sing with spirit. It was a social refuge, filled with laughter and shouts of Amen. The preacher, Jones said, had no formal training, "he just got the call."

Jones looked back, not through rose-colored glasses, but with a dose of realism. "It was the way of the times," he said. "It was history."

And although there was racial prejudice and inequity, he always remembered his grandmother telling him to be patient.

"She told me to love my neighbor. If I was treated unfairly, she said, the Lord would take care of it ... in His time, that the Lord would make a way somehow."

And somehow, the Lord always did.

Fields of learning

Jones quit school in the 10th grade to help support his family. He wasn't even 10 when his grandfather died, so at an early age Jones assumed the responsibility of providing a steady income to assist his grandmother. That included working on other farms and plantations, as well as tending his family's crops.

Grandmothers, mothers, children all working for their very existence was a picture that was firmly embedded in his mind. He could recall his own grandmother picking two- to three-hundred pounds of cotton a day. She could carry a bucket of water in each hand and one on her head for a mile and a half, Jones said, "singing a good old hymn-song while she did it and praising the Lord."

In the summertime, the heat could be blistering, the fields sizzling like a steam iron, he recalled. "Sometimes, they wouldn't even stop for lunch, just for maybe a quick snack. When you talk about a day's work, you were talking about 12 to 14 hours."

A lot of what he learned about discipline, hard work, caring, honesty and dependability came from those fields, he said.

In the simple setting of his farm home, Jones said, there was peace, joy and harmony, despite the backdrop of racial inequality beyond its walls.

"There was prejudice at the time, but we never looked at it that way. Me and the white kids would go hunting and fishing after school. We'd do things together. The only thing we never did is go to school together. But as I got older, my mind started to expand. Friends who were older went away and came back. I knew right then there was a better way of living."

A new world

It was that desire to achieve better things that prompted Jones at age 17 to go in search of new horizons. In 1955, Jones moved to New York, carrying only a shopping bag and the hope of a steady paycheck.

"I had no idea what I was going to do," Jones said. "I left the cotton field with a sack on one arm Friday afternoon, and by Saturday afternoon, I was in New York City. I had little education and little experience. I didn't even know how to use a telephone because we never had one."

A few months later, he found a job making $40 a week at a vegetable packing plant in Greenwich Village. It was the most money he had ever seen. Admittedly naive to "city ways," he laughed when recounting one of his first experiences on the job.

"My boss told me to go across the street and get the time, a bagel and a cup of coffee. I wondered why he wanted the time, since a clock was right up there on the wall. But I didn't want to look stupid, so I went on anyway. I came back, brought the coffee and the bagel. He asked me where the time was. I told him that it was 10 after eight. But he was talking about The New York Times. Back then, though, I didn't know anything about the newspaper. I was strictly a farm boy right out of the woods, and I didn't know anything about big-city life. I guess I was gullible."

The bright lights and fast-paced life of New York City was, indeed, a different world for a young man who still yearned for the starry nights and gentle pace of life back in Berkeley County. But there was no turning back.

"After I left home, I had to change my life around 110 percent because everything was completely different to me. I had never seen any building higher than one-story tall until I went to New York City."

Jones' life would change forever after an uncle took him to the old Madison Square Garden for a professional wrestling show. From that point on, he knew exactly what he wanted to do with the rest of his life.

Fortuitously, Jones had a job as an elevator operator at a four-story military surplus store on 42nd Street, less than a block from a gym frequented by pro wrestlers. He began using his lunch hour to join them in workouts, and a trainer there agreed to teach him the ropes.

At a shade under six feet tall but weighing only 160 pounds, Jones was too light for the pro ranks. Over the next several years, though, he would bulk up to a solid 210 pounds.

"No drugs, just high-protein milkshakes," he'd say, along with some grueling workouts that "separated the men from the boys."

Jones was in his late 20s before his wrestling training finally paid off, when he was hired by promoter Vince McMahon Sr. to work some shows for his Northeastern-based World Wide Wrestling Federation, a predecessor to today's WWE.

It was a brave new world for a young man who had never before even seen a wrestling match on television. He was now part of a spectacular and colorful show, one that took him to cities he had only read about and gave him the opportunity to meet characters from all walks of life.

"Burrhead" Jones

Although Jones had refused to allow race to define his childhood, it had been a way of life in the South. Blacks were constrained daily by "Jim Crow" laws enforcing segregation — elevators, buses, water fountains, restaurants and housing, all made legal by a set of Supreme Court decisions in the late 1800s that would remain valid for 70 years.

"We all knew our role," Jones said. "We didn't step across the barrier. At the time, I didn't know there was anything better out there because my mind was just focused around the little area I was raised in."

Most of Jones' early in-ring work brought him back to the South, where black grapplers weren't allowed to mix it up with white wrestlers. Too often, blacks were called on to reinforce negative stereotypes.

Wrestling under the ring name Jimmy Jones, "because it was simple and easy enough to spell," the man who had been known as Melvin Nelson was forced to bounce from territory to territory looking for black opponents to work with.

Jones wrestled in scores of venues throughout Tennessee, Alabama and Louisiana, and even had to work as a referee when his stable of black opponents ran out.

He recalled wrestler Billy Hines, promoting in Panama City, Fla., at the time, coming up with the idea of Jones going up against a white wrestler. The two devised a plan where they'd get into a pushing match after Hines accused Jones of being a biased referee. Hines set up a match between them the following week, vowing that he would destroy Jones and inciting the crowd of rabid fans.

"The matches that night in Panama City were supposed to start at 7:30, but people were still in line at 9 o'clock trying to get into the building," Jones recalled. "Billy took everything I gave him until it was time to stop. He hit me below the belt, and the house went wild. We had a near-riot, and the promoter had to call the match to keep people from getting hurt."

The two worked the successful program for several weeks. As Jones' popularity soared, so did his bookings.

Jones remembered sitting in a Baton Rouge motel room when he heard a commercial announcing the debut of a wrestler named 'Cockleburrhead Jones' at a show in Morgan City. When he arrived at the arena, fans were pointing at him, calling him "Cockleburrhead.'

"I wondered what the heck they were talking about. Billy Hines was laughing his head off. He told me that he had changed my name. I was a little mad in the beginning, because all my ring attire had 'Jimmy Jones' on it." Hines explained that an Afro hairstyle commercial had played while they were filming promos, and he thought it would be a catchy name for Jones.

"My Afro would get all tied up in knots and looked something like a pine burr, all fluffed up," said Jones, adding that the hairstyle had become popular and that those with Afro cuts were sometimes called "cockleburrheads." Although some initially interpreted his name as a racial slur, Jones says it never bothered him, and it made him money and a memorable character.

"The name stuck with me from one end of the world to another. It was a good-luck charm to me."

The Deep South

During the '60s, Jones saw a different side to race relations in the North, and he says he wasn't shocked to see that things had changed little in the South, where in some one-horse towns he could wrestle, but wasn't allowed "to sit down in the cafeteria and eat with the boys."

He recounted an incident when he and a group of white wrestlers stopped at a restaurant in west Mississippi.

"The waitress brought glasses of water to the (white) wrestlers. I told her what I wanted. She said, 'Sorry, sir, we can't serve your kind.' I said, 'I didn't order that, Miss, I don't want none of my kind, I just want a hamburger steak.'"

Still trying to get a meal, Jones went to a kitchen in the basement.

"Here were these people with their aprons that looked like they hadn't been washed in six months. One lady had her lips full of snuff, one guy had a jaw full of chewing tobacco, and one guy had a jug of corn whiskey behind the counter. I tried to see if I could find a white cook. I asked them who was cooking for the white folks. They said they were."

"I can't eat with my friends, and you all are cooking for the white folks, too?" Jones asked.

"Son, you must not be from around here," replied the elderly man, who offered Jones a slug of his moonshine.

Jones himself endured a number of stereotypical gimmicks during that time. Billed "from the cotton fields of Louisiana," he once dragged a cotton sack to the ring for a match with a wrestler named Frank Dalton in Baton Rouge, La. He worked a match in Montgomery, Ala., in which the loser got tarred and feathered. "I looked like the bird on Sesame Street," he said. "They used molasses, and I swallowed one of the feathers and almost choked. But I got $25 extra in my envelope."

The angle worked and played to sellout crowds for weeks. It all was no worse, Jones reasoned, than some of the gimmicks promoters saddled other wrestlers with. The bottom line was to make the fans feel emotion and keep the turnstiles clicking.

The business, though, ultimately accorded Jones the respect he had earned. In many ways, he says, the wrestling profession was like the family he had left behind years earlier.

"Wrestling is one big family that sticks together. I've gotten to meet many interesting people along the way. I never sensed any prejudice among the boys. Traveling was a great experience for me. I may have a 10th-grade education, but I've got a Ph.D. in common sense and knowledge. I can hold a conversation with anybody, no matter what level they're on, no matter if it's the president of the United States or a wino in the gutter. The experience of life and traveling around the world, meeting people from different walks of life, has given me that gift."

"He was truly something else," said McDaniel, now a pastor based in Seneca. "His accounts of being chased out of the shower by the original Sheik (Ed Farhat), who was holding a snake, his story of how he got the large scar on his forehead by the hands of George 'Two Ton' Harris, these were stories that made me laugh and just form a bond of friendship that I hold dear to my heart.

"His openness about how hard it was being a black man in the wrestling business and the times he was not allowed to wrestle a white guy … they were a harsh reminder of how things used to be. Burrhead was not bitter, he was not angry, and even his wrestling name, certainly not politically correct, it was how he preferred to be addressed. It was him, he was a beloved character and his stories of how he made it through all the hard times, was truly encouraging. Our world could use a few more like him."

A new career

Jones enjoyed one of his most successful runs in the business teaming with a cousin he met in New York several years before turning pro. He and Carey "Buster" Lloyd, a Dillon native who would later become Rufus R. "Freight Train" Jones, one of wrestling's most popular performers, worked out at the same 42nd Street gym.

The two first teamed in New York in the late '60s and again in the mid-'70s for Charlotte-based Crockett Promotions, becoming one of that company's top acts. One of their most memorable matches saw Burrhead Jones take a seemingly vicious beating at the hands of "bad guy" Blackjack Mulligan in a 1976 bout televised in Raleigh, N.C. It was a textbook angle that is still talked about in wrestling circles.

Jones held numerous titles during his career, but one of his biggest victories came during the late '70s in New Brockton, Ala., where he defeated a young 6-5 giant with 24-inch arms, a beach bum tan and a comic book cleft chin named Terry Boulder — later to emerge as superstar Hulk Hogan.

He began winding down his career in the late '80s, although he worked occasional matches well into the next decade. He left his home in Montgomery to return to the Lowcountry in 1991 to take care of his ailing father, the same man who had deserted him before he was born.

"My dad was in bad health," said Jones. "I had never seen him, and he never got to actually see me, since he was blind."

Like a faithful and dutiful son, Jones tended to his father until his death at age 78 of cancer.

"I got him everything he needed to make him comfortable. He never gave me a glass of water his entire life. That's where the saying comes in that you never burn a bridge behind you because one day you may have to come back across it."

Jones, who eventually pared down his ring schedule, landed a non-wrestling job at the then Standard Warehouse's branch office in Bushy Park where he worked as a forklift operator and in a non-official capacity as "security chief."

"If you want to know what's happening, ask Melvin," joked a plant supervisor at the time. "But he's one of the hardest workers we have. He's quite a colorful character."

"There is a stop sign in every walk of life," Jones would say. "I saw myself getting older and older. Wrestling wasn't going to provide for me in my old age. So I got myself another job, and   never looked back."

One of the crowning achievements of Jones' career was his induction into the Lowcountry Wrestling Hall of Fame in a 1998 ceremony at the old County Hall in Charleston.

"It was one of the highlights of my life," said Jones, who would be presented the Pioneer Award in 2002 at the Gulf Coast Wrestling Reunion in Mobile, Ala, and would be inducted into the S.C. Pro Wrestling Hall of Fame in 2012. "Very few black wrestlers, at least in the early days, had made themselves known worldwide like I had. There were no halls of fame for black wrestlers back then."

A wonderful life

It's always hard to say goodbye to a friend, especially when it's someone who has deeply enriched your life, and the lives of many others.

But it's also hard not to smile when you think about those times you've shared, the stories that still make you laugh and the memories of a life well lived.

Through the good times, bad times, and the enormous changes he had seen, Burrhead remained steadfastly optimistic. When looking back over those many years, he saw a life of joy and simple truths.

"A person can make anything out of life that he wants to," he once told me. "God has given me more than I ever expected."

Declining health, especially for someone who had battled the likes of Black-jack Mulligan, Ric Flair and Hulk Hogan, might have undone a lesser man. But Burrhead, in his typical folksy, laid-back demeanor, would always point out that there were situations far worse than his. And that he had a wonderful life that had afforded him many opportunities that he remained thankful for.

Most of all, he was able to do something he loved, and that was professional wrestling.

Two lines in his obituary described Melvin Nelson/Burrhead Jones to a tee.

"Melvin was a fun-loving man who was able to travel the world in pursuit of his life's passion. He loved, he laughed, and he lived!"

My friend Andy McDaniel and I always referred to Burrhead as "The Local Legend," a nickname that just seemed fitting. As part of the Lowcountry Legends Reunion in 1998, of which Burrhead was one of the special honorees, he stole the show in typical Burrhead fashion, taking command of the mic and interviewing everyone in sight.

Like Andy said, the world sure could use a few more like him. But then again, he was Burrhead Jones, the one and only, and there'll never be a cotton-pickin' nuther.

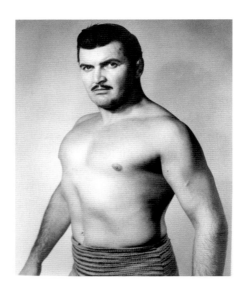

Bronko Lubich
A heel worth loving

Dec. 27, 2009

Many fans might remember Bronko Lubich as the slow-counting, slow-moving referee for the Dallas-based World Class Championship Wrestling during its glory days in the 1980s.

I'll remember him as a character who hooked me on this business more than four decades ago.

My life would never be quite the same after taking a break from a Saturday afternoon backyard football game to check out the action on my family's black and white console. It was to be my first taste of professional wrestling, and it opened up a brand new world for a 10-year-old whose horizons heretofore hadn't expanded beyond the more conventional sports such as baseball, football and basketball.

But here I was, transfixed by this grand spectacle on my TV set, with larger-than-life characters the likes of which I had never experienced before. On one team was a 600-pound Arkansas plowboy aptly named Haystacks Calhoun, sporting a massive bib overall, a lucky horseshoe and a partner not even half his size named Johnny Weaver.

It was the other team, though, that intrigued me. A pair of menacing-looking foreigners — one from Buenos Aires, Argentina, the other billed from Belgrade,

Yugoslavia — with a hickory cane-wielding manager who sported a permanent scowl and a nasty demeanor to match. The faux Kentucky colonel's name was Homer O'Dell, and his nefarious charges were Aldo Bogni and Bronko Lubich.

Lubich, in particular, cast an imposing figure. Not a large man in stature, with dark, close-cropped hair and well-groomed mustache, he moved methodically in the ring, complementing his bigger, lumbering partner. What really set him apart, though, was a hold he called the "corkscrew" that rendered his helpless opponents unconscious. And it was as painful as it sounded, with Lubich digging his knuckles into his foe's temple until the unfortunate wrestler either submitted or blacked out.

Keep in my mind, this was years before the "don't try this at home" disclaimers, and I found this neat little maneuver to be especially effective whenever pushed to do battle in the local schoolyard. This helpful bit of wrestling knowledge came in handy on more than one occasion, but was used, of course, only as a defensive measure.

As a result, Bronko Lubich soon became one of my favorite wrestlers, despite the fact that he was a despised and feared heel. But it wasn't long before I was smartened up to one of wrestling's facts of life — that the "bad guys" inside the ring were usually friendlier and more accommodating outside the ring than the so-called "good guys."

Bronko Lubich was successful in his trade because he knew how to make the fans hate him. Outside the ring was another story.

Bronko's girls

Lubich passed away more than two years ago, in August 2007, at the age of 81 of complications from a stroke while in hospice care in Plano, Texas. At his side were his three daughters. His wife of more than 50 years, Ella, had passed away three years earlier after a lengthy bout with cancer.

His three girls will tell you there was a lot more to Bronko Lubich than the fans ever saw. Those true believers of a bygone era might be surprised to know that the man they loved to hate was a doting father, a faithful soulmate to his wife, and a homebody who loved tending to his garden.

Kathy Lupsity, 56, the eldest of the daughters, says not a day goes by that she doesn't think of her dad. "He was the most gentle man I've ever known," she says, still holding back tears.

She fondly recalls being raised in a traditional, old-school family. While her father was on the road much of the time, her mother stayed at home and took care of the kids.

Maria Miller, 52, says her father was "the salt of the earth." And despite his rigorous travel schedule, he was "a real homebody" who planted a garden wherever he lived. "He traveled a lot but when he was on home, mostly on Sunday, he'd be in the backyard with us and play with us all day long."

Most fans from that era might have a hard time visualizing the rough-and-tough wrestler tucking his three young daughters in at night and telling them stories before they went to sleep, but that's exactly what he did, she says.

"He was such a good dad and such a good role model," she says. "He was such a positive person. We never heard any negative things about other people."

One of her favorite memories, she says, was her dad putting up a pup tent for her and younger sister Melanie, and spending the night with them in the tent.

"Half of his body stuck out of the tent," she laughs. "Here's a guy who rarely got to sleep in his own bed, and there he is, spending the night in a tent with these two little girls and their stuffed animals, giggling and carrying on."

"He was so wise," says Melanie Becker, 50, the youngest of his three daughters. "He didn't have a very good education because he came from a poor family, but he loved to read, loved history and invested well. He was like a sponge. It was amazing. He inspired me so much in my life. He was very hard-working."

Melanie still has an old poster that was framed by her sister. Her dad and Aldo Bogni are wrestling The Kentuckians in the main event of a wrestling card in the '60s. There are other names on the bill such as George Becker (no relation), Johnny Weaver, Big Bob Orton, Nick Kozak and George Drake that bring back memories. It hangs on her wall and is a constant reminder of the days when her dad was a big-time wrestling star.

"I saw my dad in such a different way then. He was basically a very quiet person. It always struck me kind of funny to see him get in the ring in front of all these people and wrestle and do interviews. But that never fazed him a bit."

Her mind wanders back to a time when things were simpler and life seemed so much easier. She remembers a house they lived in where there were woods in the back and a swath of undeveloped land.

Sundays with their dad were special. Ella would pack them a lunch, and they would enjoy peanut butter and jelly sandwiches near a gentle stream in the woods. There was a big vine nearby, and the girls would swing and swing while their dad pushed them. That vine once broke, but they'd always go back to the same spot. They'd go hiking and fishing. Melanie and Maria couldn't bare the thought of eating the fish, so Bronko would put the catch in their above-ground pool.

They'd cut down their own Christmas trees during the holidays. It always seemed to be on the coldest day of the year. "We just had so much fun," they recall.

As Melanie got older, she'd go to spot shows with her dad, and they'd have "their talks" on the drive home. Monday night was Fort Worth, she remembers, and they'd watch "McCloud" together. It was like clockwork. He'd get home right before the show started, go upstairs and put his suitcase up, and quickly change into his pajamas. It was their "Monday night thing."

She also fondly recalls her days living in Charlotte, where she would hang out with Wendi Weaver (daughter of wrestlers Penny Banner and Johnny Weaver) and Craig Evers (son of Harvey "Rip Hawk" Evers). "Wendi was always fun because she was a girl and we could do girl stuff," remembers Melanie. "Craig always had cool stuff at his house like Mad magazines and things like that. The moms would play canasta, and we'd read magazines."

And, for the record, Bronko Lubich was even beloved among his biggest ring rivals, behind the scenes, of course.

"He was wonderful ... a wonderful person," said Johnny Weaver, with whom Bronko engaged in many a bloodbath over the years, shortly before his death in 2008. "He never got nervous, mad or anything like that. He was always calm, cool, just a great ring general."

A wrestler's wrestler

Bronko Lubich was born Sandor Bronko Lupsity on Christmas Day 1925 in Batonja, Hungary, although after the war and the boundaries changed, his family moved to Yugoslavia. They had wanted to move to the United States, Kathy Lupsity says, but the country had a quota at the time. Bronko ended up moving with his family to Montreal, Canada, in December 1937.

A self-taught businessman, Lubich had only a sixth-grade education but left school to help support his family, who lived in a home with a dirt floor. He had a real thirst for knowledge and was an insatiable reader, says his daughter, and he loved history and theology.

His future wife's family already had come over from Yugoslavia with little but the clothes on their backs, settling in an ethnic neighborhood in Montreal with a sizable Slavic population. They worked hard to carve out a living.

"Our people would kind of get together and buddy up and help the new people get jobs," says Maria. "Their kids would teach the other kids how to speak English or be their buddies at school."

Bronko and Ella's families didn't know each other until they settled in Montreal and were attending the same church. Ella was a year-and-a-half-older, and they courted for a number of years before marrying in their early 20s.

Lubich became an accomplished amateur wrestler who was selected to represent Canada in the 1948 Olympic Games, but he was unable to compete after breaking his arm in a competition shortly before the Games. Unable to wait four years for another shot at Olympic gold, he continued to wrestle as an amateur and took a job in an aircraft factory.

The injury also proved to be a blessing in disguise for Lubich. He turned pro later that year and quickly rose to prominence as the manager of mat villain Angelo Poffo. The two eventually would form a top team, winning the Texas tag-team belts from Pepper Gomez and Dory Dixon in 1961.

"Daddy was the brains behind everything they did," says Kathy.

Lubich's first high-profile stint was serving as manager for Poffo, the father of future stars "Macho Man" Randy Savage and Lanny "The Genius" Poffo, on the Chicago and Indianapolis circuits. With the crafty Lubich using a cane on opponents, usually behind the referee's back, the two drew tremendous heat wherever they appeared. A tag-team match against Wilbur Snyder and Yukon Eric in the main event of a show at the Cincinnati Gardens in 1959 drew more than 15,000 fans and set a record for any event ever held in that building.

Melanie says it wasn't uncommon for the two to get pulled over and have their cars searched.

"They looked like gangsters," she jokes. "They were both dark-haired, muscular guys wearing these big overcoats. They were suspicious looking."

Lubich eventually settled in Charlotte, the headquarters for Crockett Promotions, and was a top star in that territory for many years. Some of his best days were in Charlotte where he was very close to promoter Jim Crockett Sr. It was a good area to raise children, and he loved the fact that he was able to take his family to the beach in the summer and the mountains in the winter. He stayed there longer than any other territory he had wrestled in, although he would travel to Florida for short stints in between.

The Carolinas-Virginia circuit was a hotbed for tag-team wrestling during the '60s, with such top duos as George and Sandy Scott, George Becker and Johnny Weaver, Rip Hawk and Swede Hanson, The Bolos (The Assassins), Skull Murphy and Brute Bernard, and The Kentuckians.

At the top of that tag-team hierarchy was the villainous duo of Bogni and Lubich along with manager O'Dell. The team held numerous tag titles, including the Southern tag-team belts, and later captured the Florida tag-team title with the colorful George "Two Ton" Harris as their manager.

Bogni, under the moniker Count Alexis Bruga, had teamed with Lubich years earlier in the Calgary-based Stampede Wrestling territory. With the always controversial O'Dell added to the mix, the combination became one of the most hated and feared forces in tag-team wrestling. And O'Dell wasn't just controversial in the ring. He was infamous for carrying a revolver, and he often shot it behind arenas to scare off fans who might pose a problem.

"Bronko and Aldo Bogni were one of the top teams in the Carolinas, and we had a lot of great teams here," recalled Weaver, who first met Lubich in the late

'50s when he was starting out in Indianapolis. "They stayed for a long time ... years and years and years. They didn't have to move to other places. The heat stayed on them. We had a lot of full houses with them."

Weaver, just days before his own passing in February 2008, reflected on his many fond memories of that era.

"I think about them almost every day. That was a very special time. Bronko was a great competitor ... one of the best I ever wrestled. He was all for the business, and that seems to be a lost art now."

Respected veteran Abe Jacobs, who met Lubich in Detroit in 1960 and worked a number of tag-team matches against him later that decade in the Mid-Atlantic area, credits Lubich for the success of his team with Bogni.

"He was the brains behind that team," Jacobs says, referring to the Bogni-Lubich-O'Dell tandem. "He made that team work. He knew how to get the heat on Homer, and he was the one who told Homer to do stuff behind the referee's back in order to get heat. He was just so smart inside that ring."

Jacobs even took his praise one step further when talking about Lubich.

"Eddie Graham was really smart and creative, but when I really think about it, I'd have to say Bronko Lubich was the smartest guy I ever met in this business. He really had an incredible grasp."

Savvy businessman

Lubich was smart in business, too, saving and investing his money wisely. Choosing not to squander his savings foolishly like many of his peers, he would encourage others not to throw their money away. O'Dell was one of the worst, and frequently would buy drinks for the entire bar. Despite Lubich's pleas, O'Dell would go through money like it was going out of style.

Lubich, though, had saved and invested throughout his career, and had an impressive investment portfolio. He was wise with his money, says Kathy Lupsity, unlike many of the younger wrestlers who were making good money but spending it on expensive cars, fancy restaurants and high-priced motels.

"He used to tell these guys to take some of that money and invest it," she says. "Don't just blow it. Something could happen tomorrow, and you might not be able to wrestle anymore," he would routinely advise them.

Much of Lubich's adult life, like most of his colleagues in the business, were spent on the road. His daughters spent most of their lives in Charlotte and Dallas, where their father was headquartered during his active career, and remain thankful they didn't have to move from territory to territory every couple of years. It was important to Bronko that this family maintained as normal a life as possible.

One thing was for certain, his daughters say, and that was that they always maintained a special relationship.

At noon every day, father and daughters had a pact. He would think about them, and they would think about him. He'd send them postcards when he was on the road.

"I think we were much closer than some families were," says Maria. "I could always go to him and talk about anything. Even when I got older, and I was troubled about something, I could go over to see him, and everything just melted away."

The best advice he ever gave Maria, she says, was encouraging her to lead her life in a way that would be an example to others. "He told me that my actions were going to follow me, and that's what people are going to think about you."

She remembers his big hands gently cupping her small face and telling her: "Honey, you're a beautiful girl, but that isn't by your choosing. That has nothing to do with the kind of person you are. You need to be good person on the inside."

It would tear him up, she says, when the sisters would argue. Bronko and his brother never had an argument in their entire life and adored one another, she says, and he couldn't understand how siblings could ever fight.

Soulmates

Both Bronko and beloved wife Ella were "old school," their daughters say, and the children learned to speak Serbian at an early age. Ella was a good listener and a people's person. Bronko was more reserved. The combination worked.

The key to their success, jokes Melanie, was that "Dad traveled all the time and wasn't home." But, she adds, they were as close as two people could be.

"In my heart and soul, I really believe there are people who are meant to be forever," says Kathy. "And Mom and Dad were two of those few people." She looks at a card with the words, "Your father is in his beloved wife's arms," and smiles. "That's truly what I believe. I just know Mom and Dad are together right now."

The last 10 years had been rough. Ella had gone fast after cancer came back with a vengeance three years after being diagnosed and going into remission. Bronko's illnesses were much slower.

"He was like the Energizer bunny," recalls Lupsity. "Bless his heart ... he just kept going on and on and on."

Ella had cancer and chemo, and the disease went into remission. Then Bronko was diagnosed with prostate cancer and underwent radiation. Ella's cancer eventually returned, and radiation treatments followed.

Bronko suffered a series of strokes, and each one chipped a little more away. It made it harder every time the girls would go to see him.

Bronko recovered from an initial stroke that he had at the doctor's office. Another stroke at a hospital was more serious. Eventually someone was hired to live at the house. Bronko, who eventually lost the use of his right arm, eventually moved to a personal care home three miles from Melanie's house.

Kathy, who had served as a caregiver, would grab her dad's hand and squeeze it. "I don't even know if he knew I was there."

"After each one (stroke), you would notice something different," says Melanie.

Throughout the hard times, the sisters say, there also were many poignant moments.

Bronko thought the world of Lou Thesz, his daughters recall, and he kept a picture of the two in a box next to his bed during his final years.

His mind had failed him in many areas, but "he always knew that was Lou Thesz."

Maria remembers her dad, following one of his strokes, asking her if her folks were still alive.

"Yes they are, and you'll be very glad to know that, because you're my dad," she told him in no uncertain terms.

His eyes beamed. "I am? That's great, because I really like you," he told his daughter.

He paused for a few moments and then asked, "Do you know Steve?" referring to his wife's brother and his best friend.

"I told him that I did," says Maria, "but we didn't see him often, because Steve was in Montreal and we were in Dallas."

"Daddy looked at me, his eyes really twinkling, and asked, 'Do you know his sister?' Dad had a crush on Mom since he was 12 years old."

When Maria told her dad that was her mother and his wife, and that she was on her way home, she recalls him barely being able to contain his excitement.

"You mean Steve's sister is on her way right now?" he gushed.

"Daddy immediately threw the covers off the bed and said he had to change his clothes," relates Maria. "She walked in that room and you would have thought it was Miss Universe. He looked at her like that until she died."

"He and Mom were soulmates. They always managed to have fun together," says daughter Kathy.

It was hard watching his health slowly decline, she says.

"I saw this man who always kept his body fit. You don't want them to go, but that's out of selfishness. You know when they go, they're going to somewhere better. It was a blessing when Daddy passed, because he wasn't in pain. He's with Mom now."

Maria, like her two sisters, has a difficult time composing herself when asked what she remembers most about her father.

"My dad always had a thing about his eyes," she says. "He could tell stories and communicate so much by just looking at him. I could just look at him sometimes and we wouldn't have to even say anything to each other, just look at each other, and we always knew what we were thinking. I just miss the look in his eyes. He'd give good bear hugs. I miss Mama too. But at least they're together now."

The Von Erichs

Lubich moved to Dallas in 1971 for his last major run as an active wrestler. He teamed with Chris Markoff to win the NWA American tag-team belts on two occasions from George Scott and Tim Woods, and later Johnny Valentine and Wahoo McDaniel.

He eventually moved from the wrestling end to the management and promotional side of the business, guiding such stars as The Spoiler (Don Jardine) and Boris "The Great" Malenko (Larry Simon) before becoming a full-time referee in 1973 when he officiated for the NWA world title match where Jack Brisco defeated Harley Race in Houston.

In the meantime, though, he formed a business partnership with Fritz Von Erich (Jack Adkisson), who was the promotion's top babyface as well as the owner of the NWA-affiliated territory. Lubich still maintained visibility inside the ring, for years serving as the senior official for the nationally syndicated World Class Championship Wrestling.

A staple at the famed Sportatorium in Dallas and the North Side Coliseum in Fort Worth, Lubich worked in the World Class office and served as referee until he retired in 1990. The years he spent with the company, though, were bittersweet.

World Class, which formerly had been known as Big Time Wrestling, had become the innovator of pro wrestling's worldwide exposure via television syndication in the early '80s. Wrestling events were like rock concerts, and Von Erich's sons and their wild, young friends were treated like rock idols. Rabid crowds, consisting mostly of teen-agers, flocked to the Sportatorium in Dallas arenas to experience the excitement of World Class.

With Von Erich's three oldest sons as the franchise stars, WCCW was one of the most syndicated shows in the world, In its heyday, WCCW had a higher TV rating than Saturday Night Live, and the show was on more than 85 stations in 25 countries.

The promotion, however, burnt out through a string of shocking tragedies. The Von Erich brothers were portrayed as wholesome, milk-drinking brothers, but the clan wasn't as wholesome as it was portrayed on TV. Living in the shadows of each other and their famous father, the Von Erich boys had problems. The office became the home base for some of the most heartbreaking stories in wrestling history.

The oldest Von Erich son, Kevin, would later say that a statue of Bronko Lubich should have been erected when they tore down the famed Sportatorium.

The sons Bronko never had

Becker, who lives in Plano and is an office manager for a manufacturing company, attended North Texas State with Kevin and David Von Erich (Adkisson). Both boys left school for the wrestling business.

Lubich was always close to Fritz Von Erich and his boys, all of whom but Kevin died tragically, and he never could forget having to break the news to Fritz when son David died during a tour of Japan. He got a call in the middle of the night about David, and he made them go back and check three times before telling Fritz.

"All of his kids, as far as Daddy was concerned, were like his sons," says Lupsity. "They were like the sons he never had. It grieved him terribly when those boys died."

Everyone respected Bronko. What he said was the law. "Kevin and David loved him like a father."

Shortly before David's death, he and brother Kevin, both of whom Lubich had helped train, had gotten into an argument in San Antonio. Bronko got mad at them and sat them down. He told them they should be ashamed of themselves.

"I would give anything in the world to have my brother back," he reprimanded.

After the talking, she says, they made up, went out and got drunk.'

"They were completely united. David went to Japan shortly after, and it was the last time Kevin saw his brother alive."

It was uncommon for Bronko to intervene. "It was a bold move for him, and for him to listen to that inner voice at that time was great," recalls Miller.

Kevin later said that he would have hated himself had they not made up.

"Those guys all went through their personal hells," says Becker. "Before he left for Japan, David had been very sick. He was throwing up blood before the matches. Everyone told him to go to the doctor, but David said he didn't have the time and would go when he returned from Japan. He would be sitting at the dinner table and just black out. It wasn't surprising that something like that happened."

The Von Erich saga remains one of the greatest tragedies in the history of the business.

The tragic story of the star-crossed family began with the electrocution of 7-year-old Jack Jr. in 1959. David, 25, died in February 1984 of an intestinal inflammation, theorized by some to be a drug overdose, during the tour of Japan. Mike, 23, died of a self-administered drug overdose in April 1987. The youngest, Chris, 21, shot himself with a 9mm pistol in September 1991. Kerry Von Erich, at the age of 33, ended his troubled life in February 1993 with a single bullet in his chest. He was the fifth of six brothers to die young. Only Kevin remains to carry on what was once the sport's most heralded dynasty.

Jim Hellwig, formerly known as The Ultimate Warrior, was one of Kerry's best friends and reflected on the tragedy shortly after his death.

"Kerry was just a big kid. His poor kids didn't think it was him (in the funeral home). They thought it was a mannequin. They think he's out on tour or something. Kerry's problem was he had a bad drug problem and he couldn't go to his father because of the respect in combination with the way they looked up to their father. He didn't want to let him down. Or Fritz denied the whole thing all the time to himself that Kerry actually had a problem."

The deaths were especially painful for Lubich.

"He knew those boys ever since they were kids. It was really hard on Dad," says Lupsity.

"I don't know how Kevin survived," says Lupsity. "There was so much tragedy all around him."

As the problems within the company worsened and the lack of discipline got out of control, it became more and more of a chore for Bronko to go to work, says Lupsity.

It had become a far cry from the days when Bronko worked in the Charlotte office for promoter Jim Crockett Sr.

"I can remember when he worked for Mr. Crockett," says Lupsity. "Daddy always wore a suit and tie. Guys in World Class wore cut-off shorts, bare-chested or wearing a dirty shirt. It was like night and day.

"I remembering him saying that Mr. Crockett was one of the most influential men in his entire life, and that he always wanted to respect him by wearing a suit and a tie. Daddy would always refer to him as 'Mr. Crockett.' And I think Mr. Crockett respected Daddy."

It was quite a different story in the Dallas office.

"It got the point where he truly hated to go to work. That's when Mom told him to get out of it. He finally made up his mind to retire. And that was it."

Rare breed

Bronko Lubich was a rarity in a cutthroat profession where slings and arrows are bandied about at breakneck speed. He was universally respected by peers, with performers from "Nature Boy" Ric Flair to "Stone Cold" Steve Austin singing his praises. Austin, who got his start in World Class Championship Wrestling, would often travel with Lubich and longtime Texas wrestling figure Skandor Akbar (Jim Wehba).

"We'd be together in one of their cars, and they'd be up front smoking big, smelly cigars and I'd be in the back seat asking them questions and soaking up everything they were telling me. That was a college degree in the old-school ways of doing things. I love those guys," Austin recounted in his autobiography.

"Sometimes they'd tell me old wrestling stories. I'd always enjoy hearing those. I didn't have any money then, and they wouldn't charge me for transportation.

I'd just sit in the back and ask them questions. Those guys were cool. They knew I was genuinely interested in learning, and they both took me under their wings."

"Both Akbar and Bronk were excellent storytellers," added Austin. "When one of them told a story, the way they laughed made me want to laugh too. It was a real good time in my life. Those guys and their wealth of knowledge about ring psychology were tremendous influences on me throughout my whole career. They also furthered my respect for the wrestling business."

As for those "smelly cigars," as Austin put it, the confines of the car was the only spot he smoked them, recalls daughter Kathy. "He never smoked one inside the house. I think he just did it to have something to do."

Bronko loved telling tales and joking with the boys. Those jokes and those tales, though, usually stayed in the locker room and the office.

"Your dad was like king of the joke-tellers in the dressing room," David Von Erich once told Melanie.

"I'm sure it was a lot different in the dressing room," she says. "He was always such a gentleman around his girls. I'm sure it was probably really hard. He touched so many people's lives. I always knew he did mine in a very special way."

A good man

I last talked to Bronko 10 years ago and invited him to a Mid-Atlantic legends reunion that was being held at the old County Hall on King Street. He had main-evented in that storied building numerous times, and I could tell he relished the thought of returning to one of his old stomping grounds.

But his beloved Ella had been ill, and even the prospect of seeing many of his old friends couldn't lure him away from her side.

We talked about the old days, that faraway time when larger-than-life heroes made true believers out of 10-year-olds, when wrestlers didn't make headlines for dying early and steroids weren't in vogue.

I've often thought about Bronko since then.

More than 45 years later, it still gives me comfort knowing that Bronko Lubich was as good a man as there was, despite making fans think he was as bad a man as there was.

A lot can be said about Bronko Lubich, but the ring-wise Hall of Famer Abe Jacobs may have given him the highest compliment a wrestler can earn.

"He was a square shooter."

Rest in peace, Bronk, and thanks for the memories.

Nelson Royal

Nelson Royal left behind golden memories

Feb. 10, 2002

My memories of Nelson Royal are golden.

If you've been a fan of the business for any period of time, chances are you've heard stories about him. And if you're a longtime follower of the mat game, you can probably tell your own stories about him.

Few men loved the wrestling business more than Nelson Royal. That's what made his passing last weekend a particularly tough pill to swallow.

"Nellie," as he was affectionately known to a generation of fans and friends, died of a heart attack at the age of 66 in his hometown of Mooresville, N.C. It had been a normal Sunday morning for Royal, one in which he attended church and had breakfast with a longtime friend, Love Valley, N.C., mayor Andy Barker. But Royal had been complaining about pain in his shoulder the past several months, and on this Sunday morning, the pain had been even more pronounced.

According to a report, Royal pulled into his driveway, got out of the car and collapsed in front of Barker's barn at approximately 12:20 p.m. Emergency personnel were called to try to resuscitate him, but by then it was too late.

Former NWA world champion Ronnie Garvin had last talked to Royal two days earlier and confirmed that his friend had not been feeling well.

"He was complaining of a bad shoulder then, but he was being treated with cortisone shots," said Garvin. "He said the shots weren't helping him one bit. That might have been a sign of a heart attack coming on."

Nelson Royal was as well-liked in this North Carolina community as he had been during his 30 years in the wrestling business. A devoted husband and father, a respected businessman and longtime owner of a western specialty store, Nellie had changed little over the years, unlike the business he had devoted most of his life to.

"But he never got to enjoy his retirement," lamented Garvin, who had planned to take Royal to the annual Gulf Coast wrestling reunion in Mobile, Ala., next month. "I guess I'll go by myself now. It just won't be the same without him."

"He wanted to go fly with me ... he wanted to go hunting," added Garvin, an experienced pilot who would occasionally take his friend on plane trips, including a 1987 hunting excursion to Colorado where they both bagged a mule deer. "He loved flying. He wanted to fly with me in a DC-3 when I went to work," said Garvin, 56, who transports cargo across the country. "But he always had to work."

Tag-team specialist

Nelson Combs (he later added the name Royal) was born in Wheelwright, Ky., on July 25, 1931. He started wrestling at the age of 17 under the watchful eye of Indian star Don Eagle. With men like six-time NWA world champion Lou Thesz at the helm of the business, a young wrestler couldn't help but be inspired, Nellie would say.

"I wrestled Lou years and years ago when I was young in the business," he once related. "He looked at me and said, 'You'd better go after me, son.' And I did. He was one of the greats."

Royal himself would achieve a level of greatness for his realistic, hard-hitting style. He once said there wasn't a rib in his body that hadn't been broken, and if it weren't for anti-inflammatories, he would never be able to sleep. Nellie, however, considered his numerous scars and ring injuries a badge of honor. He longed for the days when wrestling meant wrestling. "Few of them today know a hammerlock from a padlock," he liked to say.

Royal first arrived in the Carolinas in the early '60s as half of a heel tag team along with The Viking (Bob Morse). Sporting a black beard and black vest and billed from London, England, "Sir Nelson Royal" was a perfect complement to his white-bearded, "Scandinavian" teammate. Nellie, who would become one of the Mid-Atlantic area's top babyfaces in later years, had refined his heel gimmick working in the Pacific Northwest and the Amarillo circuit, where he feuded with the legendary Dory Funk Sr. Bringing The Viking with him to the Carolinas, the two headlined in matches against such teams as The Kentuckians and George and Sandy Scott, but eventually went their separate ways. Morse, whose late-night, hard-living style didn't mesh with the milder-mannered Royal, went to Kansas City where he became a headliner in his own right, while Royal grabbed a cowboy hat, turned babyface and hooked up with Tex McKenzie.

Royal, who became one of the top draws for promoter Jim Crockett Sr., was a tag-team specialist in a territory known for its tag-team wrestling, and enjoyed a host of successful partnerships with such stars as Paul Jones, Sandy Scott, Klondike Bill, Les Thatcher, George Becker and Johnny Weaver. His favorite, however, was with the long, tall McKenzie who, as Nellie would say, "was one big, tall sucker — he stood seven foot tall if he stood up straight," towering over the 5-9 Royal, whose hard-nosed mat style earned him the nickname "Crowbar," a contrast in technique to the lumbering McKenzie.

"He'd drive Nelson crazy," joked Sandy Scott. "Nelson would go halfway down to the ring, and Tex would just be coming out. Nelson would turn around and Tex would wave, 'Hey, Nellie.' Nelson would say, 'Can't you just walk to the ring with me?' They were really a pair."

Royal reflected on Big Tex after McKenzie's passing last May at the age of 72.

"People thought that since Tex was such a total extrovert on TV, that he would be different outside the ring. But that was him — he was truly that great person. It was a pleasure teaming with him."

Between long runs with McKenzie and Jones as partners, Royal would be involved in memorable programs with such combos as Rip Hawk and Swede Hanson, the Anderson Brothers, Skull Murphy and Brute Bernard, The Masked Infernos (Frankie Cain and Jimmy "Rocky" Smith), Aldo Bogni and Bronko Lubich, The Missouri Mauler and Hiro Matsuda, and The Masked Marvels (Billy Garrett and Jim Starr).

Royal achieved further success during the mid-'70 when he captured the NWA's world junior heavyweight title in Oklahoma, a title he held five times between 1976 and 1988.

Friend and teacher

A number of his former colleagues from the Mid-Atlantic territory last week paid tribute to Nellie.

"You couldn't find a better guy. He's probably the best human being I ever met," said Garvin, whose nickname for Royal was "Grandfather." "He's called me 'Grandson' for years," he joked. "We'll miss him."

"Nellie was always in incredible shape," said Sandy Scott. "He was a great performer. I met him in Oregon in the late '50s or early '60s. He was a buzz saw up there. He was a top guy in the Carolinas. "Nellie loved his horses and he loved his ranch."

Garvin recalled Royal holding a rodeo at his ranch back in the early '70s to benefit a child who was undergoing spinal surgery. "I remember getting up on a Brahma bull, and that big old thing sent me sailing 30 feet up into the air. I never got on one of those again. Jerry Brisco got hurt that day, and missed about a week of work."

"Nelson was a good friend, and I had known him for my entire career," said Tim Woods, the former masked Mr. Wrestling, who met Royal in Oklahoma in 1965. I always liked Nelson. He was always in tremendous condition, and he was a fanatic using the Stair-Master. He also helped a lot of guys prepare to get into the wrestling business."

"Nelson was a great teacher and a great friend," echoed Don Kernodle, who held the NWA world tag-team belts with Sgt. Slaughter during the early '80s. "I learned a lot about wrestling from Nelson, and he meant a lot to this business."

Rip Hawk (Harvey Evers) was one of Royal's fiercest rivals in the ring, but the two remained close friends throughout their careers.

"We really went at it," recalled Hawk, who once broke Royal's leg during a singles match. "When I wrestled Nelson, we really wrestled. There were no cartoons or anything like that. Nelson was great as a singles or in tag teams. He was a leader and he was fun to wrestle. It was hard, but it was fun. The people couldn't believe some of the moves we made. Nobody could 'see daylight.' It was all very tight."

"I never had an argument with him," added Hawk. "He was a great wrestler and a great friend. Not only to me, but to a lot of people. I'm really going to miss him."

"I can say one thing. He lived a full life," said David Crockett. "Nelson was one of those guys who helped build the groundwork for what it (wrestling) is today."

Royal also trained scores of wrestlers, including a young Ken Shamrock, who moved with his dad to Royal's ranch during the late '80s while Royal was training wrestlers along with Gene Anderson and running his Atlantic Coast Wrestling promotion.

Nellie, who was involved in a number of community efforts such as the DARE drug awareness program and Crime Stoppers, operated his western supply store in Mooresville for more than 30 years, selling boots, belts and saddles, and raised horses "until the town got bigger and a five-lane highway came through." He lived for the outdoors, although most of his last years were confined to running the store with wife Karen. For years, his dream had been to sell the property and "move across the road and go back out to the country."

Unfortunately Nellie never made it across that road.

But what he left behind is a treasure chest of golden wrestling memories — the kind that will never die.

George Scott
A legacy of greatness

Jan. 26, 2014

I t's probably a safe bet that most younger fans of today's version of professional wrestling aren't familiar with the name George Scott.

And that's a shame.

Scott, who passed away last week at the age of 84, was one of the most influential men in the business for several decades.

During the '50s and '60s, Scott was a top-flight wrestler, forming one of the sport's most successful brother duos, The Flying Scotts, along with younger brother Sandy.

During the '70s, Scott used his considerable talents as a booker to turn the storied Mid-Atlantic territory into one of the hottest promotions in the country.

During the '80s, Scott played a key role in Vince McMahon's national expansion of the WWF and the creation of Wrestlemania.

George Scott did all this and much more during a career that spanned from 1948 until his retirement in the early '90s.

"George Scott took a kid who was rough around the edges and molded him into a champion," said 16-time world champion "Nature Boy" Ric Flair. "He was the biggest influence in my career. He was totally responsible for my makeover after the (1975) airplane crash."

Scott, indeed, modeled Flair after close friend "Nature Boy" Buddy Rogers, helping the young Minnesotan fine-tune the gimmick and elevating him to main-event status early in his career in the Carolinas.

"My career took off with George's help and guidance, and I owe much of my success to him," adds Flair.

Scott also was responsible for bringing in a greenhorn named Richard Blood, billing him as Ricky Steamboat and matching him up against Flair, the territory's top heel. Their rivalry would become legendary, and Steamboat would become one of the top babyfaces in wrestling history.

When Scott, having retired from the ring due to a broken neck and other linger-ing injuries, took over as booker in 1973 following the death of longtime promoter Jim Crockett Sr., he infused the Mid-Atlantic area with new talent.

WWE Hall of Famer Jerry Brisco, younger brother of the late great Jack Brisco, was one of those Scott turned to.

"George gave me my first big break when I came into the Carolinas," says Brisco. "He made me a star in the territory and booked me with all the great workers that he had brought in."

The Carolinas had been known as a hotbed for tag-team wrestling during the '60s. But into the '70s, headliners had grown older, talent had become stale, and crowds had declined.

Scott decided to take an entirely different approach when he brought in a number of top singles stars to help jump-start the promotion.

Main-event performers such as Johnny Valentine, Wahoo McDaniel, The Super Destroyer (Don Jardine) and Blackjack Mulligan slowly but surely began popping the territory.

And with the rapid development of young talent such as Flair and Steamboat, the Mid-Atlantic area became a wrestling fan's paradise with a "who's who" of grappling talent.

"George really helped advance my career by giving me the opportunity to work with guys like Johnny Valentine and The Super Destroyer," says Brisco. "I just had tremendous respect for his knowledge of the business, how he handled himself, how he handled talent."

Ironically, adds Brisco, "When Rip (Hawk) met me in Australia in 1970, the whole premise of me coming to the Carolinas was to take George Scott's place. And I ended up teaming with Sandy."

The Scotts, in fact, had provided the blueprint for top babyface brother duos — such as Jack and Jerry Brisco — to follow.

"What people forget is that George was a great worker," says Brisco. "He made that great transition long before it was popular for a wrestler to come into that position. He became a highly successful booker and matchmaker. Both George and Sandy were very creative in the business. They were the model of a tag team that many aspired to be."

"George really re-invented the Carolinas and the Mid-Atlantic area to be the great territory it became," says Brisco. "He was the architect of Mid-Atlantic."

Flying Scotts

While George and brother Sandy (Angus Scott) both played key roles in the promotional and creative end of Mid-Atlantic wrestling during the '70s and '80s, it was inside the ring where they had become the darlings of a generation of fans in the Carolinas and Virginia.

George, already an established star at the time, helped break Sandy, five years his junior, into the business in the early '50s.

With youthful good looks and polished mat skills, the brothers were dubbed "The Flying Scotts" due to their speed and aerial antics, which included dropkicks and flying head scissors.

They spent nearly six years as tag-team headliners in Stu Hart's Calgary-based Stampede territory where they won the Canadian tag-team belts within months of their arrival. Torrid matches with another top team of that era, the Miller Brothers, set records at the Calgary Stampede, an annual festival and rodeo that featured wrestling spectaculars, in both 1957 and 1958.

The Scotts, main-eventers everywhere they went, bounced from western Canada to Toronto and Buffalo, adding to their tag-team title collection at every stop.

But it was a warmer climate and another veteran promoter, Jim Crockett Sr., that lured the Scotts to an area they would eventually call home and achieve their greatest success, both as wrestlers and as bookers.

Born in Scotland and raised in Hamilton, Ontario, Canada, the Scotts would settle in the Carolinas-Virginia area, where Jim Crockett Sr. told his headliners that they had a home for life.

The Scotts also found an abundance of top-tier teams to feud with in the Mid-Atlantic area during the '60s. For a decade the Scotts battled the likes of such heel tandems as Rip Hawk and Swede Hanson, The Assassins, Skull Murphy and Brute Bernard, Aldo Bogni and Bronko Lubich, Bob Orton and Boris Malenko, and The Andersons.

The Scotts became involved with every aspect of the promotion, and were responsible for giving a number of young stars their first break in the business.

"George Scott is the only father I've ever known," says WWE Hall of Famer Tony Atlas, who was "discovered" by George and brother Sandy at a YMCA in Roanoke, Va., during the early '70s. "He was a wonderful man. Everything I learned I learned from him. He always took care of me. He and his brother were both wonderful people."

Veteran fans who were weaned on the old days of Carolina wrestling also recall George Scott with fond memories.

"George Scott 'booked our youth,'" wrote Dick Bourne of the popular Mid-Atlantic Gateway website. "He was the man behind the scenes during our favorite years in Mid-Atlantic wrestling."

"He made me a fan. Best eye for detail ever (along with Les Thatcher)," said filmmaker Richard O'Sullivan. "He was one of those visionaries who will never get the credit he deserves. If not for him, they'd be calling Wrestlemania 'the Colossal Tussle' (and no one could do that with a straight face). Best of all time."

Wrestling historian and author Bill Murdock remembers going to the Asheville Civic Center on Wednesday nights to see his hero in action.

"We'd stand at the front door just waiting for them (the Scotts) to walk out. They would be three feet away from us, and we just couldn't speak."

To Murdock and thousands of other fans, the Scotts were matinee idols, larger-than-life heroes who represented virtue and battled the bad guys on a weekly basis for mat supremacy.

"Sandy would put the abdominal stretch on one guy, and George would put the sleeper on the other," says Murdock, referring to the Scotts' trademark one-two punch.

George Scott didn't need a gimmick or a flashy name.

"Why would I change my name and want to make somebody else famous?" he'd wryly ask.

Sandy Scott died at the age of 75 on March 11, 2010, from pancreatic cancer.

WWF expansion

Brisco, a Tampa resident, would remain friends with Scott, who moved nearly 25 years ago to nearby Indian Rocks Beach.

Years after Scott brought him to the Carolinas as a rising young star, he would return the favor by helping bring Scott into the WWF fold as Vince McMahon was beginning his national expansion of the company.

"When Jack and I decided to sell our stock to Vince (in 1984), Vince asked us who we would recommend to be his booker when he took it over." Both immediately suggested George Scott.

"George got the job and went on to help create the first Wrestlemania. He was a very creative guy and he gave everything he had to the business. "

Scott booked the first show, as well as some of WWF's weekly programming, but he had a major problem with the proposed name for the inaugural mega-event.

"They were going to call it 'The Colossal Tussle,' notes Murdock. "But George said no way are we calling it that."

The rest, of course, is history, and three decades later the annual show is the biggest event in professional wrestling. A lot of the credit goes to Scott.

So entrusted by the McMahon family was Scott that, in later years, he would proudly display a letter from company owners Vince and Linda McMahon declaring that, if anything ever happened to them during that period, Scott was to take control of the organization.

But he eventually became disenchanted with the changing tide of the wrestling product. Less and less emphasis was being placed on traditional wrestling as Scott had known it.

Along with an increased spotlight on what many traditionalists called "cartoon characters," drug problems began to crop up on the WWF roster, and Scott grew wary of dealing with talent he deemed neither dependable nor accountable.

A few brief stints in the business followed, including a run as WCW booker, but nothing would ever recapture the magic Scott had enjoyed in earlier decades.

Pro wrestling had changed forever, and Scott knew when it was time to leave.

He finished up his career working for a regional outfit called South Atlantic Pro Wrestling.

'Always a wrestler'

George Scott also was instrumental in the early development of the Asheville, N.C.-based Eblen Charities, an organization that benefits thousands of needy families in western North Carolina.

"George helped grow that organization. He helped put together the first golf tournament. It's now one of the biggest charities in the nation," says Brisco.

To Bill Murdock, executive director of Eblen Charities, George Scott was a boyhood hero, mentor and close friend.

"Where everybody else had (heroes like) Joe Namath and Pete Rose, I had George Scott. I had George and Jack (Brisco) and Dory (Funk Jr.). But George was my first sports hero. He'll always be one of my heroes."

Their relationship extended beyond a professional one.

Scott was one of the first "celebrities" to help the Eblen organization its in early days as a mere fundraiser.

Murdock recalls reaching out to the local wrestling community, and being told by Ricky Steamboat to give George Scott a call.

Initially, says Murdock, he was in awe of actually calling someone he had idolized as a youngster growing up in Asheville.

"For three weeks I wouldn't call him. I'd call the president or the pope before I'd call George Scott. I was actually holding George Scott's phone number."

Murdock eventually mustered the courage to call his boyhood hero and found Scott as engaging and pleasant as he had imagined.

"He was just so nice. He invited me to come down to Spartanburg that Friday night. We went out to eat afterwards and had a wonderful time."

Scott helped recruit a group of pro wrestling stars for Murdock's first celebrity golf tournament, and the event has been going strong ever since.

An avid golfer, Scott enjoyed participating in the annual auction and golf tournament, which greatly added to the star-studded atmosphere, says Murdock.

"He had a good time with everyone. When Jesse Ventura was here for the event, George smiled and pointed out, 'I used to be his boss.'"

In 2004 Scott received the Frank Gotch Award recognizing individuals for bringing positive recognition to professional wrestling through work outside the ring.

"All of his accomplishments in the ring, in the office, paled in comparison to the man that he was and the wonderful heart that he had for others. He was a world champion in a lot more ways than in the ring," says Murdock. "I will forever be in his debt."

Murdock says he admired how Scott understood all sides of the wrestling business.

"George had such a love for the sport ... and for the guys. He was respected by so many people in this business. Being a wrestler, he understood the talent he was dealing with (when he became booker).

"No matter what position George had in the industry, as booker or matchmaker, he was always a wrestler. He took such pride and honor in that. I think the product he put out from behind the desk reflected that. He loved and understood the sport, he loved the fans and the towns, and he understood what the boys had to go through."

Scott, who had been diagnosed with lung cancer in November 2011, passed away on Jan. 20.

He left the wrestling profession with a legacy that will never be forgotten.

"George was a great wrestler, world champion, businessman, promoter and philanthropist. What an honor it was to have known him," says Murdock.

Sandy Scott
Saying goodbye to Sandy Scott

March 14, 2010

Forever young.

That's how I'll always remember Sandy Scott.

In that bygone era of professional wrestling, long before the Hogans, the Austins, and the Cenas, fans flocked to arenas large and small to see their hometown heroes do battle with all shapes and sizes of dastardly heels.

In this area of the country, specifically the Carolinas and Virginia, no one was more popular and beloved by the wrestling crowd than a pair of Canadian brothers named George and Sandy Scott.

Sandy's recent passing leaves a void in the hearts of those who cherish the magical memories of an era of wrestling when the lines were clearly drawn between good and bad, and there were no shades of grey.

Sandy, a fan favorite his entire career, wasn't just a good guy inside the ring. That clean-cut persona followed him outside the squared circle as well.

Sandy, who was diagnosed late last year with pancreatic cancer, passed away at the age of 75. The deadly disease did what time never could. Sandy never seemed to lose that special spark, that zest for life, those same qualities that endeared him to a generation of wrestling fans.

I was one of those fans, long before I was a friend, and I'll remember Sandy as that ageless hero I rooted for on Friday nights at the arena and Saturday afternoons on black and white television, as he waged war against the bad guys.

That was nearly 50 years ago, but some things never change. Good guys like Sandy Scott are golden.

The Flying Scotts

Few individuals played a bigger role than Angus "Sandy" Scott in the success and popularity of the Charlotte-based Jim Crockett Promotions and Mid-Atlantic wrestling during the 1960s. That influence continued into later decades when he transitioned from the ring to behind-the-scenes roles that included a variety of front-office duties.

But it was inside the ring where Sandy and older brother George became the darlings of a generation of fans in the Carolinas and Virginia.

George, already an established star at the time, helped break Sandy, five years his junior, into the business in the early '50s. They spent nearly six years as tag-team headliners in Stu Hart's Calgary-based Stampede territory where they won the Canadian tag-team belts within months of their arrival. Torrid matches with another top team of that era, the Miller Brothers, sets records at the Calgary Stampede, an annual festival and rodeo that featured wrestling spectaculars, in both 1957 and 1958.

The Scotts, main-eventers everywhere they went, bounced from western Canada to Toronto and Buffalo, adding to their tag-team title collection at every stop.

But it was a warmer climate and another veteran promoter, Jim Crockett Sr., that lured the Scotts to an area they would eventually call home and achieve their greatest success, both as wrestlers and as bookers.

The brothers from Hamilton, Ontario, Canada, with their youthful good looks and polished mat skills, made an instant connection with the fans in the Mid-Atlantic territory, whose major cities included Greenville, Charleston, Columbia, Charlotte, Raleigh, Greensboro, Asheville, Richmond, Norfolk, Roanoke and all the smaller towns in between.

Tag-team wrestling reached an apex during the '60s, and the Carolinas-Virginia area was the hottest tag-team territory during that period. And the hottest team was the Scott Brothers.

For nearly 20 years the Scotts faced the top duos in the business. Many of those teams were other sibling acts, which made the match-ups particularly appealing, and were big draws at the box office. Among those brother (and pseudo-brother) teams were Gene, Lars and Ole Anderson, Bill and Danny Miller, Chris and John Tolos, Ronnie and Terry Garvin, Maurice "Mad Dog" and Paul "Butcher" Vachon,

Art and Stan Neilson, Al and John Smith, Mike and Doc Gallagher, and Ivan and Karol Kalmikoff.

The Scotts also found an abundance of top-tier heel teams to feud with in the Mid-Atlantic area. Some of the biggest wrestling crowds ever at the old County Hall on King Street packed the building week after week to see George and Sandy battle the bad guys of the day. There were bloodbaths with the likes of Rip Hawk and Swede Hanson, The Assassins, Skull Murphy and Brute Bernard, Aldo Bogni and Bronko Lubich, Bob Orton and Boris Malenko, and The Andersons.

The brothers were dubbed "The Flying Scotts" due to their speed and aerial antics, which included dropkicks and flying head scissors, and the two were silky smooth in the ring, with George using the sleeper as his finishing hold and Sandy applying the abdominal stretch as his coupe de grâce.

What many fans didn't know, ironically enough, was that their smooth in-ring teamwork belied a strained relationship between the brothers in real life.

Throughout the '60s the Scotts shared main-event babyface tag-team status with the equally popular tandem of George Becker and Johnny Weaver. One team would cover the southern part of the territory, while the other would go up north. They would switch off every four or five weeks. The formula worked to perfection.

Behind the scenes

Sandy Scott, like brother George, wore many hats in the wrestling business. Wrestler, booker, matchmaker, agent, public relations man, front-office worker.

George was offered the booking job in Charlotte shortly after breaking his neck in 1972 and retiring from in-ring competition. It wasn't long before Sandy followed his lead.

Jim Crockett Jr. offered Sandy a position working in the office and handling some of the towns on the circuit, with Greenville being his home base. Much of his duties involved interacting with fans, dealing with building managers and basically doing PR to hype Crockett's shows.

Sandy was tailor-made for that role. His honesty shone through in all of his dealings, and his easygoing approach endeared him to the public, much like it had during his wrestling career.

While George helped turn the territory around by building new stars such as Ric Flair, Ricky Steamboat and Roddy Piper, and by bringing in older talent such as Johnny Valentine, Wahoo McDaniel and Blackjack Mulligan, Sandy knew the value of strong television exposure and strengthened the product's reach across the circuit.

Like George, Sandy had a great mind for the business. While George's major strength was the creative end, Sandy was more of a pragmatist who dealt with the day-to-day responsibilities of running a wrestling office.

It wasn't an easy job, said longtime friend Danny Miller, who took the reigns of the Greenville operation from Sandy in 1977.

"Sandy just had that natural ability to make it look easy," said Miller, a top star in his own right who quit wrestling in 1977 at the age of 45 to help the Crocketts in the office.

"I had known Sandy as a wrestler for many years. My brother, Dr. Bill Miller, and I wrestled the Scotts many times in Canada during the '50s. Sandy was working in the office when I came to the Carolinas in the '70s. I stopped wrestling, and was asked to come in and work in the office also. I first worked with brother George, who was doing the booking at that time in Charlotte, for several months. Jim Crockett wanted Sandy to move from Greenville, the South Carolina-western North Carolina section of his area, to the area between Charlotte and Roanoke."

Miller jumped at the opportunity to get into the promotional end in Greenville.

"Sandy spent a few weeks with me showing me exactly what needed to be done. I ended up doing it there for eight years. Sandy had done an excellent job there in Greenville. I had a very easy job because Sandy had it all set up the way it should be run, and I just followed his suit. Sandy always did a great job wherever he went."

One of Sandy's greatest attributes, pointed out Miller, was his ability to connect with the fans.

"Sandy was a good friend. I always enjoyed being around him, and wrestling with him and sometimes as partners. But one of his greatest attributes was how he related to the fans. He was always casual and cordial with them. In the promotions field, you have to be able to talk to everybody and not only conduct business, but to be there for them. You have to listen to what they say."

Even-keeled and seemingly unflappable, Sandy also had a lighter side he would occasionally spring on friends.

"He'd like to rib you occasionally," laughed Miller. "If you didn't know Sandy, you might get the impression that he wasn't being too friendly. But if he knew who you were, he was a great guy."

"He was a great ribber. He was really good at that. He was better at giving them than taking them," joked longtime Mid-Atlantic star Don Kernodle.

"Sandy was a genuinely nice man who was so easy to respect and to want to be around," said WWE Hall of Fame announcer Jim Ross. "While so many ex-wrestlers from Sandy's generation, and after, are bitter about their careers, about not saving their money or preparing for their future, Sandy was a joy to be around and he rarely had a cross or negative word to say about anyone."

A different era

Those in the business aren't always as good as their word. Sandy Scott always was.

"Sandy was a great guy, a great promoter and a good friend," said Miller, who went to work for Hiro Matsuda and Duke Keomuka in the Tampa-based Florida Championship Wrestling office in 1985 after leaving Charlotte.

George helped book the territory until 1981 when he left following a pay dispute. Two years later he was enlisted by Vince McMahon to help with the WWF when his father, Vince McMahon Sr., became deathly ill. Scott went on to become lead booker and was instrumental in the national expansion of the WWE during the mid-'80s when he booked the first two Wrestlemanias and NBC's Saturday Night Main Event.

Sandy remained one of the Crockett family's most loyal employees, booking towns and venues and handling advertising and public appearances, and was there until the end of the company's run in the late '80s when he took a similar position with the Ted Turner-owned World Championship Wrestling. He even added the role of on-air host of WCW World Wide to his duties.

He booked towns and venues, and handled advertising and public appearances. He took part in angles and served a role on-camera as a special representative of the NWA.

Like many from his era, however, his style didn't mesh well with the corporate mentality of the Atlanta suits, and he eventually left in 1991.

It wasn't surprising that his last major run in the business came with Jim Cornette's fledgling Smoky Mountain Wrestling. In many ways it had modeled itself after the old territories, and was the antithesis of what had become a corporate-run industry that favored style over substance. He most recently had made appearances for the ACW promotion in Rocky Mount, Va.

He was inducted into the Lowcountry Wrestling Hall of Fame in 1998 a ceremony at the old County Hall, then renamed the King Street Palace, and the NWA Wrestling Legends Hall of Heroes in 2008 in Charlotte.

To know Sandy was to like him.

"I will never forget how friendly and professional Sandy was to me when I first went to work for Jim Crockett Promotions, and that fact alone put Sandy on a short albeit unforgettable list," said Ross.

"He was a good boss and a good friend," said Burrhead Jones (Melvin Nelson). "He gave me an opportunity in North Carolina. Rufus (R. Jones) and Blackjack (Mulligan) spoke up for me because Sandy and George didn't know me. Sandy gave me a chance and took real good care of me. We met up again in recent years at some of the reunions, and we rekindled our relationship all over again."

"Sandy Scott was a great man and a great mentor," said Kernodle, who first met Sandy in 1973. "He helped me a lot and he helped a lot of young people. He was great like Johnny Weaver was in helping folks and giving them a lot of confidence about the business. He had done everything in the business, and he taught us so much. He was a master in the psychology of wrestling. He was as good as anyone I've ever met. He was top of the line."

Many of the younger wrestlers of that generation owe a great deal to Sandy Scott. He took a young Jerry Brisco under his wing in the early '70s, lent his expertise to the amateur standout, and pushed him to main-event status as a tag-team partner.

I knew Sandy had a keen eye for talent and the business when he was the first to tell me that a 20-something Ric Flair would be world champion one day. It would be a good five years before the Nature Boy would win the gold. But sure enough he did. Again. And again. And again.

Getting to know Sandy over these many years, I think if he could send out a final message to his fans, it would be to convey his appreciation for their loyalty and friendship. Rarely in conversation concerning the business did he fail to mention the folks whom he felt were responsible for his success in life.

Sandy Scott was part of an era that, sadly, is gone forever.

"It'll never be like it was when we were there," said Miller.

But the memories remain.

For the 72-year-old Jones, as one door closes, another one opens.

"We all have to cross that road one day or another. That's one match we all have to show up for," said Jones. "I suppose Rufus is getting more and more friends each and every day. There'll be a lot of guys up there, and more to come. I'm sure Sandy's up there now with some of the guys he worked with on this side ... Wahoo McDaniel, Johnny Weaver, Johnny Valentine. Make room for the rest of the boys, Sandy, they're coming. I don't know when, but they'll be there to join us. It'll be one heavenly wrestling reunion."

Johnny Weaver

Memories of Johnny Weaver and Saturday afternoons

Feb. 24, 2008

Turn out the lights, the party's over, they say that all good things must end..."

- Willie Nelson

Whenever I think about Mid-Atlantic Wrestling and Jim Crockett Promotions, my mind invariably takes me back to the days when County Hall was the place to be on Friday nights and the black-and-white Saturday afternoon wrestling show emanated from a small TV studio in Raleigh.

From Charleston to Norfolk and all points in between, it was a territory that thrived on unique characters who could make people believe and have them coming back each week for more. Many of those names from that bygone era are gone now, leaving behind memories that will last a lifetime for those who were lucky enough to be around that special time.

No name was bigger, and no wrestler was more beloved, than Johnny Weaver. Weaver, who passed away at the age of 72 at his home in Charlotte, was to wrestling fans in the Carolinas what Mickey Mantle was to baseball and Johnny Unitas was to football. He wasn't particularly flashy, but that was part of his appeal. He was a genuine everyman's hero who related to the predominantly blue-collar audience that followed the sport religiously back in those days.

One of those fans was me.

Watching the Saturday afternoon wrestling show was a ritual for me and my grandmother, a sweet, soft-spoken, little Greek lady who turned into a rabid fanatic whenever one of her favorites was on the receiving end of the bad guys' underhanded and devious tactics. With her wooden cane taking dead aim at the television set, she would yell and scream in a mixture of Greek and broken English, as if she could somehow get the attention of the hapless referee who never could quite catch the villains in the act.

Granny had her share of favorites, but no one could touch Johnny Weaver.

It's been nearly 45 years since I first saw Johnny Weaver wrestle, and I've often told him the story about my Greek grandmother. He'd always laugh, wondering how he could have that kind of effect on a fan. To be honest, though, he had that kind of effect on a lot of folks. And he did until the day he died.

Becker and Weaver

Billed from Indianapolis, but actually born in East St. Louis, Illinois, Johnny Weaver was the biggest fan favorite to ever come through the Carolinas. He arrived in Charlotte, headquarters of Crockett Promotions, in 1962 and made it his home. He occasionally appeared in other parts of the country, but only for limited amounts of time, always returning to the area that adopted him and the fans who made him their local hero.

During the '60s, if you mentioned the name Johnny Weaver, the name George Becker was usually in that same sentence. The two were virtual bookends and the territory's top team in those days.

While Becker at that time was the ringwise veteran and elder statesman of the territory, Weaver proved to be the ideal complement as his young babyface partner. It was a match made in wrestling heaven, especially since the Carolinas-Virginia territory was a hotbed for tag teams during the '60s, and the majority of main events consisted of tag bouts featuring some of the best combos in the business.

Becker and Weaver ruled the roost, holding the Southern and Atlantic Coast tag-team belts and enjoying profitable programs with such formidable duos as Rip Hawk and Swede Hanson, Skull Murphy and Brute Bernard, Aldo Bogni and Bronco Lubich, The Masked Bolos, The Andersons, The Masked Red Demons, The Masked Infernos, and The Missouri Mauler and The Great Malenko, just to name a few.

The team also set attendance marks throughout the area, including a record at the old County Hall for a match with The Red Demons in which the champions put their belts and their hair on the line against the masked pair's hoods and identities. Becker and Weaver had Klondike Bill in their corner to neutralize Demons' manager George "Two Ton" Harris. The popular champs kept their straps and their hair, while The Demons unmasked and were revealed to be Billy and Jimmy Hines.

Weaver was only 26 when he first came to the Carolinas from Indianapolis, and once said that Becker's experience helped him immensely.

"George was a great partner and a great man. He was also a very good tutor. I was the 'young blood' so I did most of the wrestling, and I'd tag George when I'd get in trouble."

There were other partners along the way with whom Weaver shared success and titles — stars such as the popular Cowboy Bob Ellis, 601-pound Haystacks Calhoun, strongman Sailor Art Thomas, rugged Art Nelson and the acrobatic Argentina Apollo. His final tag-team reigns were with Dewey Robertson and Jay Youngblood in 1981.

But none clicked the way Becker and Weaver did.

"George Becker and Johnny Weaver were it," said respected veteran Abe Jacobs. "Johnny kept the team together."

Weaver could only chuckle when thinking about the many tag matches they won with him using the sleeper hold and Becker, all 5-8 and 185 pounds of him, and jokingly referred to by his opponents as "skinny legs," applying his vaunted abdominal stretch. "I can't count that high," he would say.

But he also admitted that Becker was unflappable and a steadying influence on him. Nothing bothered him, according to Weaver, and the two never had an argument during all the road trips they made together. That unflappable nature eventually extended to Weaver.

"I don't think I ever remember seeing the guy upset or anything like that," promoter Greg Price said of Weaver. "He was just as cool as a cucumber. What a guy."

Mid-Atlantic hero

A generation of Mid-Atlantic fans grew up watching Johnny Weaver battle the bad guys. To longtime pundits like Dick Bourne, Weaver was a sports star of the first order. He was a good-looking, smooth-working babyface with an All-American smile and an easygoing personality. He was, in wrestling parlance, "over."

"He was such a household name back then," says Bourne, who runs the Mid-Atlantic Gateway site. "As a kid in the '60s and early '70s, I could list on one hand who the real sports stars were. There was Johnny Unitas, Pete Rose, Wilt Chamberlain and Johnny Weaver. That's how big he was to us."

Although Weaver's specialty was tag-team wrestling, he also was an accomplished singles performer who held a slew of titles and was a top challenger to every NWA world champion from Lou Thesz to Gene Kiniski, Dory Funk Jr. and Jack Brisco.

"There's a lot of people who came through this territory and worked the towns, and it seemed like Johnny was here forever," said Price. "Johnny knew wrestling like the back of his hand. Not only the wrestling part, but the promotion part, too. You see a lot of guys who leave wrestling and try to promote shows and book, but it's like apples and oranges. It's two different things. But Johnny was so good at both. He was equally as good at promoting as he was wrestling. He knew every back road and every contact. He had relationships with everybody — every building, every town. The only person I can compare him to, as far as that aspect, would be (longtime Charleston promoter) Henry Marcus."

Fan Rusty Loudermilk of Pittsburgh, who grew up in Charlotte, said Weaver will never be replaced.

"Respect in wrestling is not given — it is earned — and he had the respect from all of us. He was more than a wrestler to me. He was more than 'one of the boys.' He was a great friend to me doing my childhood and most of my adult life as well."

Loudermilk, who suffers from cerebral palsy, fondly remembers Weaver clowning around with him, playfully applying his signature sleeper hold.

"He was the kind of guy who just related so well to his fans. It's no wonder that people still fondly remember him to this day."

"He was special," said Price. "When you talk about heroes and Mid-Atlantic Wrestling, Johnny Weaver was right there at the top of the list."

Weaver was universally respected by those he worked with in the business.

To longtime star Blackjack Mulligan (Bob Windham), Weaver was the anchor for Mid-Atlantic Wrestling, a steadying force who knew the territory better than anyone else.

"Johnny had the greatest mind in the business," said Mulligan, who added that his friend had a book of finishes that covered every match he had ever worked. "One night I asked him if he would decode that thing. He was the best finish man in the business. He was a master at this business."

The loss saddened an entire community of wrestlers and former wrestlers. One of the hardest hit was Jim Nelson (Jim Harrell), who began his career in the early '80s as Private Jim Nelson in Sgt. Slaughter's "Cobra Corps" along with partner Don Kernodle.

"I got sick when I heard about Johnny's passing on my way home. I had to pull over and sit on the side of the road for a couple of hours. I just wasn't expecting it."

"Johnny was Mr. Mid-Atlantic Wrestling," added Nelson. "There's no doubt about it. Everybody knew who Johnny Weaver was. He helped me so much when

I came here and taught me stuff in the ring. He was a super guy, a great friend, and God, I'm going to miss him. When Don and I got together, he helped both of us tremendously. It was stuff you never forgot.

"He always went out of his way to put guys over. As far as he was concerned, he had been made a long time ago. He always worked for the wrestling match. He once told me that you're only as good as the guy you're in the ring with. He believed that with all his heart."

"It's still hard to believe," said Price. "It's hard to imagine that he's not here anymore. He was part of us for so long. I don't think there'll ever be another one like him."

Jody Hamilton remembers starting out in the business with Weaver in the mid-'50s in Hamilton's hometown of St. Joseph, Mo. The two youngsters pulled the rings for promoter Gust Karras and worked out in the ring after setting them up. Soon Weaver was teaming with local veteran Sonny Meyers as the Weaver Brothers.

"Sonny Meyers had a lot of influence on his style of work. He copied Sonny quite a bit, and Johnny turned out to be a premier performer," said Hamilton.

A few years later, both Weaver and Hamilton would be headliners in the business, their paths meeting again in the Carolinas and Virginia, with Weaver one of the circuit's top babyfaces, and Hamilton and partner Tom Renesto two of the top heels as The Masked Bolos (also known as The Assassins).

"We worked with Johnny lots of times when he was with (Haystacks) Calhoun, and worked with him when he was with George Becker," said Hamilton. "At Becker's age, of course, Johnny carried the team. As a worker, Johnny was in the upper echelon. As far as his contribution to the business, he was always the ultimate professional. I had nothing but respect for his uncanny ring ability. At one time, he was one of the elite performers in the business. He was a credit to this profession."

Johnny Weaver was all of that for sure.

Just like old times

Weaver filled many roles in the wrestling business — as a main-event performer, a booker and office man, a color commentator in the announce booth, and a mentor to many. Affectionately known as "the dean of professional wrestling," his storied career spanned more than four decades.

Weaver told the Mid-Atlantic Gateway site in an interview last year that he could tell when his in-ring days were numbered.

"You know how I knew time was passing me by? I was always fan friendly, and I would get dressed and go out and talk to the people all the time during all of the matches up until it was time for me to go on. I did that for years and years and years. The girls would all run up and hug me. And then finally, they started running up to me, the girls, and they'd throw their arms around me, about a hundred of them, and they'd whisper in my ear, 'Go get Ricky Steamboat.' And then I knew I was over the hill."

When his wrestling career officially ended in 1989, he took a position with the Mecklenburg County Sheriff's Department, a job he held until his death. In his 50's at the time, Weaver became one of the oldest people to take the basic law enforcement test, even though he was tougher, stronger and in better shape than some officers half his age.

Longtime Cauliflower Alley member Al Mandell, who had worked at the department for 10 years under a previous administration, helped get Weaver the job.

"He called me up when Turner let him go. He called me and told me he needed to talk to me, so we met at Valentino's Restaurant," recalled Mandell. "He told me he wanted to go to the sheriff's department. The chief deputy was a very good friend of mine, and I introduced him to him and the sheriff. And that was it."

Weaver spent most of his 19-year second career transporting prisoners on the same back roads he'd traveled as a wrestler and promoter.

Like most heroes, though, Weaver wasn't perfect or infallible, nor did he hold himself up as a role model. His 35-year relationship with women's wrestling star Penny Banner was far from the ideal marriage, with the two separating more than a dozen years ago. Both would readily point out, though, that something wonderful came out of it, and that was their daughter Wendi.

Weaver had attended Greg Price's inaugural Mid-Atlantic Wrestling Legends Fanfest in 2004, and was looking forward to being inducted into the Hall of Heroes at this year's event in August. What made it even more enticing, says Price, is that Weaver was going to be inducted by old ring rival Rip Hawk.

"He was so looking forward to that," said Price. "Rip was inducted last year and had told Johnny what a great experience it was, and apparently that was the key to the whole deal. He was very happy when I told him that I wanted Rip to be the one to induct him. I just hate that it didn't work out. It's something I definitely was looking forward to."

Weaver also attended a "Johnny Weaver Weekend" event last November in Rocky Mount, Va., that brought together some of his old fans and friends who threw him a surprise birthday party.

Two of those who attended were Sandy Scott, who first worked with Weaver in the Carolinas in the '60s, and Jim Nelson, who worked with Weaver two decades later.

Nelson, like many other aspiring wrestlers, had grown up idolizing Weaver. It was a dream come true when he actually had the opportunity to team with him briefly in the early '80s. It was yet another honor for Nelson when he got to get in the ring with him for an angle at the November show.

"Me and Johnny Weaver were in the ring again like a tag team. We had tagged up years ago when I turned babyface against Slaughter and them. It was just like old times. It was a great night."

Nelson said he almost forgot what he was doing when Weaver clamped his sleeper hold on an opponent as he was applying the cobra clutch.

"Johnny was so excited when he got in the ring that night. It was like he hadn't missed a step. I was supposed to get the cobra clutch on the manager, and I got so caught up watching Johnny, I almost forgot about what I was doing. I had goosebumps."

"As far as I know, that was the last time Johnny ever used the sleeper," added Nelson.

Nelson said it was a night he'll never forget.

"He was just like a little kid back there in the dressing room that night. He was so excited about being there and talking about wrestling and kicking stuff around. He was so creative. He had an unbelievable mind for the business. We were in awe in the dressing room that night as he talked about all these finishes. He was so wound up. It was like we had stepped back in time 20 years and were back in Charlotte."

It was the first time Scott had seen Weaver in nearly 15 years.

"We really enjoyed getting together. It was great seeing him again," said Scott. "We had some long talks, and we sat down and caught up on things. It brought back some good memories. It seemed like we had just seen each other a couple of weeks ago."

Not only did Scott team on occasion with Weaver in tag matches and in six-man bouts with Becker and Weaver, the two were pretty good at handball. "He was a handball partner of mine, and we played two or three times a week. We took on all comers, and we were pretty good at it," laughed Scott.

If there was a team that rivaled Becker and Weaver, it had been Sandy Scott and brother George.

"One team would never cover the south, and the other team would go up north, to towns like Norfolk, Richmond, Hampton and Roanoke. And we would switch off every four or five weeks," said Scott.

Weaver had learned how to operate a computer in recent months, thanks to longtime Mid-Atlantic fan Peggy Lathan, and was enjoying exchanging correspondence with fans, friends and former colleagues. Bourne and Carroll Hall also set up a website for him.

"I had gotten an e-mail from him a day or two before he died," said Nelson. "It's still hard for me to believe."

Weaver and Mulligan also had recently communicated. Mulligan had asked

Weaver to spend this past Christmas with him and his family in Texas.

"We spent Christmas with the family sitting on the Saba River, cooking out and having the greatest time," said Mulligan. "I asked Johnny to fly on down to San Angelo, and I was going to pick him up. We'd have a great Christmas with roasted hens and dressing and stuff, and I told him he'd love it here. I called him a week in advance and told him we were going to do something a little different. But he said (daughter) Wendi was coming over, and he was expecting her. I never did find out, but I really hoped she did come over that day."

The final chapter

I talked to Johnny a couple of weeks before he passed. He had just been sworn in again as deputy sheriff and was looking forward to his retirement in October from the Mecklenburg County Sheriff's Department.

We talked about the "glory days" in the Mid-Atlantic area, and I asked him if he thought much about them.

"Oh, God, almost every day," he said without a hint of hesitation.

We also talked — again — about how my late grandmother loved watching Johnny Weaver every Saturday afternoon. "God bless her soul," he laughed wistfully.

Of course, the entertainment quotient wasn't as high back in those days, but Saturday afternoon wrestling was still appointment viewing.

"I've had many people tell me, 'Boy, Daddy worked us hard, but at 5 o'clock in the afternoon we were in front of the TV and we had to be quiet.' There wasn't much around back then, and we didn't have basketball, football and all that we've got now," said Weaver. "Outside of racing, which was seasonal, we had wrestling. And that would come on every Saturday, and it was done in little studios in High Point, Charlotte and Raleigh."

We also talked about all "the boys" we had lost over the past few years. Especially the ones who had made the Mid-Atlantic area one of the top territories in the country. Weaver noted Mid-Atlantic legends like Nellie (Royal), Swede (Hanson), Gene (Anderson), Mr. Wrestling (Tim Woods), Two Ton (Harris), Klondike (Bill). "All from right around area," he noted.

He was counting down the working days until his retirement in October. "I work a crazy schedule. Twelve hours a day," he said, reciting a portion of his breakneck schedule.

But it was not to be.

Just days later, he failed to show up for work, which was highly unusual for the punctual and dedicated lawman. Fellow deputies went to his home to check on their colleague, and found him dead.

He reportedly had taken a physical a few days earlier, and had checked out OK.

His death was attributed to natural causes.

Weaver was buried Wednesday in Forest Lawn East Cemetery in Matthews, N.C. "Ironically," noted Dick Bourne, "he was buried less than 15 yards from where another legend of wrestling was laid to rest 16 years ago — his friend Gene Anderson."

Wrestlers past and present, law enforcement officials, friends, family and fans turned out to pay their last respects.

"I had never been in a funeral procession for someone in law enforcement before," Bourne posted in a blog. "One of the lasting memories I will have of that day was topping each hill on the way to graveside and seeing, stretched out before me, a line of seemingly endless patrol cars with blue lights flashing, slowly winding through Mecklenburg County, on their way to see Johnny laid to rest. It was a jolting reminder that a brotherhood of officers had lost one of their own. And they were there in force to say goodbye."

Don Kernodle, who broke into the business working for Crockett Promotions in the late '70s, spoke of his longtime friendship with Weaver during the service.

"Have any of you ever loved someone before you even knew them?" Kernodle asked. "That is what it was like for me with Johnny Weaver. I loved him as a child growing up watching wrestling."

When I think of Johnny Weaver, I'll think about that everyman's wrestler who always showed up at the arena with a smile, always had time to sign an autograph or take a photo, and the enjoyment my grandmother got out of watching him every Saturday.

And I'll also think about the times, as the color man alongside Rich Landrum, David Crockett and Bob Caudle, he'd launch into, "Turn out the lights, the party's over," as a match neared its finish.

All good things, indeed, must come to an end, but the memories of Johnny Weaver will last forever.

Tim Woods
Always 'Mr. Wrestling'

Dec. 8, 2002

The trademark white mask, white trunks and white boots spoke volumes about the man. But it was his name — Mr. Wrestling — that told the story.

From collegiate champion to professional wrestling star, Tim Woods embodied the spirit of the game — so much, in fact, that he adopted the name "Mr. Wrestling" 37 years ago. While the billing may have initially appeared presumptuous and even arrogant to some, it didn't take long for Woods to make believers out of the skeptics. No one was ever more tailor-made for the role than the man who would end up carrying it straight into the annals of wrestling history.

To a generation of fans, Tim "Mr. Wrestling" Woods epitomized wrestling. To those fortunate enough to have known him, he represented the best the sport had to offer. So when Tim passed away last Saturday evening at the age of 68, it was hard not to feel that a little bit of the business we loved died with him.

Woods' achievements in both the amateur and professional ranks were monumental. Before turning pro in 1962, he had been one of amateur wrestling's most decorated athletes, having won a number of state and regional titles in high school and later as a star at Michigan State, where he captured two Big 10 titles and twice finished second in the NCAA championships, along with being a three-time AAU national champion.

One of an elite few to master both disciplines, the Ithaca, N.Y., native seamlessly bridged the gap between the amateur and pro styles. His decision to don a hood, conceal his identity and work as a fan favorite after only three years as a pro was a risky move. Few in the '60s would have imagined a masked grappler as a babyface, since hoods in those days were exclusive to the profession's most hated heels. Then again, few had the credentials that Woods brought to the table.

His approach to professional wrestling was simple, and he stuck with the basics.

"He is poetry in motion," said the late Gordon Solie. "What he is doing out there is what the Greeks had in mind when they invented the sport."

Although he would eventually drop the mask, the name would stick. Woods, whose given name was George Burrell Woodin, was a hero to a legion of fans who spoke of him in the same reverential tones reserved for such legendary stars as Johnny Valentine, Lou Thesz and Ric Flair. Between his pro debut in 1962 and his retirement in 1984 before a sellout crowd at the Omni in Atlanta, Woods held a slew of prestigious titles and became one of the most respected professional wrestlers of his era. He held victories over every world champion over a two-decade span, a lofty list that included names like Thesz, O'Connor, Kiniski, Race, Funk, Brisco and Flair. Named wrestling's most outstanding performer in 1974, Woods held then-world champion Harley Race to a draw in October 1973, marking the first sellout in Atlanta's Omni.

Woods also was a major force in the resurgence of Mid-Atlantic Wrestling in the '70s. It was while working for the Charlotte-based Crockett Promotions that Woods was involved in the 1975 plane crash that ended the career of Valentine — with whom he had engaged in a torrid feud at the time — and broke the back of future legend Flair. In a crafty move that may have saved business in the territory, an injured Woods wisely gave authorities his real name and listed himself as a promoter so fans wouldn't discover in newspaper reports that he had been on the same flight as his "hated" ring rival.

The highlight reels Woods leaves behind will forever be etched in the memories of longtime fans. There were the brutal matches with Johnny "The Champ" Valentine over the thousand silver dollars; the classic pairing (and later feud) with Mr. Wrestling No. 2 (Johnny Walker); the bloodbaths with Ric Flair and Blackjack Mulligan over the U.S. title; the "amateur rules" matches with Jack Brisco and Baron Von Raschke; and his unique standing cradle finishing hold, a three-quarter nelson where he would pin his opponent while standing on his head. Fans will always remember popping when Woods took a baseball bat to Jimmy Snuka and manager "Nature Boy" Buddy Rogers more than 20 years ago.

One of Woods' personal highlights was being inducted into the prestigious George Tragos-Lou Thesz Professional Wrestling Hall of Fame last year in Newton, Iowa (in 1996 he had been inducted into USA Wrestling's Hall of Fame/All-American Club at the World Championships in Atlanta). Woods, who considered his entry into the Thesz shrine as one of his greatest honors, had been longtime friends with the six-time world champion, who died in April at the age of 86.

"Lou was the greatest wrestler of all time," Woods said earlier this year. "I was scared to death the first time I wrestled him (in 1965). Lou would test you and decide whether he would beat you like a dog or give you a little more respect. We worked a match five minutes, and I think he realized I had some wrestling experience. Since that time, we've been very, very close friends."

A man of diverse talents, Woods was an accomplished musician and photographer, and also raced drag-type cars and motorcycles. After retiring in 1984, he developed several patents dealing with air conditioning, heating and refrigeration, and later managed a consulting business in Charlotte.

All-around good guy

One of wrestling's real "good guys," he worked tirelessly for a number of charitable organizations, including the Asheville-based Eblen Foundation, which assists families in western North Carolina deal with chronic illness.

"The only thing, I believe, that could eclipse Tim's accomplishments on the mat or in the ring is what he accomplished out of it on behalf of countless children, adults and families who were battling illnesses, disabilities, and may have been less fortunate than others," said Eblen Foundation executive director Bill Murdock. "Tim, selflessly, used his celebrity to advance the cause of many charitable endeavors and would always go to great lengths to ensure that the events and causes that he lent his name to had total access to him and his assistance at every level.

"He would never just 'show up,' but would continually be in contact with the organization to offer anything he could to make the event and the organization a success. Tim helped establish the Eblen Charities and the Eblen Celebrity Golf Invitational and was one of our most popular celebrities since its inception. Everyone wanted to golf with Mr. Wrestling."

Nearly 40 years have passed since I witnessed my first live wrestling match that featured Tim as a newcomer to the business. It was, of course, a very different business back in the '60s, when ring ability, grit and toughness separated the men from the boys. But it was easy to see then that the wrestling prodigy was destined for stardom.

I last heard from Tim via an e-mail note he sent on Thanksgiving Eve, just three days before he was stricken with a massive heart attack at his home in Charlotte. I thought at the time how the inspirational message so beautifully reflected how Tim lived his life.

"As you go through your life, take the time to live. Take time to appreciate and enjoy the beauty that surrounds you, to make a difference, to do something that you truly care about."

I also remember the words he spoke to me during our last conversation: "Be thankful. Enjoy life, be thankful for your friends, be thankful for what you have and what you're able to share with other people. There are some awfully nice people in this world."

On Wednesday morning at a Church of God in Charlotte, there was a service for Tim. Not surprisingly, it was a "celebration of life," for a man who had achieved everlasting fame.

Jay Youngblood
A daughter remembers

Nov. 14, 2015

There's not a day goes by that Ricca Jonas doesn't think about her dad.

She was only three years old when her father, the late Steven Nicky Romero — better known as pro wrestling star Jay Youngblood — died on Sept. 2, 1985, in Parkville, Victoria, Australia, a suburb of Melbourne, during a tour of the South Pacific.

His death at the tender age of 30 was attributed to a heart attack that had been precipitated by hemorrhagic pancreatitis. He was in a coma for nearly two weeks before passing away.

"He and his brother Mark were on tour and my dad told him he needed to go to the hospital," relates Jonas. "He was diagnosed with pancreatitis when he first went into the hospital, and they did a laparotomy to confirm the diagnosis."

Jonas believes her dad, who was experiencing pronounced abdominal pain, realized the severity of his condition but didn't want to disappoint his fans.

"He started to get better and actually thought he was going to get out of the hospital ... then his organs started to fail."

The official coroner's report listed a series of physical breakdowns that led to the young wrestler's death: acute hemorrhagic pancreatitis (one month), acute renal failure (one week), abdominal sepsis (two weeks), pneumococcal septicemia (four days), and finally, cardiorespiratory arrest.

"He was really sick for a week, got better and had surgery," says Jonas. "He had a series of heart attacks and had hemorrhagic pancreatitis. He developed septicemia and other abdominal problems. He thought he was getting better, and then it happened. I think he probably knew what was going on."

Steven "Nicky" Romero's final resting place is a spot near his parents, Ricky and Stella Marrujo Romero, at a family gravesite in Amarillo, Texas. The elder Romero, who passed away in 2006 at the age of 74, also was a pro wrestling great and one of the top stars for Dory Funk Sr.'s Amarillo-based promotion during the '60s and '70s.

Two more sons, Mark and Chris Youngblood (Romero), would follow in their father's footsteps and step into the squared circle.

Jay's pro career lasted only 10 years, but in that one decade he earned a spot among wrestling's hierarchy.

Portraying a Native American, though actually of Hispanic descent, Youngblood hit his stride in the late '70s when he formed one of the top teams in the profession with partner Ricky Steamboat. With good looks and ability to match, the two would quickly be regarded as one of the greatest babyface teams in the business.

Jonas, a 33-year-old dark-eyed, dark-haired mother of two whose striking features resemble those of her dad, was just a toddler when Youngblood was stricken overseas. All she has to remember him by are photographs and stories from her mom.

A self-described "ghost hunter," she admits that her search may never be over.

"No matter where I look, how deep I go, I just can't seem to find it," she wrote in an essay on her dad. "I'm not even sure what ghost I'm chasing. My father is out of my reach. An enigma, an actual legend, a flicker on my TV screen. A ghost that so many others have seen, witnessed, communicated with. He's brought light and happiness to others. He brings me questions, emptiness."

For most of that last year, she says, her father was gone. "I only know what my mom and others have told me."

YouTube, she says, has been a tremendous help, allowing her to see footage of her dad in his prime. "I'm lucky I have the Internet to fall back on," she says. Along the way, other wrestlers would tell her stories about her father, and how he loved performing and loved his fans.

But those stories, like the images, are all fleeting.

"Others recall how his eyes lit up when I was around. He mentions me in his letters, yet he's still just a spirit I'm chasing after, yearning to make a connection with. He is the ghost of the past. My memories of laughter, joy and unapologetic happiness have made me who I am today. I hold onto these memories like artifacts, able to connect me to the legendary apparition of my past."

Dynamic duo

Youngblood broke into the wrestling business in 1975 in the Amarillo territory. Working under a mask as "Silver Streak," he moved to the Pacific Northwest before becoming a main-event act in the Carolinas teaming with the popular Steamboat.

The two clicked like a well-oiled machine and were considered one of the best teams in the business. And they left a lasting impression on fans in the Carolinas.

"Jay and Ricky were both laid back, and they made an excellent tag team," recalls longtime Mid-Atlantic wrestling photographer Eddie Cheslock. "They did some unique stuff in the ring that was unbelievable."

Steamboat, a WWE Hall of Famer, thinks often about his late partner. The two were inducted as a team this summer into the Mid-Atlantic Legends Hall of Heroes.

"Jay was the best tag-team partner I ever had. We were like brothers. We could translate information to one another without having to speak it. All we had to do was look at one another during a match. I'd give him a nod and would say, 'I know what you want brother, I know what you want.' And we did it together for almost five years."

Two of their most remembered programs would take place in the Crockett-run territory with the teams of Sgt. Slaughter and Don Kernodle, and Jack and Jerry Brisco.

A classic bout on March 12, 1983, with Slaughter and Kernodle — part of a program billed as "The Final Conflict" — drew 15,000 fans to the Greensboro Coliseum, with thousands more turned away and traffic backed up for miles off I-85 and the streets lined up with fans hoping to scalp a ticket at the eleventh hour.

Photographer Cheslock was on hand that night.

"I was in the back with Susan (Romero/Youngblood) and Susan (Blood/Steamboat). We all three had a group hug. It was such an amazing event. The police told me that they had turned away almost 20,000 cars. It was just unbelievable."

The two teams worked every night for a month and set records everywhere they went.

So strong was the duo's popularity that promoter Jim Crockett was convinced to allow the Briscos to turn heel for a program with Steamboat and Youngblood.

Jerry Brisco, now a talent agent for WWE, recalls that it took a lot of goading from him and his brother, along with Steamboat and Youngblood, to get Crockett to go along with the plan.

"We had a lot of conversations with Jimmy Crockett trying to get him to approve," recalled Brisco. "Jack and I had been strong babyface draws for so many years. Jimmy didn't think it would work. But we assured him we weren't really going to change our wrestling styles. We were just going to be more aggressive."

"Of course we had the perfect foes in Youngblood and Steamboat," he added.

"They had just come off that big run with Don Kernodle and Sarge. We stepped right into it because they were still real hot from that."

"How in the world are you going to be able to even come close with Jack and Jerry Brisco?" Steamboat recalls Crockett asking him.

It wasn't an unfair question. The Briscos were the No. 2 babyface team behind Steamboat and Youngblood in the Carolinas.

The switch from fan favorite to hated heel came subtly when Jack "accidentally" injured Steamboat's leg by falling on him while Steamboat was trapped in Jerry's figure four leglock.

The fans blamed the Briscos for purposely injuring Steamboat despite the brothers' denials.

An all-out war between the two teams broke out when the brothers swiped Youngblood's Indian headdress and claimed it for their own.

The Briscos achieved their goal of winning the world tag-team belts when they won took the straps from Steamboat and Youngblood on two occasions during 1983 before losing them to the popular duo for the final time on a Thanksgiving Day show at the inaugural Starrcade in Greensboro, N.C.

"Those guys told Jay and I after it was all said and done that it was the most fun they had in their entire careers," says Steamboat, who shared the NWA world tag-team title with Youngblood on five different occasions.

"The matches that we had with Sgt. Slaughter and Don Kernodle, and later when we turned the Brisco Brothers into heels, you can't dispute the crowds we drew and the accolades we got," added Steamboat. "There wasn't a lot of tape on those matches; many were at house shows. But we had tremendous matches with these guys.

"It was so much fun during that tag-team time in my career. I learned so much. Even though I was a main-event guy, there was stuff going on in the ring while I was standing on the apron, and I'm watching Jay sell or Jay fire back and the heels are getting heat. And I'm standing there so close, and I'm still learning. It was a lot of fun."

Youngblood went to Florida Championship Wrestling in September 1984 where he and brother Mark captured the Florida version of the United States tag-team title. He would wrestle in Memphis, Mexico and for Pro Wrestling USA that next year prior to his final, fateful tour in Australia.

Daddy's 'princess'

Ricca Jonas spent her first 23 years in North Carolina before moving to Independence, Mo., outside the Kansas City limits, with her husband Adam. Her mother, Susan, remained in North Carolina and didn't remarry until 15 years after Jay's passing.

Now 33 and a mother of two (son, Caleb, 15, and daughter, Taylor, 11), Jonas works as a laboratory technician involved in medical research.

A self-described Kansas City Royals baseball fanatic, she is well-versed in everything having to do with history ("especially JFK and Lincoln") and is an accomplished painter. She "adores" animals and loves playing most any kind of sport with her family.

Bright, talented and attractive, she's the embodiment of the all-American girl.

When Ricca was young, she would spend summers with her grandparents in the Texas Panhandle.

Her grandfather, "Rapid" Ricky Romero, was a professional wrestler for more than 50 years and was well known for throwing miniature sombreros to fans at matches. A close friend and frequent tag-team partner of Amarillo promoter and wrestling great Dory Funk Sr., Romero was one of the most popular stars in the southwestern United States and Mexico during the '60s, '70s and '80s, battling the likes of Lou Thesz, Gorgeous George and Jack Brisco.

A consummate professional and affectionately known as "SuperMex," Romero was one of the first Hispanic wrestlers in that area of the country.

Romero, who had played minor league baseball in the New York Giants organization, retired from wrestling in 1985 after the death of his son. He died in 2006 at the age of 74 after years of complications from diabetes.

"I absolutely adored my grandfather Ricky and grandmother Stella," says Jonas. "I went to Amarillo every summer as a kid to stay with them, the last time was when I was around 12 years old. They loved telling me stories about their 'Stevie,' how he got along with all of his siblings, how he liked to go to the lake in the summertime. But mostly they told me over and over again how much I look just like him and how much he loved me. We actually didn't really talk much wrestling, which seems kind of funny considering almost the entire family was in the business."

Uncles also lived in the area, and Jonas says she still keeps in touch with her cousins.

She has an older sister (Tiffany, 39) and brother (Daniel, mid-30s), and a younger sister (Kaylee, 29).

Ricca also has fond memories of seeing her godfather, Ricky Steamboat, when he made an appearance at Harley Race's wrestling school in Missouri a couple of years ago.

"I had on my Jay Youngblood shirt and my mother-in-law Tammy, father-in-law Franny and my two kids were standing in line with me to get his 'autograph.' I handed him a photo of my father and he and looked up at my shirt and just said 'Jay ... haven't seen that in a long time.'"

"He hadn't really looked up at my face yet, and as he was signing my picture, my mother-in-law couldn't hold it in anymore," says Ricca.

"This is Jay's daughter," she told the surprised wrestler.

"He actually looked at me, really looked at me, and sat back and said 'Ricca!?' I'm pretty sure it took him a good long while for the shock to actually wear off."

Ricca knows her dad shared so many great times with Steamboat.

"I wish I could have spent more time with him. I really would love to actually sit down and talk to him about my father. After all, he is the one person that really, honestly knew my dad and who he was on the inside."

People reach out to her, she says, and now that she's older, she sees what an impact he made on others.

"I think the greatest and most important thing that I've about my father is that while he wasn't perfect — he had his issues just like we all do — he did do something meaningful with his life the short time he was here.

"I have so many people reach out to me and tell me how much they loved watching him wrestle, that he was truly an artist at what he did, but the thing that means the most is when they tell me how kind he was."

"Jay was one of the most down-to-earth people you'd ever want to meet," echoes Cheslock. "He was always kind and respectful. When my wife was pregnant with our son, every time we saw him he'd rub her belly and say that he couldn't wait to see the baby."

Sadly, though, it never happened, says Cheslock, whose son was born the week of Youngblood's passing. "He never got to see my son. I really regret it."

"All he ever talked about was Ricca," says Cheslock. "He was always talking about 'his princess.' He would have been so proud. She turned out to be such a beautiful and talented young lady. She and her mom were downright angels. You couldn't ask for two nicer people."

"The entire Romero family ... they're just great," added Cheslock. "Mark and Chris are also super guys."

Tying the knot

Susan Nessell was introduced to pro wrestling at a young age. She remembers her father watching the weekly matches on TV and cheering on favorites like George Becker and Johnny Weaver. She would later tag along with him to the Tuesday night shows at Dorton Arena in Raleigh where he had weekly reserved tickets.

Although she didn't consider herself an avid fan, her main job was keeping an eye on her younger half-brother, who wasn't much older than a toddler, and keeping him occupied while her dad watched the matches and mingled with fellow fans at the concession stand.

"I mainly went so I could help him," she says. "But I enjoyed the matches too."

It was at one of those shows where she caught the eye of a handsome young wrestler named Jay Youngblood.

"I had been running after my half-brother," she recalls. "It was before the show started, and he was walking across the arena. He struck up a conversation, and that's where it all started," she laughs. "At Dorton Arena."

Both were in their early 20s, and an immediate connection was made.

"I thought he was handsome. He just seemed like a good fellow. He asked me for my number. I really didn't expect him to call, but he did."

The two dated, off and on, and she eventually made the move to Charlotte where Youngblood was headquartered.

"Jay came from a long line of wrestlers. I wanted to marry him, but I didn't know if I could handle that lifestyle," she says. "That's one of the reasons I moved to Charlotte and lived with him."

They were together several years before finally tying the knot on Halloween of 1981.

Ricky Steamboat and his then-wife Susan were best man and maid of honor. Paul Jones smoked a turkey for the reception.

"I still remember that smoked turkey," she laughs. "It's just one of the things I'll never forget."

Before Ricca was born, Susan and Jay moved from territory to territory, living the nomadic life that wrestlers endured during that era. From Charlotte to Oregon to Tampa and back to Charlotte.

She also came to understand some of the unwritten codes of wrestling.

"When I would ride with Jay, I would usually go shopping, go eat or sit out in the car. I felt like that (wrestling) was our bread and butter, and I didn't want to interfere with that. A lot of the fans — especially the female ones — weren't crazy about girlfriends or wives."

Like his colleagues, Youngblood was often on the road. He broke his foot prior to his final overseas tour, and got to spend some quality time at home.

It was a rare occasion when Jay had the opportunity to take time off from work and spend time with his family. He and Steamboat went on an extended tour of Japan just weeks after Ricca was born.

In addition to his wrestling duties, Jay ran a juice bar — aptly called "The Reservation" — at a gym Steamboat owned in Charlotte.

But Jay was passionate about the business, and was regarded as one of the rising stars in the profession. "A great, great worker with lots of fire," whose comeback was second to none, Steamboat would reflect.

Susan knows that while Jay and Steamboat were as close as brothers, a tension existed. As Jay's drinking increased, Steamboat's tolerance grew shorter.

Steamboat would later say that he became like a "baby-sitter" as Youngblood battled problems with alcohol abuse. "It just became too much for me to even try to watch him."

Susan recalls the fateful final month of her husband's life.

"Jay was drinking a little bit more then. I don't know if Rick was in the dark like I was, because no one knew he was sick. I think Rick didn't understand. You can't help somebody if they don't ask for it. When Jay was in Australia, he was in so much pain they put him in the hospital."

Even she had no clue that her husband was battling pancreatitis.

"There were several things that the doctor later told me that might have attributed to it — things like alcohol, seafood. I don't think the licks (bumps) he took helped at all. I think he was in a lot of pain and just didn't tell anybody."

"I think a lot of people could have understood and not have felt as disappointed or angry if they knew," she says. "I know I could have helped a lot more if he had told me that he was hurting."

Jay didn't know of the condition until he was hospitalized, she says. She recalls that he had been in a cage match where he suffered an infection after being cut on the forehead.

"He was on some really strong antibiotics. I think he had had that condition for quite a while."

"He loved his family," she adds. "He would go up and see them as much as he could. He liked people. He really enjoyed what he did."

Today she lives in Rockingham, N.C., and works for the Chesterfield (S.C.) County Public Defenders' Office.

She remarried her "first love" 15 years later. The two had been friends since high school.

She sometimes wonders what Jay might have become had he lived the 74 years his dad had enjoyed.

"He talked about wanting to be a butcher. He said they made good money, and it was a steady job. I know he would have gotten into something he enjoyed. Jay would have been good at anything he did."

Photographs and memories

Jay Youngblood would have turned 60 years old in June. Tag partner Steamboat, who turned 62 in February, only got better with age and looked as good the day he retired as he did when he came in.

There's no reason to believe that Youngblood would have looked his age either. He had reached a wrestling zenith in his mid-20s, and his potential seemed unlimited.

The "what ifs" and "what could have beens" still haunt family and friends.

While his daughter is grateful for the time she got to spend with him and the memories he left behind, she will forever lament that she didn't get "the Jay Young-blood the world got."

"I didn't have that much time with him," she says. "But I am so honored and beyond grateful to have had the chance to share him with the fans."

For Ricca Jonas, Jay Youngblood's legacy will always live on.

"His light shines brightly and his love is always here, and I will forever be his daughter."

She gazes at an old scrapbook that contains priceless images of her and her dad.

"I definitely resemble my dad in my looks," she says. "Even as a newborn, we could have been twins, between our jet black hair and dark brown eyes."

Ricca is personable and funny, traits that she attributes to her dad.

"I also think I got my sense of humor from him. There's nothing that makes me happier than a giant belly laugh, even if I'm only making myself giggle. He was determined, hard-headed and very passionate, traits he definitely passed on to me."

There is one memory of her dad, she says, the one where he's standing in the bathroom with a hot rag covering his face. The toddler goes in to watch, unable to say any real words, but she remembers her dad looking down and smiling after she takes the rag off his face.

"Do you want to try Mija?' he asks. "Mija" (shortened from "Mi hija") is Span-ish for "My daughter."

The image is permanently etched in her mind.

"I remember him putting the rag on my face and telling me to breathe in the warmth. I of course didn't understand, but it didn't matter because he then tickled me and I ran out of the bathroom giggling, with him laughing and running right behind me."

Those are the memories Ricca holds on to. It makes her happy when she thinks about those times back in North Carolina. It also makes her happy thinking about how he made others feel.

"He was always willing to talk with a fan ... he made them feel like they were the most important person in the room and it's something they always remember. His gift was not only the athleticism of doing what he loved, but that he was loved for being himself. And I'm extremely proud of that."

Part V
BRAINTRUST

Jim Barnett

Bobby Heenan

Oliver Humperdink

Henry Marcus

Lance Russell

Gordon Solie

Jim Barnett
'An unforgettable figure'

Sept. 26, 2004

J ames E. Barnett may be the most unlikely entry in professional wrestling's hall of fame.

A man of diminutive stature who wore stylish three-piece suits and horn-rimmed glasses, his sentences usually began with the phrase, "Oh, my boooooy," a line imitated by a generation of wrestlers who loved impersonating the flamboyant promoter. His passion for fine art, Mozart and penthouse living would lead a fellow Georgian, Jimmy Carter, to appoint him to the National Council for the Arts during the 1970s. More significantly, in a business that was hardly open to change, Barnett was openly gay.

But Jim Barnett, who died recently at the age of 80, was one of wrestling's most influential figures over a period that spanned the past half-century.

"He was an unforgettable figure, as much as anyone I ever met," former NWA world champion Jack Brisco wrote earlier this year in his self-titled autobiography "Brisco."

Barnett died in an Atlanta hospital on Sept. 17. The official cause was pneumonia, but the promoter had been battling cancer and had never fully recovered from surgery after breaking his arm in a fall.

The erudite Southerner was a creative, behind-the-scenes power broker who worked alongside most of the post-World War II era's most influential promoters. A former board member and secretary-treasurer of the National Wrestling Alliance, at the time the most powerful governing body in the industry, Barnett became an outwardly wealthy man who lived large and owned substantial stock in the lucrative Georgia and Florida promotions. But according to those who worked closest with him, Barnett's millionaire persona was more style than substance.

"He tried to portray someone who came from 'old money.' I have no idea if he did or not, but I do believe it was more of an act than reality," recalled Brisco. "Jim looked like a character out of a Noel Coward play. He would always come up to me and say, 'Jack, my boy, how are you today?' When he had all the wrestlers together, he would say, 'When I look at my boys, I see stars.' He was quite a character."

"At first we all thought he was a multi-millionaire," said former mat star and booker Ole Anderson (Al "Rock" Rogowski), who added that the rarely photographed promoter sometimes would purposely leave outlandish stock notes on his desk so his staff would think he was making a killing in the market. "He created that illusion by having apartments in Louisville and Atlanta, and by frequenting a ritzy hotel out in L.A. He had a chauffeur in a Rolls Royce who drove him up to the office every day. It was all designed to make everyone think he was a multi-millionaire."

But things weren't as they appeared, according to Anderson, who says he was among many who made financial loans to Barnett over the years.

"I'm sure at one time he had a ton of money," said Jody Hamilton, whose association with Barnett dates back to 1957. "I'm not sure what he did with it, nor does anyone else. Knowing Jim and knowing how he liked to live, I would dare say that he probably didn't have as much money as a lot of people thought he did."

There was, however, no denying that Barnett's scope of influence in the wrestling business was far-reaching. He was an integral part of pro wrestling's national television boom in the '50s, oversaw the golden age of wrestling in Australia during the '60s, and worked with Ted Turner in the '70s in bringing the sport to a new cable audience. Brokering some of the biggest transactions in wrestling history, including the sale of Crockett Promotions to Turner in 1988, Barnett also was in on the grand floor of Vince McMahon's national expansion in the mid-'80s.

Few figures in the history of the business were part of as many pivotal events as Jim Barnett.

Impact on industry

It seems as if everyone who ever worked with or for the promoter had their own unabashed opinions of Barnett. Some, like Ron West, a booker and referee who worked for Barnett for 15 years in the Atlanta and Knoxville offices, remember him as a thoughtful individual who would go out of his way for friends and employees.

"Jim was a very good businessman, and he treated my family very well," said West. "There are many others in the business who also appreciate what he did for them. He knew the wrestling business and he put good people around him."

"Back when I had my heart attack, when Ole (Anderson) ran me crazy," said West, "Jim came to the hospital several times. Out of all the people in that company (WCW) in management, Mr. Barnett was the one to come and see me. I have nothing but respect for him."

And in the 31 years he knew Barnett, West says he never missed a Christmas without calling him.

"He was one of the most influential people I ever dealt with in the NWA," said 16-time world heavyweight champion Ric Flair. "He was a very good friend to me, and was an old-school guy who paid me a lot of respect. At one time he had as much political stroke as anyone in the industry, and he was a very good payoff man who made a lot of people a lot of money."

"Jim helped me tremendously in my career," Brisco said Friday. "Jim gave me one of my first big breaks in Australia. If you look back on his career, I would think that he has to go down as probably the greatest promoter of all time. He did just about everything in this business that could be done. A big part of this business is gone forever."

For a number of wrestlers who claimed he unfairly pushed his favorite performers, Barnett was an easy target.

Jim Wilson, a former NFL player and All-American at the University of Georgia, claimed in his 2003 book, "Chokehold," that Barnett irreparably damaged his promising wrestling career after he turned back the promoter's sexual advances during a 1973 tour of Australia. Barnett, who claimed he sent Wilson home from the tour because Wilson, then 32, was having an affair with a stewardess whose airline was a sponsor for Barnett's company, denied the allegations.

"The reason that Jim Wilson didn't become champion was because he couldn't work and he had no charisma," argues Hamilton, a major star in the '60s and '70s as one of the masked Assassins along with the late Tom Renesto. "I knew and worked for every promoter in the country, and if they thought they could have taken Jim Wilson into their territory and made money with him, they wouldn't have paid any attention to Jim Barnett. By God, Jim Wilson would have been there, and he would have been working on top. They (promoters) thought more of money than they did personalities."

"Jim Barnett had a long life and did a lot in the business," said Wilson, who has spent the past 30 years fighting unsuccessfully for the unionization of pro wrestling. "But there are no hard feelings. They saw things the way they did, and I just believed in another way. I've always tried to walk a couple miles in somebody else's shoes, but it was what it was. I went through a lot of hardship. The business does funny things to people. But I hope he didn't suffer, and I sincerely hope he's in a better place."

Politics of wrestling

Although Barnett's sexual persuasion was well known inside the business, former pro wrestling star and promoter Cowboy Bill Watts said he never heard of Barnett "crossing the line into wrestling." He was discreet about his private affairs, said Watts, and didn't mix his sexual life with business.

"Jim would get very infatuated with a piece of talent as far as who he liked and who he didn't. He never came on to me. He loved Dusty Rhodes, but he never came on to Dusty. The same with guys like Ric Flair, Robert Fuller, Cowboy Bob Ellis and Mark Lewin when they were young stars. But I never heard about anything like that happening, and this is the wrestling business, where it would be very hard to keep a secret like that."

Watts said he first met the promoter in 1962 when Barnett owned a part of the Detroit and Indianapolis territories. It was then that Watts, who was looking to break into the wrestling business, learned of a relationship that Barnett allegedly shared with Hollywood actor Rock Hudson when he lived in Louisville during the '50s.

"Sam Menaker, who later became my television announcer and taught me to fly, was Barnett's commentator at the time," recalled Watts. "Sam had a Rolls Royce and Jim didn't drive. But Jim would borrow Sam's Rolls Royce whenever Rock was in town for a week, and he'd hire a driver."

The fact that Barnett was gay ultimately limited his achievements in a business that socially was well behind the times. A president and chairman of Georgia Championship Wrestling who also booked appearances of the NWA's world champion for a number of years, Barnett also served as NWA secretary-treasurer during the '70s and had the connections to be president of the organization. Board members at the time, however, argued it would be bad for their image to have a homosexual as president.

"I know the wrestling profession inside and out, and I know the people that were involved in the wrestling profession, and I know Jim Barnett. And in all the years I knew Jim Barnett, I never knew him to make a pass at a wrestler," said Hamilton. "Jim never tried to hide the fact that he was gay. But he didn't cross the line between business and his own personal life."

Dick Steinborn, who wrestled for Barnett during the '60s in Indianapolis and in Australia, claims there was another side to Barnett.

"He was a fan of the business who could be a very vicious guy. He made a lot of promoters uneasy," said Steinborn, who claims that Barnett paid Harley Race 15 thousand dollars to drop the NWA title to Barnett's hand-picked successor, 24-year-old blond heartthrob Tommy Rich, in Augusta, Ga., in 1981. Rich, one of the NWA's top drawing cards at the time, dropped the strap back to Race just days later.

"That was quite a deal," Steinborn said wryly. "By the time the other NWA promoters had time to think about what happened, Harley had the title back."

That's not, however, the way Hamilton saw the title switch.

"It was Harley's idea to put the strap on Rich," said Hamilton. "He may have promoted it to get Tommy over and he may have promoted a 15 grand payoff, because Barnett was certainly not above doing things like that, but sexual favors had nothing to do with it. It was to get the guy over. To have been the NWA world champion, even for four days, had a lot of prestige. At that time they were running the Ohio and West Virginia towns and were starting to branch out. They needed to add some emphasis to Tommy."

"A lot of people were envious of Jim and were willing to start these unfounded rumors because they were jealous of his position and the money he was making and the power that he had," Hamilton added. "They were going to do anything they could to destroy his reputation. The only thing I can go by is my personal experiences with Jim and my association with him over a period of nearly 50 years — longer than all these other guys put together. I had never known him to cross that line."

Anderson says he simply learned to get along with Barnett. To the burly Minnesotan, it was merely a matter of him handling the wrestling operation while Barnett tended to the office details, and keeping their personal lives separate.

"I knew what he was like, and he knew what I was like," said Anderson, who worked with Barnett in Georgia Championship Wrestling from 1974-83 and in WCW during the '90s. "But he knew I could do a good job. So every time I quit, he'd hire somebody. When those people ran everything into the ground, he'd hire me back. It went back and forth."

"Jim was difficult to work for at times," Hamilton agreed. "I liked Jim, but working for Jim as a booker was a nightmare. Jim didn't know much about booking, but he would criticize everything you did. It was his psychology of trying to keep his foot on your back to make you try to be the best you could be every day. But watch out if you did something and it didn't quite work out."

Barnett surrounded himself with quality talent, said Hamilton, which made booking the territory far from rocket science.

"Ole was so brash and overbearing that Jim was about half afraid of him," said Hamilton. "But he was giving Ole a free hand. We had the greatest talent in the country at the time. It didn't take a genius to put together cards that would draw money. Consequently the territory was doing well and drawing money, and Jim was willing to put up with Ole's brashness and BS because of the fact that he was drawing money."

Master manipulator

Barnett owned pieces of the promotion in such territories as Detroit, Indianapolis, Louisville and Atlanta, where his Georgia Championship Wrestling show was the flagship program for Turner's "SuperStation," becoming the first professional wrestling operation on national TV since the DuMont network in the mid-'50s, which Barnett also ran along with wrestler-turned-promoter Fred Kohler and Verne Gagne, the future AWA founder and world champion whom he helped break into the business.

Barnett had entered the profession in the early '50s as the right-hand man of Kohler, who at the time was the most powerful promoter in the country. After splitting from Kohler, he established strong wrestling bases in Detroit and Indianapolis. Selling the Detroit operation to The Sheik (Ed Farhat) and Indianapolis to Wilbur Snyder and Dick "The Bruiser" Afflis, Barnett finally got to run his own national promotion when he opened up Australia in 1964. After business partner Johnny Doyle's death in 1969, Barnett promoted five more years Down Under, assembling a stellar cast of touring performers that included most of the top names in the United States at the time.

"We had some great times over there," said Jack Brisco. "I was as green as could be, and there were so many big stars over there. I was in awe of all those guys; I had never met any of them, but had followed them for years in magazines. I was like a kid in a candy store."

Brisco recalled one particular incident when Dr. Big Bill Miller, a 6-4, 300-pound former collegiate star at Ohio State, botched the finish of his match with Spiros Arion. "It was in front of a sellout crowd in Melbourne, and Jim went running to the ring, shaking his finger at Miller. He chewed his (behind) all the way back down the aisle to the dressing room. All the boys laughed like crazy at this big monster getting chewed out by Jim."

Watts, who owned part of Georgia Championship Wrestling, brought Barnett in from Australia in 1973 to help in the Georgia wrestling war with Ann Gunkel. To entice Barnett, Florida promoter Eddie Graham sold Barnett 10 percent of the Georgia and Florida promotions.

"I learned a lot from Jim," said Watts. "One of the most important things I learned was to cultivate relationships with the station managers who controlled your television show."

Barnett was a master manipulator, in the same league with Vince McMahon and Sam Muchnick, and knew like few others how to play both ends against the middle. Barnett, who had introduced Gunkel to her late husband, Ray, would later get Gunkel to indemnify him in her antitrust suit against Georgia Championship Wrestling.

"Jim was very savvy as far as connections," added Watts. "He tried to continually maintain strife among people and pit them against one another. But he had a certain knack. He was very fickle. But he was extremely successful in the business for a lot of years."

"Jack Brisco and I once were so mad with each other that we were going to get into a fight," recalled Watts "We had known each other since high school. We finally compared notes and began laughing. Barnett had caused it."

Thanks to the tremendous reach of WTBS, Barnett was one of the most powerful promoters in the country.

"In his heyday, he was the man," said Hamilton. "When he was promoting Georgia Championship Wrestling, he was probably one of the biggest men in wrestling at the time. Jim was the guy who really took advantage of Channel 17 (WTBS) as far as branching out. He was the forerunner of what wrestling has evolved into today. It was the beginning of a central-based wrestling promotion that promoted everywhere. Everywhere that Channel 17 went, they went."

Barnett rubbed elbows with some of the state's leading figures in politics, business and the arts. Those relationships helped him immensely with his wrestling business, to the point where few would challenge him.

"He had a lot of political connections," recalled Hamilton. "He always maintained a working relationship with the police department, which was very important, and he always made sure that certain judges got very nice gifts, along with senators and state reps. That's why he was so successful all these years keeping the athletic commission out of here."

Legend in the business

Barnett was a pivotal figure in some of pro wrestling's fiercest turf wars. But he also had the uncanny ability of landing on his feet and living to fight another day. Whether it be as an ally of Ted Turner, Vince McMahon or Jim Crockett, or running promotions with Bill Watts, Verne Gagne or Fritz Von Erich, Barnett was a survivor.

Barnett, who was instrumental in the first three Wrestlemanias, had been a key man for McMahon during the wrestling boom of the mid-'80s due to his many television connections dating back to the '50s on the DuMont network. Senior vice president of the WWF from 1983 to 1987, Barnett brokered the McMahon-

Crockett deal for the coveted TBS time slot in 1985, with Crockett paying McMahon $1 million.

Perhaps getting a glimpse into the future, McMahon told Crockett, "You'll choke on that million."

While Barnett was working for McMahon in Connecticut, he had also kept in back-channel contact with Crockett, still confident in his ability to work both sides of the street. Shortly after Wrestlemania III in 1987, the most successful event in company history, McMahon called Barnett into his office, demanded his resignation and ordered him out of the building. Barnett, who had been one of Vince Sr.'s best friends, promptly went home and overdosed on sleeping pills.

Although the family sent flowers and Linda McMahon sat at his hospital bedside, there was no offer to come back. After he recovered, Barnett picked up and moved to Dallas, and started working for the Crocketts in the fall of 1987. Less than a year later, the Crockett family signed over their assets to Turner.

Barnett, again landing on his feet, would finish his final decade in the business working for Turner's new Atlanta-based company, WCW, and later McMahon's WWE, where the lifelong family friend was invited back as a consultant. In the interim he would be fired by then-WCW boss Eric Bischoff.

"He was yet another guy Bischoff aced out of his job," lamented Flair. "Bischoff got him fired because he knew Jim could always go over his head."

Hamilton said the two talked on the phone at least once a week over the past couple of years. He first found out about Barnett's condition several months ago.

"Jim was a very proud man. Unless you made it obvious that you wanted to contact him or wanted to associate with him, he wasn't going to initiate it," said Hamilton. "He had often commented to me that nobody called him anymore. It was sad because at one time Jim was one of the most important people in the business. He made a lot of people a lot of money."

Out of the 20 or so who paid their final respects to the promoter Friday, Hamilton was one of only several wrestling personalities who attended his funeral service.

"The rest of the people that came were office people and a couple of friends. I thought it was rather sad, a man who made such an impact on the sport of pro wrestling not to be honored by more wrestlers that he made big stars of on Channel 17. It seems as if there is no gratitude anymore," said Hamilton.

"I had a great deal of respect for Jim and I had a great deal of affection for him, especially toward the end, because I really felt sorry for him, having been the icon in wrestling that he was at one time, and then almost to be a forgotten man."

But not everyone forgot.

"That's one thing I'll say about Vince McMahon," said Hamilton. "He had been in touch with Jim right up to the end."

Those who worked with the promoter over the years will never forget Jim Barnett.

Bill Watts will remember the days when he and cohorts like Dusty Rhodes and Jack Brisco would slip past the security guard during late-night binges, barge into Barnett's luxury apartment and drink up his cognac. Or when he once locked the promoter out of his office for an entire week.

"He complained to Eddie Graham, who died laughing," said Watts. "Eddie finally talked me into letting Jim back into his office. But I guess I was just making a statement."

Oddly enough, the man who was the butt of more than a few jokes probably saw those as acts of endearment.

Watts and Brisco say they'll all agree on one thing.

"Jim Barnett was a legend in this business."

Bobby Heenan
Bobby 'The Brain' Heenan
was gold standard in pro wrestling

"When someone you love becomes a memory, that memory becomes a treasure."

– Steve "Brooklyn Brawler" Lombardi on Bobby Heenan

It was almost a rib that Bobby Heenan proclaimed himself "The Brain."

"I don't look at myself as a hero or smart person. I have a seventh-grade education," he would say.

"But," he'd quickly add, "I've had a lot of fun."

Truth be known, millions of fans throughout the world had fun watching Bobby have fun for several decades.

It would be difficult to encapsulate his importance to the wrestling industry in a mere column, but to say that Bobby Heenan was one of the most influential figures in the modern era of professional wrestling would certainly not be a stretch.

Widely regarded as the best of his generation, Heenan was the blueprint for great managers. "He formed in my mind as a fan and performer what I thought a manager should be. Best ever," said Jim Cornette. "He was even better than me when using my own gimmick."

Heenan, though, was much more than an outlandish, heat-seeking mouthpiece for star performers. He was an extremely entertaining color commentator whose humor and wit were unparalleled in the business. And, early in his career, Heenan was a bump-taking machine whose injuries cut short a promising career in the ring instead of outside it.

Raymond Louis Heenan passed away Sept. 17 at his home in Largo, Fla., at the age of 72 due to complications from throat cancer and other health issues.

But his humor, his wit and his zest for life will never be forgotten.

Gift of gab

He had few equals. Full of bombast and bluster, Heenan never failed to make an impression.

"I'm a legend in this sport," Heenan once said in typical flamboyant fashion. "If you don't believe me, ask me."

Always the funny man, Heenan brought that humor into his act, as he explained in his 2004 WWE Hall of Fame induction speech.

"To be able to work and do prime time, and to be allowed to express myself and bring my comedy into a business that I thought needed a kick in the pants and a couple of smiles, rather than a guy blowing his nose and belching and spitting. I mean, if you want to see that, come to my room. And that's just my wife!"

His 20-minute speech left the fans howling. And he did it without a single scripted note. Few could elicit boos, jeers and laughter like Heenan.

No less than Arn Anderson, once part of the infamous "Heenan Family" as a member of The Brain Busters tag team along with Tully Blanchard, acknowledged Heenan's quick wit and exceptional comic timing.

"Bobby has the best wit of anybody I've ever met. He's as good as any stand-up comic on television."

Sixteen-time world champion Ric Flair called Heenan the greatest manager ever.

"One of the funniest people I've ever known, and the greatest manager of all time. As a worker, a manager, an announcer, he did it all and at a very high level."

Heenan's early in-ring career was overshadowed by his later legendary status as a manager and commentator. He broke his neck during a tour of Japan in 1983 and didn't have it operated on until 1995 because it was the first time he had insurance. It was an injury that plagued him for the rest of his career.

"He was a phenomenal performer and he was unselfish," Flair wrote in a 2004 book titled "Chair Shots and Other Obstacles: Winning Life's Wrestling Matches." "He got beat up every night, got up and did it again the next night."

In an earlier era of "true believers" where Heenan was particularly adept at drawing the ire of the crowd, the slippery manager not only endured catcalls and curses, but escaped thrown chairs and attempted knifings and at least one shooting.

"I've been shot at and stabbed. I've had people throw rocks, batteries and cups of urine and beer at me," Heenan wrote in his 2002 book 'Bobby the Brain: Wrestling's Bad Boy Tells All.' "They even spit right in my face. That's because they hated me. And I was good enough at what I did to make them do that."

Flair says Heenan had a major impact on him as a rookie in the business.

"He was managing Blackjack Lanza and Blackjack Mulligan against The Crusher and The Bruiser, and he caused a full-scale riot. Bobby was a professional all the way, and I always respected the way he was able to separate his personal life and his professional life. Bobby was an original, and there'll never be another quite like him."

'Set the standard'

Billed from Beverly Hills, Heenan was actually born in Chicago, the son of a railroad worker and hotel manager. He quit school at the age of 15 in order to support his mother, his grandmother, and his aunt, and broke into the business as a 17-year-old in 1965, working as a stagehand and later a wrestler for Dick "The Bruiser" Afflis' WWA promotion in Indianapolis.

Former pro wrestling standout and longtime trainer Les Thatcher recalled Heenan as young, energetic fan who carried the wrestlers' jackets from the ring back to the locker room in those early days.

"I remember going to Calvin Pullins, who was to work with Bobby in one of his earliest matches, and asking him to tell Bobby he was just ribbing about stretching him that night as the rookie was a bundle of nerves because of it. I'm not sure how many of us are still around that remember those days."

"Bobby Heenan was a one of a kind multi-talented human being that will never be topped or duplicated in our lifetime," added Thatcher. "He should automatically be inducted into every hall of fame and placed high on any top 10 listing, and his name will be mentioned in any conversation involving greatness in pro wrestling. His passing is leaving a great void in the wrestling world. But to me I will always remember with fondness the young man that worked at the Ford dealership and carried jackets who became my friend all those years ago."

"We would go to the matches periodically," former CBS Late Show host and Indianapolis native David Letterman said on a 1989 appearance on "Later with Bob Costas." "They always had a big Thanksgiving card. Even then I thought it was a real touch of genius (for) Bobby Heenan to be introduced as being from Beverly Hills. You couldn't have said anything more irritating to these people."

Not that Heenan didn't try, as he coined the terms "ham-and-eggers" and "humanoids" to describe the working-class, blue-collar fans who loved to hate him.

Along the way he managed some of the greatest in the game. He was the driving force behind one of the most well-known matches in wrestling history, as he managed Andre The Giant in his colossal battle with Hulk Hogan at Wrestlemania 3 where a reported crowd of 93,000 packed the Silverdome in Detroit. His last protégé would be Hogan rival Ric Flair, and it marked one of Heenan's finest efforts in a star-studded managerial career.

In writing the foreword to Heenan's first book, Hogan said Heenan "set the standard for professionalism behind the scenes and was the consummate professional in front of the camera."

Manager of champions

Heenan would make the monikers "The Brain" and "The Weasel" household names in the sports entertainment industry. No veteran mat fan can forget the on-camera bantering and bickering between the bombastic Heenan and the late Gorilla Monsoon (Gino Marella) on WWE's "Prime Time Wrestling" show.

Their adversarial relationship in the broadcasting booth, in which Monsoon played straight-man to Heenan's over-the-top shtick, was purely show; the two were close friends behind the scenes and respected one another greatly. Heenan broke down at the end of his WWE Hall of Fame induction speech during Wrestlemania XX weekend, lamenting the fact that Monsoon, who passed away in 1999 at the age of 62 following complications from a heart attack and diabetes, wasn't there to share the moment with him.

As a constant foil to Hogan, Heenan also was an important ingredient in the early success of the transformation of the wrestling industry when he left his longtime home in the AWA in 1984 to join Vince McMahon's burgeoning juggernaut and pop culture phenomenon in New York. But unlike many other colleagues who immediately jumped to McMahon's company, he refused to leave Verne Gagne's AWA until his contract was up.

It was in the then WWF that he received his greatest exposure with a laundry list of clients that included a parade of championship-caliber heels. Over the years his "family," not the more commonly used "stable" as he was wont to point out ("A stable is where you find fly-infested horses," he told Bob Costas in 1989. "I have a family."), included the likes of Ray Stevens, Nick Bockwinkel, Blackjacks Lanza and Mulligan, Jesse Ventura, The Valiant Brothers, Big John Studd, Ravishing Rick Rude, King Kong Bundy, "Mr. Perfect" Curt Hennig, Andre The Giant and Flair, who would be his last charge before Heenan turned full-time on-camera commentator when neck problems forced him to avoid physical contact.

"Bobby is such a well-rounded guy. He was wild like I'm wild," said Flair in writing the foreword to Heenan's first book. "But I know that when he went home and took off that Superman cape, he was one hell of a father and husband."

Valiant battle

While Heenan's exploits in the wrestling business are well documented, what many friends will remember him for is the courageous battle he waged with health issues the last part of his life.

Those challenges dated back 15 years when he was first diagnosed with throat and tongue cancer. It would cost him his greatest attribute: his money-making voice. He had several surgeries to repair his jaw and also had fallen a number of times in recent years, suffering broken hips on more than one occasion. He broke his shoulder several years ago.

He had trouble swallowing and couldn't open his mouth very wide. With his speech considerably slowed and having difficulty talking, he would joke, "But that's why God gave us fingers."

Heenan eventually lost the ability to talk after multiple surgeries on his tongue and the reconstruction of his lower jaw. It seemed a cruel twist of fate for a man who was one of pro wrestling's legendary talkers.

No one ever doubted that the wit was still there, though, as he regaled thousands of fans over the past decade with a twinkle in his eye and a mischievous grin. While his speech was affected, his charmingly sarcastic sense of humor was not.

Cancer was a disease he battled with that same sense of humor.

"Not humor at someone else's expense, but humor that makes each day better, no matter what situation I find myself or someone else in," he once said. "There's no right or wrong way to face possible tragedy. I live with it by telling jokes about it."

Finding dignity

WWE Hall of Famer Superstar Billy Graham (Wayne Coleman) recalled a brief but memorable encounter he had with Heenan and his wife of nearly 40 years, Cindy, at an autograph convention several years ago in New Jersey.

Having not seen him in some time, it was unsettling for Graham, who was among the list of champions that Heenan managed over the years, to see his old friend in such a state.

"I was sitting at a table signing autographs and Bobby walks over to my table," Graham recounted. "I immediately stood up, walked around my table and gave him and his wife a big hug. I was stunned at the devastating effects his battle of throat and lung cancer had taken on him physically. He was paying a heavy toll in his fight to stay alive.

"He was talking to me and I could hear his voice but could not understand what he was desperately trying to tell me. His wife recognized my difficulty and began to basically interpret for me what he was saying. She said, 'He is trying to tell you that not long ago he fell and broke his shoulder.' I just kept listening as he passionately was telling me his stories. I was speechless yet managed to utter the words, 'I love you brother,' and we hugged again and he walked away."

It was a far cry from the man who was once recognized for his flashy appearance, blond pompadour and sequined jackets, along with his silver tongue, sharp wit and endless stream of one-liners and insults.

"I saw a man in despair, disfigured and ravaged by this deadly disease from the pits of hell," said Graham. "He was fading away at an agonizing slow pace. He was a man of unspeakable sorrow. Yet, he was a man who was carrying himself with dignity. I was shaken by this brief encounter, but I was also proud to have this mammoth fighter as my friend. Bob Dylan wrote and sang a song called 'Dignity.' It could be about Bobby Heenan."

Graham recalled some of the lines from that song.

Sick man lookin' for the doctor's cure
Lookin' at his hands for the lines that were
And into every masterpiece of literature
For dignity

Englishman stranded in the blackheart wind
Combin' his hair back, his future looks thin
Bites the bullet and looks within
For dignity

So many roads, so much at stake
So many dead ends, I'm at the edge of the lake
Sometimes I wonder what it's gonna take
To find dignity

"Well Bob Dylan, I knew a man who found DIGNITY," said Graham. "His name is Bobby Heenan."

Indeed the world of professional wrestling was a better place for having Bobby Heenan in it.

"There's a case to be made that Bobby 'The Brain' Heenan is the best all-round performer in wrestling history," Chris Jericho said last week. "From a commentating standout: the best. From a managing standpoint: the best. From a promo standpoint: the best. From a wrestling standpoint: he could work better than 90 percent of the boys."

"He was the best ever at what he did," wrote Wrestling Observer's Dave Meltzer. "Nobody ever did it better than the Wease," tweeted Jim Ross. And now he belongs to the ages.

Sir Oliver Humperdink
The House that Humperdink built

March 27, 2011

" Time to go home."

In pro wrestling jargon, the expression is used as a form of communication to signal that it's time to go to the finish of a match. A savvy veteran always knows when it's time to go home.

For John "Red" Sutton, it was an easy call. He had gamely fought the good fight. But at the age of 62, with the end in clear sight, the man known to his many friends as "Hump" called his own finish.

Given the option of going through grueling rounds of chemo to combat a late stage of bladder and kidney cancer, and already greatly weakened by heart disease and a bout with pneumonia, Hump decided to let nature take its course and said his final goodbyes.

A game warrior to the end, the legendary wrestling manager known as Sir Oliver Humperdink passed away in St. Paul, Minn., during the early-morning hours of March 20.

Hump, upon making the decision to go into hospice, reassured friends that he was at peace and ready for the next stage. He was a lucky man, he said, who had enjoyed not one, but two, great lives — both in and out of wrestling.

"Happy Thanksgiving," he greeted one his oldest wrestling friends, former AWA announcer Mick Karch, in a phone conversation near the end.

"Now I know what he meant. No more pain and suffering," said Karch. "I will miss him very much, but now it's time for him to hang out with (late wrestling promoter) Wally Karbo and share a lifetime of stories."

As the delightfully captivating character Sir Oliver Humperdink, Sutton enjoyed a colorful wrestling career that allowed him to see the world and do what he did best. And that, simply, was being one of the greatest managers in the business.

Throughout the '70s and '80s, the bug-eyed, red-haired, red-bearded manager incurred the wrath of fans from coast to coast, putting together an infamous stable of heels known as "The House of Humperdink." They were brawlers, misfits and outcasts, men like Bruiser Brody, Abdullah The Butcher and Bam Bam Bigelow, who were meticulously guided by the conniving, fast-talking Humperdink, whose vocal skills added even more depth to his notorious charges.

Sir Oliver's unique appearance, which included outrageous ring outfits and apparel, once prompted fellow manager Bobby Heenan to describe him as "looking like he fell out of a box of cards."

His accomplishments in the wrestling business are well-documented. He managed The Hollywood Blonds (Jerry Brown and Dale "Buddy" Roberts) to stardom during the '70s. His decade-long feud with "American Dream" Dusty Rhodes cut a torrid swath through Florida. He was known as the manager of champions, and that list included a "who's who" of mat ruffians.

It may seem odd that a man so hated in the wrestling business could also be so loved and respected, but as the walls of kayfabe came crashing down, many of those same fans became some of Hump's biggest admirers. In later years he became an immensely popular regular at wrestling reunions, fan conventions and other gatherings and, through social media, attracted a vast legion of followers.

It didn't matter to Hump if you were in the wrestling business, or if you were a ditch digger or a bank president. The jovial and engaging man never met a stranger.

Tobias McGregor of Charleston recalls meeting Hump in Key West, Fla., where both were living during the '90s.

"Hump was a truly wonderful guy. If you didn't know him from the wrestling business, you'd still think he was a wonderful guy, because he really was."

Hump, says McGregor, was a fixture at the famous Sloppy Joe's bar.

"We used to hang out there, and we just became great friends. He'd come into Sloppy Joe's bar, which was the biggest bar in town, and everybody took notice. He'd walk in the place, and he just had a presence that lit up the entire room."

Donning his ever-present Hawaiian shirt, shades and shorts, the lifelong bachelor loved the island charm and laid-back atmosphere of the Keys, even though he had spent most of his life in the cold climes of Minnesota. The area's gravitational pull on artists, writers, musicians, nonconformists, free-thinkers and other assorted eccentrics seeking to escape from the urban world held a certain appeal to Hump.

He was a natural for the Keys, says McGregor, a painter, musician and self-described "old beatnik from way back" who lived there for nearly 30 years before moving to Charleston four years ago. It was a close-knit community where everyone knew each other.

McGregor says he really didn't pay much attention to pro wrestling until he met Hump and another local wrestling friend, referee Mickey Jay (Mickie Henson), a longtime Keys resident.

"We were like brothers ... we were naturals. Hump fit right in. It was funny that some of the folks who met Hump knew him from somewhere, but they couldn't figure out that it was from wrestling."

Knowing Hump, says McGregor, sparked an interest in a profession that had been foreign to him until that time.

"Then I saw the human side of it, and it became a really wonderful thing to me."

Hump truly was a man for all seasons who could be comfortable in just about any setting. He was well-versed in a variety of topics. Among his many interests, he was a blues aficionado, and could talk for hours about that genre of music.

"He could handle himself really well with any type of conversation. He was a lot more than many people even realized," says McGregor.

Hump had dodged death a number of times. He survived a serious accident in the late '60s when a ring truck he was driving hit a snow bank in Minnesota. Ten years ago he underwent emergency surgery to replace an aortic valve and had a pacemaker installed. Two years ago he was hospitalized after developing pneumonia due to complications from congestive heart failure. He was once declared clinically dead on the operating table.

McGregor recalls when the Key West crowd held a benefit for Hump in 2001 when he developed serious heart problems.

"Everybody showed up. They loved Hump. When he made his presence in Key West, he became a celebrity figure, an icon, you name it," says McGregor. "He loved the gals ... he loved the young ladies. He just had that presence about him."

It's true that Hump made an indelible mark on the business he loved. But he made an even bigger one on the many fans and friends he touched.

The House that Humperdink built was more than a rogue faction of wrestlers. It was a fraternity bonded by respect and admiration for a man who enriched those lives around him.

I suspect there was a reason Hump made a concerted effort to attend as many reunions and fan gatherings as he could in recent years. He understood so well that life is precious, and that it's a gift not to be taken for granted.

And he knew when it was time to go home.

Henry Marcus
Last of the old-time promoters

Aug. 1, 2004

I can't help but think about Henry Marcus whenever driving past the old County Hall on King Street.

Now an affordable housing complex known as the Palace Apartments, the building is long removed from the days when it was the place to be on Friday nights, wrestling was the ticket and Henry Marcus was the ringmaster.

To thousands of wrestling fans in these parts, he was as much the building as the mortar that held it together. He was a promoter extraordinaire who dabbled in everything from the Royal Canadian Ballet to the Ice Capades. But pro wrestling was his bread and butter. It's what endeared him to mat fans throughout the state for half a century.

The news of his passing last Sunday at the age of 93 leaves a void not only in the wrestling business, but also in the rich cultural fabric of our town, which counted Marcus among its unique group of engaging and colorful personalities. A master storyteller who was gifted with razor-sharp wit and an amazing sense of recall, he was the last of the old-time promoters.

Born to promote

I first crossed paths with Henry Marcus in 1964. It marked my indoctrination into the soap opera gone mad known as professional wrestling. By that time he had been in the promoting business for more than 20 years. What I first noticed about him was that he stood in stark contrast to the burly behemoths who worked on his shows. With thinning hair swept straight back over his head, thick glasses and trousers hitched up to his belly button (which earned him the name "High Pockets"), the nattily attired promoter was not an imposing physical presence by any stretch of the imagination.

One thing, though, was for sure. This was his show. You'd see him handing out tickets at the box office. You'd see him taking tickets at the door, with his "Hold your own ticket!" refrain providing a familiar backdrop for the bustling County Hall throng. He'd occasionally do the ring announcing, giving the festivities just the slightest sense of decorum and an added dose of legitimacy. And, what the fans normally didn't see, was the promoter working the backstage area, making sure the performers showed up on time and going over the intricate details that fill out a wrestling card.

Back in those days, County Hall was a mecca for wrestling in this area, and Marcus brought them all to his mat shrine. From Jim Londos to Gorgeous George to Lou Thesz to Ric Flair, they all graced the hallowed hall at 1000 King Street. Henry Marcus was the common thread that tied this unique form of entertainment to the Lowcountry, although the man was about much more than professional wrestling.

Like any promoter worth his salt, Marcus knew how to relate to people, which included the largely blue-collar wrestling audience. Whether holding a dinner in honor of Jack Dempsey at the old LaBrasca's restaurant across from County Hall, or dining with Irving Berlin at the old Lindy's on Broadway, Marcus always found a comfort zone.

"He was probably the smartest person that never graduated college you'd ever meet, anytime or anywhere," Eric Marcus would say about his dad.

The son of a railroad man who died when the Hartsville native was only 3, Henry Marcus was a familiar figure in Columbia and Charleston, where the storyteller routinely held court with local businessmen, politicians, newshounds and practically anyone who appreciated his unique gift of gab. His scope of acquaintances, however, extended far beyond the Lowcountry and the state, as he rubbed shoulders with the likes of actor Tyrone Power and President Harry Truman, and was personal friends with such sports figures as boxing greats Jack Dempsey and Joe Louis, and basketball coach Frank McGuire.

Lucrative left turn

Marcus got into the promotional field purely by accident. As he would tell the story, he was headed on his way to the post office when he made "a left turn instead of a right one," and ended up bumping into a sports editor at The Record newspaper in Columbia who offered him a job writing publicity for the local wrestling shows for $3 a week.

The relationships he forged with building managers led to Marcus's entree into the promoting business, and he was doing it full-time by 1944, eventually expanding his entertainment repertoire to ice shows, stage shows, athletic events and everything in between.

Marcus promoted his first wrestling show in Charleston around 1950, a decade after he began in his home base of Columbia. His primary promotional lesson was simple: The customer is always No. 1.

While the wrestling business was Marcus's forte, there wasn't much he didn't promote. "From the Royal Canadian Ballet to wrestling," as he was wont to say, he dabbled in a little bit of everything. Boxing stars Jack Dempsey, Joe Louis, Rocky Marciano, Jimmy Braddock, Jack Sharkey and Primo Carnera all worked for him. He brought in such big-band greats as Jimmy Dorsey, Benny Goodman, Duke Ellington, and Xavier Cugat. Dick Clark of "American Bandstand" fame emceed many of Marcus's rock and roll revues.

He liked to tell the story about when he booked the late George Reeves as "Superman" at the Township Auditorium in Columbia, and nearly 3,000 children showed up for the matinee.

"Lois Lane came out singing torch songs with her dress split up the side," he'd recall. "All the children wanted to see Superman fly, and they had to sit through nightclub entertainment beforehand. When Reeves finally appeared, the kids still only yelled, 'Fly, Superman, fly'! Well, I knew Superman couldn't fly, and Superman sure knew Superman couldn't fly. But try telling 3,000 screaming kids."

Then there was the time he had Olympic track legend Jesse Owens race a thoroughbred horse through Columbia's Capital City Park.

He remembered promoting when wrestling tickets were a quarter. He recalled promoting band and dance shows when entertainers showed up, had a couple of mikes set up, performed for several hours and left.

"Now you have to meet them at the airport and they show up with 18 trucks," he'd later lament.

Marcus was a jack of all trades, but what he was first and foremost was a promoter.

The changing times

"Knowing a man like Henry Marcus is one of those things that people like me keep in their minds forever. He's one of the famous people that I know," said Dave Spurlock, former athletic director at St. Andrews High School, who helped give Marcus a place to hold his wrestling shows when County Hall closed down in the mid-'80s.

Spurlock said he was more than happy to bring wrestling to the then fairly new gym at St. Andrews. "Not only did I have a chance to make some money, but I got to actually see wrestling on a weekly basis," said Spurlock, a lifelong wrestling fan. The school would get the concessions money along with a cut of the gate, while Spurlock received $80 at the end of the night for being the "key man."

He can't help but smile when talking about the time Marcus let Spurlock's young son and his friends come in for free for a birthday party.

"We had my son's birthday party right there at the wrestling show, and the kids got to meet some of the wrestlers. They had a blast. We still have pictures in our old album."

"I learned a big part of promotion from him," said Sandy Scott, a former wrestling star who worked with Marcus in the office during the '70s and '80s. "When he told you something, you could take it to the bank. He was an ace of a guy."

"Henry was a wonderful promoter to work for," said Rip Hawk (Harvey Evers), who was a headliner for Marcus during the '60s and '70s. "He was a very nice man and could take a heckuva rib. "Swede (Hanson) and I used to rib him like crazy. He really and truly enjoyed it, though, and he could come back with some pretty good shots of his own. We had a lot of fun with him. I'll guarantee you he was a legend down there."

Attendance and business dropped for the aging promoter with the decline of Crockett Promotions during the late '80s. Times had changed, and Marcus wasn't part of the new WWF empire that Vince McMahon had built, nor did he fit into Ted Turner's plans for a national wrestling company, which had absorbed the Crocketts' NWA operation. A terse, two-paragraph letter written in November 1989 commended Marcus on his contribution to the sport over a 50-year period before informing him that the company was terminating its agreement with him. It wished him well in "future endeavors."

It certainly wasn't the way Marcus had envisioned going out. But he was realistic enough to know that the industry had passed him by. It was changing fast, and he didn't like that it had become more of a pay-per-view spectacle than a show that passed through all the towns on a regular basis.

He would promote his final show in 1990 for the short-lived North American Wrestling Association.

Taking it home

His retirement years, which basically didn't begin until shortly before his 80th birthday, were punctuated by times of both great joy and great sadness. He and his wife, Marguerite, moved to a beach home in Cherry Grove, near Myrtle Beach, which proved to be a refreshing change of pace from their many years in Columbia. (The two lived in the Hickory Hill subdivision of Charleston for a brief period during the 1970s, but moved shortly after they were robbed at gunpoint after a wrestling show).

A special ceremony — titled "The Night The Legends Return: A Tribute to Henry Marcus" — was scheduled in honor of the promoter on May 30, 1998. Tragedy, however, struck when his wife of 48 years died suddenly of a heart attack a month before the event. Twenty years his junior, she was 67, and her passing hit the promoter hard.

"Marguerite was Henry's life from the day he laid eyes on her at the restaurant where she was working. From the day he saw Marguerite until the day she died, she was his life," recalled Valerie Warren of Charleston, who along with husband Earl and daughter Patty, attended Marcus's wrestling shows at County Hall beginning in the early '70s.

The promoter was crestfallen and canceled plans to attend the event. Without her, he said, it wouldn't be the same. A number of friends and former colleagues from the wrestling business, however, convinced him that she would have wanted him to be there. He acquiesced and attended the show.

Fittingly the tribute was held at the former King Street Palace and the site of the old County Hall. Also quite appropriately, it was one of the last events ever staged at the building, and Marcus was there to see it for the final time. After all, as some reminisced, it was "the house that Marcus built."

Pastor Andy McDaniel, who helped organize the event, called the promoter an important influence in his life.

"He was part of my childhood. Wrestling was part of my life, and Friday nights at County Hall was a special time of bonding between my father and myself ... When he did the event in 1998, it was truly an honor for us to honor him. It takes on even more significance now."

Into his late 80s Marcus was traveling around the world by himself. He made visits to Israel, Egypt, Canada, China, Italy and the concentration camps in Germany and Poland.

He passed on walking The Great Wall of China, preferring to view it from a tour bus. His get up and go had got up and gone, he'd laugh.

He loved his visit to Israel, the land of his ancestors, and was delighted when a soldier visiting one of the pyramids in Egypt recognized him from his promoting days in Columbia. The soldier once had been stationed at Fort Jackson, and had been a regular at the promoter's Tuesday night wrestling shows at The Township. "It really is a small world," the promoter would say.

He loved his family, which included sons Eric, Jerry and Barry, and eight grandchildren. He loved his close friends and his faith.

And he loved his independence. Even in his advanced years, he'd drive his car to Charleston, pick me up and we'd go out to dinner at some of his old haunts, where invariably he'd recognize veteran restaurant patrons, proprietors and even some of the waitresses. He could crack a joke without cracking a smile. If he didn't have an answer for everything, he certainly had an opinion.

But when he lost total vision in one eye nearly two years ago and was no longer able to drive a car, the world as he had known it was gone. A fall in early 2003, when he was 91, led to another more serious fall several months later that resulted in a broken arm and rib. At that point basically bedridden with little more left than his mind, which remained amazingly sharp, the old promoter knew that the finish was near.

His final six months were spent rotating between the hospital and a nursing home. A lethal combination of a viral infection and double pneumonia spelled the end.

"If it had been boring up there for anyone lately, it got real interesting Sunday morning," said son Eric. "They've got a real card up there now to keep them in stitches."

We said our final goodbyes when I visited him a year ago in Sumter, where he had been living with his niece and her family since his wife's death in 1998. I thanked him for the years of wonderful memories he had given me, and for his unfailing friendship over the years. He asked me again, as he had in the past, to write his obit when that day came.

Perhaps the most impressive thing about Henry Marcus that some might not have known was that he had a heart of gold. Beneath the gruff exterior of an outwardly crotchety old-time promoter who could drive the hardest of bargains was a kind-hearted soul who quietly touched the lives of many.

"He was so kind and generous," recalled Valerie Warren. "There was a restaurant in Columbia where there was a young waitress who was raising children by herself. Henry ate there often and always left a very good-sized tip for her because he knew she needed help with her children. But that was Henry."

Eric Marcus probably summed up his father best.

"There aren't many people like that in this world these days."

Lance Russell
'The Voice of Memphis wrestling'

Oct. 8, 2017

The professional wrestling community lost not only one of its greatest broadcasters, but one of its greatest friends, with the passing of Lance Russell last week.

The voice of Memphis wrestling since the late 1950s, Russell provided the soundtrack to a glorious era that showcased such legendary figures as "The Fabulous" Jackie Fargo and Jerry "The King" Lawler, star performers whose acts would never have shined as bright without the steady hand and unflappable voice of the venerable announcer.

"Without Lance there would have never been a Jerry 'The King' Lawler," said the WWE Hall of Famer. While Lawler may have been the signature star, Russell was the show.

Many say he made Memphis wrestling what it was. To thousands of fans over several decades, Lance Russell was Memphis wrestling. He became as much of a star among Memphis wrestling fans as the wrestlers themselves.

Russell, who died at the age of 91, was a major factor in the success of the city's weekly televised wrestling program. No grappling show in the United States over the past 50 years had the viewership that Memphis wrestling enjoyed week in and week out. And it was all a result of Russell having the vision to take a chance on an 11 a.m. Saturday morning time-slot.

As the station's program director at the time, Russell made the call to put the live wrestling show in a timeslot to draw in adults who weren't watching cartoons. But few believed adults would watch wrestling at a time when kids' shows cornered the market.

Russell made believers out of all the naysayers, though, when Memphis wrestling became the most popular local show in the country.

At the height of the show's run, nearly half of those watching TV tuned in on Saturday mornings — the highest local market penetration in the country — while fans would line the sidewalk outside WMC-Channel 5 studios waiting to get a seat for the matches.

And the man who made it possible was a masterful storyteller who could verbally convey the magic that was Memphis wrestling.

"Lance Russell was the heart and soul of Memphis wrestling," said mat historian Mark James. "Without Lance (and Dave Brown), there's no way Memphis wrestling could have gotten over so well with the fans. Lance's sincerity and believability were paramount to the success of Memphis wrestling."

Voice of reason

And as wild as Memphis wrestling was — and it was plenty wild — Russell, the consummate professional, always provided a sense of sanity to a sea of madness.

The affable, easygoing broadcaster, whose calming voice resonated like a soft summer breeze, had a unique ability in not only relating to his audience, but also in communicating disgust at the heinous acts perpetrated by the dastardly bad guys who crossed paths with him every week on the popular Saturday morning show.

His one-liners, which would become known as "Lance-isms," were reserved for mouthpieces like Jimmy Hart, along with other nefarious sorts, who would instigate outlandish shenanigans in a studio that sometimes didn't seem big enough to contain the out-of-control action.

Russell, who somehow managed to always maintain his cool while approaching his job with the utmost seriousness, was no stranger to calling out the heels — with a bit of feigned indignation and exasperation — when warranted.

"Don't start with that smart stuff!"

"What in the Sam Hill is that?"

"Will you guys just stop and get out of here?"

And it didn't matter if Russell was having his Baxter suit torn off by heels like Lawler and Sam Bass, flour dumped on his head by motor-mouthed manager Hart, or other indignities.

He remained the voice of reason.

He gave Memphis wrestling credibility.

Dream team

From 1959 until 1997, Russell's voice was as familiar as anyone in the region. Along with the town's Saturday morning wrestling broadcasts, Russell served as a programming executive with several area stations.

One of his hires along the way was Dave Brown, a University of Memphis student and a kid disc jockey at WHBQ radio in 1967 when Russell tapped him as his sidekick for studio wrestling.

"I needed a guy to work with me because the guy that I had was dropping out of it," Russell said in a 2015 interview. "I was looking for an assistant. I got to know Dave around the station and was really impressed. When he said he would do something, he did it. Dave was just a very conscientious guy who was an extremely dependable man of his word. That attracted me to him. He had a great personality and a great sense of humor."

Brown gladly accepted Russell's offer, and a dream team was born.

"Davey came on over and worked with me on wrestling. It's amazing how it affected his career, and I'm glad that it did. He's one of the great guys around. He's just a super, super person. It's amazing how things turned out when I look back."

The duo stayed together for about a quarter-century, the longest-working tag team in the annals of wrestling broadcasting.

Russell also would give Brown his most famous role at the station — that of weatherman.

"I remember asking Dave if he knew anything about the weather," recalled Russell. "He said, 'Well, I think it's raining outside.' Davey was my kind of guy. He not only wanted to do it, but whenever he tackled a subject, he tackled it with vigor."

Their partnership lasted for decades.

Brown retired as chief meteorologist at WMC-TV in Memphis in 2015 after an incredible 53-year run in radio and TV. Regarded as one of the region's most respected and trusted news personalities, Brown also would host Memphis wrestling from 1967 to 2002, 27 of those years alongside Russell.

"I cried all the way home. It was tough," Brown told WMC-TV after learning of Russell's passing. "Lance and I were friends, coworkers, partners for 53 years, and in all that time we never had a single cross word between us."

Changing landscape

One of the iconic voices of pro wrestling's territorial era, Russell saw his role change as the territories gave way to Vince McMahon's WWF in the mid-'80s. As the wrestling business changed, so did the style of announcers who would call a new brand of sports entertainment. Like the legendary Gordon Solie and others, Russell found it increasingly difficult to compromise his smooth and distinctive style for one more suited to a shill or pitchman.

One of his final broadcasting jobs in the industry was as commentator for the NWA World Wide Wrestling show, which would become part of World Championship Wrestling. He also produced the popular WCW hotline.

After several years, though, he returned to Memphis, which had been one of the last holdouts of the territorial age, where he would finish his career in commentary once again alongside Dave Brown and Corey Maclin. He also worked as an announcer for Smoky Mountain Wrestling in that promotion's latter days.

It had been a long journey for Russell, who began his foray into wrestling in Jackson, Tenn., where he was asked in 1955 if he wanted to announce wrestling matches for a local TV station.

"I've never done it, but I feel like I ought to be able to do it," he told the station owner.

"I started doing commentary on it, and just loved it and had a lot of fun doing it."

Russell moved from Jackson to the much larger Memphis market where he continued as a wrestling commentator, first at Channel 13 and later, beginning in 1977, at Channel 5.

Those who knew Lance Russell considered him one of the finest men in the business. What you saw was what you got with Lance. He was the same person off camera as the one you saw on camera.

Always warm and personable, he had that special ability to make those around him feel like they were his best friend.

Steve Beverly, a longtime news director in Jackson, Tenn., and former wrestling newsletter editor, called his longtime friend "one of the masters."

"You felt like you were getting a textbook education in one conversation. He was that kind of guy."

"To say that Lance Russell was everyone's friend is really an understatement," added Beverly. "But for those who came just within inches of a touch of him, and had the opportunity to watch his work, and then saw him at an arena at an event, in a public venue, you know that Lance treated you like you were the most important person in the room."

More than anything, though, Russell added warmth to the show. He never spoke over the fans' heads.

"Lance gave us many Saturdays where we had extraordinary entertainment, and I can tell you it wouldn't have been nearly so had he not been the catalyst and the traffic cop to make it all happen," said Beverly. "He gave us a personality that reached out to other people, and when you saw him in person, he'd extend that hand and he'd look at you, and you felt like you were the most important person there."

Former wrestling announcer and veteran broadcaster Chris Cruise also recalled the influence Russell had on him while both were working for WCW.

"My father and I were not close. His father had deserted the family and my dad didn't really know how to be a father. But he was a good man. He was born in 1925 and was a World War II veteran, the generation of men that did not express their feelings. His mother was 17 when he was born, out of wedlock, and she never let him forget the (negative) effect he had on her life. So I didn't benefit from a demonstrative, communicative dad.

"All the time I spent with Lance Russell I never stopped thinking how great it would have been if he had been my father. I wish I had told Lance that, but it was kind of a weird thing to say to a man. I always looked forward to spending time with him. He always had something nice to say about life and people. What made him who he was? I'd like to know."

"It was great to meet him in person at the 2016 CAC (Cauliflower Alley Club) reunion in Las Vegas," wrote fan Brian Westcott. "Talking to him was like talking to my late grandfather. It was just like I knew him all my life. Incredible individual."

Fans indeed knew they were among friends when Lance Russell opened his show with his signature line: "Yello (Hello) again everybody!"

"I didn't realize that was the way I said it," Russell laughed. "Now every place I go people have to hear it. They even did a T-shirt with that on the front."

Lance and The King

Perhaps no wrestler had a closer connection to Russell than Jerry Lawler. It was Russell who gave Lawler his first big break in the business. A teenager and avid wrestling fan at the time, Lawler would draw caricatures of Jackie Fargo and other Memphis-area wrestlers and send them to Russell, who doubled as program director and wrestling announcer at the TV station.

The friendship stood the test of time.

"I started with Jerry when he was 14 years old and drawing those first pictures," recalled Russell. "People got such a kick out of seeing those things (sketches). He went from absolute nowhere to star of the promotion."

Lawler, who was responsible for Russell's nickname, "Banana Nose," told WMC-TV: "I don't know anyone who could say something bad about Lance Russell."

None were more destined for fame than Lawler.

"He had that natural ability to not only talk — and he's as good as there is — but he was a guy who was a lot different than those who were into themselves," said

Russell, who was a major part of Lawler's famous 1982-83 feud with late actor and comedian Andy Kaufman. "Jerry never took a drink. And rarely did he work out in the gymnasium. He was just an amazing star and a very nice guy."

"I learned so much from him over the years," Lawler told the Memphis Commercial Appeal. "I was honored that he asked me to come to Las Vegas last year to induct him into the wrestling commentators hall of fame."

"We so were so close," said Lawler, who had visited with Russell and his family just days before Russell's death, at the wrestler's barbecue restaurant in Memphis. "It was like losing my dad again."

Saturday morning at 11

Russell broke his hip in a fall on Sept. 29, shortly after his daughter, Valerie, a beloved school principal, died in a Memphis hospital following a long battle with cancer. She was buried just hours after her father's passing.

As the saying goes, behind every good man is a good woman, and that was Audrey Russell. And only death could separate the earthly bond the two had shared for more than seven decades. Audrey passed away on June 29, 2014, on the date of their 67th wedding anniversary.

"That was my girl," Russell said. "People used to ask how two people can stay together that long. You have to work on it, of course, but you also have to hope that the good Lord has pointed you to someone you love, and someone with whom you can develop an even deeper love. And that was Aud."

In 2015, Russell moved to Pensacola to live with son youngest Shane.

A great husband, great father, great friend. That was Lance Russell.

Lance is survived by his two sons, William Lance Russell and his wife, Debbie; Shane Russell and his wife, Debra; eight grandchildren; eight great-grandchildren; and his faithful dog and best friend Buddy.

"He had a lifelong passion for golf and the inexplicable ability to frighten fish away, which never dampened his attempts to catch them," read his obituary.

And his memorial service? Saturday morning at 11. It was a fitting final act for a friend so many fans had invited into their living rooms every week.

Gordon Solie
So long from the Sunshine State

July 30, 2000

When Gordon Solie talked, people listened. Especially wrestling fans, a generation of which were weaned on the gravel-voiced Solie's unique call of the action inside the ring and unparalleled commentary on the business.

Gordon Solie was, simply put, the sport's greatest ambassador and the voice of professional wrestling for four decades. He was the standard by which wrestling announcers were judged, and he humbly accepted the honorary title "dean of wrestling announcers."

Solie, who had battled cancer for the past year, passed away last week at the age of 70 at his home in Port Richey, Florida. His body was found Friday morning by family members, and it was believed that Solie had died either late Wednesday or Thursday. His condition had taken a sharp turn for the worse several weeks ago.

The loss shook the wrestling community.

Longtime friend Don Curtis of Jacksonville said Friday that he last saw Solie just two weeks ago and had planned to visit him again this weekend.

"What a shock to lose him," said Curtis. "We had a little party with him a couple of weeks ago. We picked up him up, put him in the car, and drove over to our favorite dining and drinking place."

Curtis said the group, consisting of "people who really loved each other," included Curtis and his wife, Mr. and Mrs. Lou Thesz, and Jack Brisco.

Curtis and other close friends confided that Solie had unofficially "given up" after his wife, Eileen "Smokey" Solie, died several years ago.

"When she died, he just didn't give a darn anymore," said Curtis. "He would talk about how he wanted to be with his wife. I guess he wanted to be in heaven with her."

Solie underwent an operation late last year to remove his larynx after doctors discovered a growth on his vocal chords that was reportedly so large it had displaced his heart and lungs. It seemed like a cruel twist of fate when Solie, who for years entertained fans with his smooth-as-silk delivery, was fitted with an artificial voice box.

"He said (last year) that this was ridiculous," said Curtis. "He was fed up. He hurt all over."

There were, however, other physical factors that led to the decline of his health, most notably Solie's well-documented addiction to cigarettes.

"It was that cotton-picking smoking that got him," said Curtis. "He was a smoking nut, and you couldn't stop him."

Great ambassador

Solie's voice automatically gave career boosts to hundreds of performers, including The Funks, The Briscos, Dusty Rhodes, Ric Flair, Mr. Wrestling No. 1 and 2, Tommy Rich, Ole Anderson, Thunderbolt Patterson, Roddy Piper and Don Muraco.

And if Flair was the consummate professional wrestler, it was Gordon Solie who was the consummate professional wrestling announcer. Ironically, Flair may have been the last person to talk to Solie before he died. Flair said he told him he loved him at the end of their phone conversation Wednesday night.

"He was a great friend and, in my opinion, the greatest play-by-play man to ever hold a microphone in his hand," said Flair. "He was a great ambassador for our sport."

Gordon Solie was, indeed, a class act. He made fans believers. They trusted him. He gave wrestling the dignity of a legitimate sporting event that few in the modern era, with the notable exception of Jim Ross, have been able to come close to replicating.

Solie was perhaps as responsible as any one for WCW. Ted Turner often credited Solie with the success of "rasslin" - as Turner labeled it - on his station. And he would be right.

Turner counted Solie among his valued friends and had many conversations with him at the old Channel 17 studio in Atlanta. Solie was an integral force behind the 1977 emergence of SuperStation TBS, a Turner brainchild, and helped oversee a cable television ratings explosion. "Georgia Championship Wrestling" was the lead-in show to the Atlanta Braves and Solie was its voice from 1974-85, often doing double duty with his popular "Championship Wrestling from Florida" program that he presided over from 1960-87.

Many of Solie's colleagues saluted their friend upon learning of his passing. "He was absolutely the best commentator that I ever heard call a match," said Superstar Billy Graham. "He was the premier commentator in the business. His words were flawless and smooth as silk. There was no effort to his commentary. He was heads above anyone I've ever heard. He was a close friend and an incredibly nice person. We lost the best."

Veteran announcer Lance Russell, the voice of Memphis wrestling, and Solie had collaborated on many occasions over the years from their respective Memphis- and Tampa-based territories.

"I never stopped learning things from the guy," said Russell. "It was always great to work with Gordie. He had an attitude that paralleled mine in terms of what we thought about wrestling."

Russell fondly recalled his stint with Solie and veteran announcer Bob Caudle a decade ago in WCW.

"That was great fun. I loved it. Getting to work with them was great."

Top-rated host

Originally from Minneapolis where he attended high school and college, Solie, born Jonard Sjoblon in 1929, went to work for a small radio station in Tampa, Fla., in 1950, following a stint with Armed Forces Radio.

"I used to do a radio talk show, and because wrestling was very big in Tampa, I would interview the wrestlers every Monday night before the matches," Solie said in a 1990 interview. "Cowboy Luttrall (former Tampa promoter) lost his ring announcer and asked me if I'd like the job. I told him I'd be very interested, and he offered me $5 a night. Since that was 10 percent of what I was making salary-wise, I was quick to jump on the offer."

Solie, who also assisted Luttrall with publicity and advertising, began doing wrestling commentary on television in 1960. With his inimitable style, Solie gained enormous popularity in Florida and became as well-known as some of the top wrestlers on the circuit. His knowledge of the sport and straightforward approach helped make "Championship Wrestling from Florida" one of the top-rated telecasts on the air.

Small in stature but big in desire, Solie was determined to give the fans the best commentary possible. So he learned the ropes firsthand - on the mat.

"I had two great teachers - Eddie Graham and Coach John Heath," Solie said. "I felt if I was going to do an accurate job of reporting what was going on in the ring, I should at least know what it feels like. And, unfortunately, I found out."

During the mid-'70s, Solie was asked to take on the additional job of serving as host of "Georgia Championship Wrestling" out of Atlanta, the first "international" wrestling program via the WTBS satellite. It also became the world's most-watched wrestling show, due in no small part to Solie.

Solie rated a classic best-of-three falls, one-hour world title bout between Dory Funk Jr. and Jack Brisco during the '70s as the greatest match he ever witnessed.

Solie returned to the NWA in 1989 after working for a Florida-based independent promotion. He joined Ross, Russell, Caudle and Tony Schiavone on the WCW staff.

"I admire Jim Ross and Tony Schiavone tremendously," Solie said. "Lance Russell and I have worked together over the years, and you won't find a finer gentleman or any better announcer than he is. And with Bob Caudle, I think we have a very well-rounded team. We've got two guys with lots of fire (Ross and Schiavone), and Lance, Bob and myself have the historical background."

Solie, however, could see that the wrestling business was changing - and changing fast.

"I think, like everything else, the changes have been made for the better. With technology having come along the way it has, we're able to do things today that were impossible years ago. I'm sure a lot of people will say that it's not like the 'good old days,' but really nothing's like the 'good ole days.' Everything changes."

Solie understood the cyclical nature of the business, but he never quite embraced the fact that the philosophy of wrestling had changed. He once called it a "damn shame" that wrestlers had turned into 'roid freaks and lamented the lack of respect for the history of the business.

In recent years Solie had worked for New Japan Wrestling as a commentator for overseas tapes and videos, and had served as an official with the NWA/Florida promotion.

The man who put wrestling on the map on TBS was unceremoniously dumped by WCW after "philosophical differences" with then-WCW executive vice president Eric Bischoff, a man Solie later called a "corporate assassin," in 1995. His last show was a Saturday morning edition of WCW Pro with colleagues Dusty Rhodes and Larry Zbyszko. No attempt was made to promote his farewell appearance, but Gordon got in the final shot.

Responding to a typically sloppy match on that final Saturday, "the dean" said to Zbyszko, "And they wonder why I'm leaving?"

The End

Acknowledgments

First, I'd like to thank my longtime employer, The Post and Courier, for providing a weekly home for what has become the longest-running column on professional wrestling in the country.

Former executive news editor and publisher Larry Tarleton green-lighted this column 30 years ago, and it has been a staple in the newspaper's Sunday sports section ever since. It was through Larry's vision and innovation that made it all possible.

Thanks also to the staff at Evening Post Books — Kristen Milford, Shaun Stacy and Robie Scott — for recognizing the value of this work and seeing the project through.

Special thanks to my longtime friend Ken Mihalik for his yeoman's job in editing this book. Ken's writing skills and knowledge of the subject were invaluable throughout the process.

I'm both honored and humbled by the forewords written by Les Thatcher and Jim Ross. They are masters of their craft, and valued friends whose contributions are sincerely appreciated.

To Gill Guerry, our designer, a great job as always. Thanks for making the book look good, just like you made our stories look better for many years at The P&C.

Thanks also to those who graciously provided photographs from their collections for this volume. They include Chris Swisher, Dr. Mike Lano (wrealano@aol.com), Pete Lederberg (plmathfoto@hotmail.com), Eddie Cheslock and Scooter Lesley.

I'm thankful to my P&C friend Kurt Knapek for his help in facilitating this project. His support and encouragement were important in making this book a reality.

And, of course, my everlasting appreciation goes out to the faithful readers of this column. We have shared many moments and memories, and it has been a privilege and pleasure writing this column for you over these many years. You've all shown your support by making it one of the best-read columns in the newspaper, and for that I'll always be grateful.

Last but certainly not least, this book would not have been possible without the love, support and patience of my wife, Ruth, who has been my rock over the years as well as a more-than-capable copy editor and budding author. You are my inspiration, and I dedicate this book to you.

– Mike Mooneyham